TEACHER

career starter

2nd edition

Joan DellaValle and Emmett Sawyer

with Mary Masi

LearningExpress

New York

Library of Congress Cataloging-in-Publication Data:
DellaValle, Joan Chandross.
    Teacher career starter / Joan DellaValle and Emmett Sawyer with Mari Masi—2nd ed.
      p.   cm.—(Career starters)
      ISBN 1-57685-399-3
      1. Teaching—Vocational guidance—United States. 2. Teachers—Training of—
United States. 3. Teachers—Employment—United States. I. Sawyer, Emmett.
II. Masi, Mary. III. Title. IV. Series.

  LB1775.2 .D45 2002
  371.1'0023'73—dc21

2001038952

Printed in the United States of America
9 8 7 6 5 4 3 2 1
Second Edition

ISBN 1-57685-399-3

For more information or to place an order, contact LearningExpress at:
  900 Broadway
  Suite 604
  New York, NY 10003

Or visit us at:
  www.learnatest.com

Contents

Contents

Introduction

Why Enter the Teaching Field?

TEACHING GIVES you the ability to touch the future by positively and dramatically influencing the lives of the young people you teach. Indeed, teaching is one of the most challenging, yet immensely rewarding careers you can choose. For some, the desire to become a teacher has always been there. When they were children, they dreamed about the day they would stand before a busy classroom full of children learning and growing. For others, the allure of teaching crept up on them. They saw friends who were teachers who loved talking about their students and being involved in a cause bigger than they were. Whatever your interest level in the teaching field may be, this book can help you to find out if teaching is the career for you. Once you determine it is, this book will also give you the inside scoop on how to prepare for and achieve success in your teaching career.

Now is an excellent time to enter the teaching field because the job opportunities for teachers have never been better. Indeed, more than two million teachers will be needed to fill positions over the course of the next decade. Whether you want to become an elementary teacher, a special education teacher, or a high school math teacher, there are many jobs out there for you.

Whether you are choosing your first career, or are considering a career change, this book can help you to evaluate your options and plan the best route to becoming a teacher. This chapter will guide you through each step along the path to the teaching profession. In addition to explaining the traditional route to becoming a teacher, this book includes plenty of advice for those who may want an alternate route to teacher certification.

Also, you will find out how to choose a teacher education program and how to pay for it. You will find the latest tips and techniques for conducting a job search, impressing your interviewers, and landing a great job. Surviving as a first year teacher is also discussed—you will get lots of practical guidance on how to thrive in your new environment.

Becoming a certified teacher is a complicated process. You can use this book to get the vital information you need to make the appropriate choices throughout that process. Take a look at the following brief descriptions of what you will find in each chapter to get an overview of how this book can help you.

Chapter	Description
One The Hottest Jobs for Teachers	This chapter gives you an inside look at the many different types of teaching jobs out there from music teacher to reading specialist to distance education teacher and more. Learn the difference between public and private schools and how substitute teaching can help you gain valuable experience. You will also find current salary tables and teacher supply and demand charts.
Two All about Teacher Education Programs	This chapter describes typical teacher education programs, the kinds of requirements that you must meet, and tips on how to choose the best program for you. Sample bachelor's and master's degree teacher education programs are included.
Three How to Find Teacher Education Programs and Financial Aid	After you decide which type of teacher education program you want to pursue, this chapter gives you the tools you need to locate the different types of programs: bachelor degrees, graduate degrees, distance learning courses, and alternative forms of education. You will also find out how to locate and apply for a wealth of financial aid options.
Four Teacher Certification	This chapter clearly spells out the steps needed to achieve teacher certification via both traditional and alternative routes. You can also find a list of the specific certification requirements needed in your state, along with contact information for each state's department of education.
Five Finding Job Openings and Creating Your Resume	This is the chapter that can help you launch your job search. It's full of practical ways to find out about available teaching positions. Then, it helps you to craft a high-quality resume by completing an in-depth resume questionnaire.

CHAPTER one

THE HOTTEST JOBS FOR TEACHERS

Teaching is an interesting and challenging profession. Few other careers can provide the satisfaction that teaching does. This chapter introduces the many career options open to teachers: early childhood, elementary, middle, and secondary levels; specialized areas, such as ESL (English as a Second Language), bilingual, and special education; and public and private school settings, including charter schools.

THE OPPORTUNITIES available for teachers today are many and varied. According to estimates by the U.S. Department of Education, two million new teachers will be needed in the next ten years to teach our nation's children. If you love working with children, elementary education offers many rich rewards. Or perhaps you have a passion for a particular subject, such as English or science, and want to spend your days imparting your knowledge to high school students. Quality teachers of all subjects and levels are needed across America.

Depending on your personal interests and talents, you can obtain one or more certifications to teach at the early childhood, elementary, middle school, or secondary level, and for specific instructional areas that span pre-kindergarten through high school. You may wish to specialize and work with physically, emotionally, or intellectually challenged children. In addition to your regular teaching assignment, you may get the opportunity to sponsor an extracurricular activity or student club—an assignment that you may find rewarding and one that can supplement your income.

THE REWARDS OF TEACHING

Teaching can be a very rewarding career. Indeed, most teachers believe that the positive effect they have on their students' lives is one of the most rewarding aspects of the job. It is also why the general public considers teaching to be a well-respected profession.

In the past, teachers were more focused on imparting their knowledge to students. However, now teachers no longer only convey knowledge; their job is to facilitate learning. In other words, teachers now teach children *how to learn*. Most educators agree that before a teacher can do this, he or she must first help their students to believe that they can do the task. This is accomplished by building the students' self-esteem.

Viki Masi, an elementary school teacher in Brooklyn, New York, says, "I became a teacher so that I could have an influence on helping children to be smart and confident. Some of the biggest rewards of teaching are the thank you notes from the students at the end of the term, when a student says: 'I want to be a teacher too,' and when a laid-back student becomes a learner."

Donna Gespari, a high school English teacher at William Floyd High School in Mastic Beach, New York, says, "I have always wanted to be a teacher—from the time I was five years old. The teachers in my life were extremely influential and positive role models. I enjoyed the idea of teaching English because of the influence my high school English teachers had on me. They affected me greatly."

Jacqueline Gruhler, a resource center teacher in a New Jersey middle school, says she got interested in the education profession because "I admire many of the teachers I have had, I like the educational setting, and I like being around children." She recalls the day when one of her students "called to me in the morning and gave me a rose. . . . It was very touching."

Many teachers find that a career in education allows time for personal and/or professional development. Schools often offer incentives or tuition reimbursement to teachers who want to take continuing education classes. For example, Rashelle Woodward, an elementary music teacher at an urban private school in Detroit, earned her Masters in Music Education from Wayne State University while she was teaching. "I was a specialist, so I often wouldn't have classes for several hours during the day, or I would have classes only before or after school. I arranged my school schedule around my teaching schedule, which was fairly easy to do. At first I was teaching just to make some money while I earned my degree, but when the administration saw how much my students were improving due to my improved teaching methods (I was using everything I was learning in my masters classes), they offered to pay for my degree."

Woodward loved the practical experience of teaching and learning at the same time. "It really helped me understand what worked in teaching and what didn't. I would bring that information back to my classes, and my professors and other students would give me feedback and suggestions. I felt support from all sides, my professors, my colleagues, my administrators, and especially my students."

Mary Elaine Elia, a special education teacher who has taught all the grade levels from kindergarten to fifth grade, says, "I chose this profession because I like to work with children." She also liked that teaching allowed her "to be home when my own children were home." Many parents find it hard to balance time spent at work with time spent with their kids. Therefore, a trend in teaching is that many professionals decide to switch careers once their children are school-aged and become certified or substitute teachers so that they can spend more time with their children. Another option is classroom sharing. Carla Mastronardi, a fifth grade teacher in Dayton, Ohio, wanted to go back into the classroom after her third child was born, but wasn't ready to go back full-time. Her district allowed her to share a class; she teaches in the morning, and another teacher and mother takes over the class for the afternoon session.

For some education professionals, teaching is a lifelong dream. Sharon Anderson, a pre-K teacher from Jersey City, New Jersey, says, "I always wanted to be a teacher, for as long as I can remember. Even when I was a young girl, I always played 'school'; the other kids in the neighborhood were my students." She says, "It's always nice when the students and their parents come back to visit me year after year."

Do You Have What It Takes to Become a Teacher?

To help you determine if teaching is a career for you, consider these questions:

- Do I have a passion for education and the future of the next generation?
- Do I like working with children or young adults?
- Do I communicate well with people?
- Do I want to teach children or young adults to appreciate their own worth?
- Do I like to design and plan individual programs for reaching a common goal?
- Am I a nurturing and encouraging person?
- Am I a problem solver?
- Do I rise to a challenge?
- Do I like working with people, young or old, who are difficult to get along with?
- Can I expand my direct assignment, working with the students, to include working with their families?
- Do I want to feel tremendous personal reward and satisfaction at the end of my workday?

If you answered *yes* to most of these questions, then teaching is probably a good choice for you. You must be a people person and a good problem solver to be a good classroom teacher.

If you answered *no* to several of the questions above, you may want to think more about what draws you to the teaching field. There are all kinds of related jobs you can do if the checklist above doesn't seem to point you toward a traditional teaching career. For instance, if you don't like to work with large groups of children, consider a career as a reading or a resource room specialist, where you work with students one at a time or in small groups. If you want to teach because you love English literature, for example, think about teaching in a private college preparatory high school, where you can indulge your scholarly interests. There are many ways in which you can build a satisfying teaching career, so rest assured that you will find one that's right for you.

TAKE A CLOSER LOOK

Once you have decided to make teaching your career, try to make arrangements to spend some time in a school. One way you can experience a classroom from a teacher's perspective is to go back to your own elementary, middle, or high school and ask to spend a day or an hour with a favorite teacher. If that isn't possible, consider asking any teachers you know if you can be an observing guest in their classroom. If you have children in school or know of a friend who does, consider contacting that child's teacher—it's always helpful to have a contact in common with someone when asking for a favor.

In some states, you can work as a substitute teacher before you graduate from college. Substituting is a wonderful opportunity to visit several grade levels and get a feel for different teaching environments. For more information about substitute teaching, see the section later in this chapter entitled "Substitute Teacher."

CAREER-CHANGERS WHO WANT TO BECOME TEACHERS

Many people are now entering the teaching field who previously held one or more jobs in other careers. Due to the large demand for teachers in many areas, special programs have been created to recruit people from other occupations to become teachers. Due to the high demand for teachers, if you are considering changing careers to become a teacher, you've chosen a good time to make the switch. In the past decade, the number of teachers who obtained certification through an alternative route doubled. You will learn more about alternative education and certification options in Chapters 2, 3, and 4. If you hold a bachelor's degree from an accredited college or university, you may be able to begin your teaching career as soon as you can apply for and land a job. Then, you can complete specific teacher education requirements while you are teaching.

Many people are making the switch from another career to teaching. Jacinta Perini, a first-grade teacher, gave up her career as a commercial artist (which included designing CD covers for rap groups) to become a teacher. Why? "I asked myself, how is this work that I'm doing changing the world?" When she couldn't come up with an acceptable answer for herself, she decided to become a teacher. Martin Boettcher, a third-grade teacher, left his job as a research analyst to work with children. His wife, also a teacher, was having more fun at her job than he was, so he changed careers.

AREAS OF SPECIALIZATION FOR TEACHERS

Here's a look at several different areas you can choose to specialize in as a teacher. Keep in mind that you may be able to combine some of these areas of specialization. For example, you can become certified as a high school teacher in science and also gain certification in special education. Or perhaps you want to become an elementary school teacher in a bilingual classroom. To compete for the best jobs in the best school districts, or to advance your salary level, you may want to obtain certifications in one, two, or more of these areas. A teacher from Long Island, New York, says, "I love going to school and learning new things, so I just kept getting more teaching certifications over the years. I started as a high school teacher teaching Spanish. Then I gained certification in Italian, French, and bilingual education. My salary kept going up with each additional certification I received."

For each of the following areas of specialization, keep in mind that most teachers do not teach all day with no breaks. They are given planning and conference time during the school day and may use this time to develop lesson plans, grade papers, set up for lessons, contact parents, or meet with colleagues.

Early Childhood Education

If you enjoy working with very young children, you may want to become an early childhood education teacher. Public elementary schools are adding early childhood education programs to their schools at a fast rate and are in dire need of certified teachers in this growing area (often referred to as pre-kindergarten, or P-K). Most P-K programs are for three- and four-year-olds; however, some special education P-K programs include children from birth to age five. In addition to teaching opportunities in public schools, a wide variety of private schools run by religious organizations, hospitals, colleges, and large corporations also have openings for qualified teachers.

As an early childhood educator, you would select, create, and plan age-appropriate activities to help students develop motor skills, counting skills, and literacy skills. Your day would have a lot of variety due to the limited attention span of very young children. Activities include small group art projects, large group story times, outside play, nap time, meals and snacks, quiet-time, games, and creative play.

Check with your state department of education to see if they offer a certificate in early childhood education. Additionally, you can earn certification from the National Child Care Association as a Certified Childcare Professional. For more information, visit the National Child Care Association's website at www.nccanet.org.

Elementary School

The elementary level usually includes grades 1–6. In some districts, kindergarten (K) is included, on a half-day or full-day schedule. Sometimes, the elementary school has been further divided in a primary school (grades K–2 or Pre-K–2) and an upper or intermediate school (grades 3–6). Many districts have adopted a middle school philosophy in which grade 6 (sometimes grades 5 and 6) is housed in the middle school.

Regular Elementary Education

The elementary license usually covers K–6, sometimes K–8. Elementary school teachers are generalists who must be prepared to teach science, social studies, mathematics, and language arts. Art, music, physical education, library science, and technology may be part of their responsibility, or a specialty teacher may handle these areas. Elementary school teachers also must be prepared to accurately diagnose learning problems: A developmental problem will disappear, with additional help, as the student matures. However, a student who is disabled will require extra attention from special education teachers.

In some elementary schools, all teachers on a grade level have the same conference period, so they can plan instruction collaboratively. Others are departmentalized, so a teacher who is interested in and prefers math and science may teach math and science to all the second graders and another teacher may handle the reading and language arts instruction. Also, you can move within up to seven grade levels (depending on how the district is organized) in an elementary school. For example, if you would like a change from the curriculum you teach and want variety, you can switch from grade one to grade four if an opening exists and the principal approves it.

Teaching at the elementary level provides great satisfaction. Children grow up before your eyes. They stay in your school for five to seven years, and their older and younger siblings often know who you are. Janelle Barnow said, "When you are an elementary teacher, you are also a parent, a nurse, a bookkeeper, a disciplinarian, and a comforter." In the classroom with these youngsters every day, you become like a family for a year. You take your students on field trips, catch their colds, and worry with them about everything. Teachers can become very attached to their students, and that bond is wonderful and enriching. Some of your former students will even come back to visit you many years later due to the strength of a warm relationship.

Parent participation varies quite a bit of course, but elementary school is the level at which most families are involved with their children's education. Positive interaction with parents can support and reward your efforts in the classroom, but it is also very time consuming. In a large urban setting, you may become frustrated because the children have more problems and fewer involved parents. In a rural or suburban district, where parental involvement and support are high, you may be expected to attend evening meetings with parents and numerous PTA (Parent Teacher Association) functions.

As an elementary teacher, you spend the entire day with your class, which can be exhausting. Although you are given a planning period and time to eat lunch, the bulk of your day is spent with young people, who can be very demanding. You have very little interaction with other adults during the day, yet you must be able to cooperate with specialized teachers—the reading specialist, the art teacher, and so on—who are involved with students in your class. You must be able to work with children at different levels of development and from many different backgrounds, and you have to teach every subject that the state requires. All of this can add up to a demanding work schedule.

Even if you prefer a specific grade level in the K–6 school, you are likely to be placed wherever there is an opening for you that first year. Remember, as the new teacher in the school, you may have to take on the type of assignments that the teachers with more seniority don't necessarily prefer. Teaching any of the elementary grades will give you tremendous experience, even if you are teaching ten-year-olds when you actually prefer to build a career teaching first grade and specialize in reading. Chances are, if you perform well with the classroom you are given, your preferences will be taken into consideration as you build tenure at your school.

Primary Education

Primary education is offered as a separate license from elementary education in some states, giving you the chance to specialize in one of the following grade levels:

- ▶ pre-K
- ▶ kindergarten
- ▶ grade one
- ▶ grade two
- ▶ grade three

Primary education is similar to elementary education, but the young ages of the children make for unique challenges that a fifth or sixth grade teacher in an elementary school would not have to face.

At first glance, many people think primary education is easy, but this level can be the most challenging one in the system. If you are considering a specialty in primary education, visit a kindergarten or first grade class for a day—just for a quick reality check. It takes a special kind of person to organize these youngsters and to give them the tools to learn—first to read and then to find the information they need. Primary teachers often have to teach children how to put on and take off a coat, never mind reading, writing, and arithmetic.

Picture this: It is the first day of school. Your class consists of four- and five-year-olds. Some of them are very nervous about being away from home. One or two might be clinging to a parent, not willing to let go. Children may be crying—moms and dads, too. Your job is to line up the children to bring them into your classroom. You announce, "Line up, please," and nobody pays attention. The concept of lining up needs to be taught—forget about the first alphabet lesson! Some children even forget they are toilet trained, and others spill their lunches all over your new sweater. And to complicate events further, a few parents have decided to videotape this occasion for posterity.

Within a few days, however, the students are all seated at desks, learning letters, numbers, and your name—the magic has begun! In grade one, you are expected to teach students to read, write, and compute as well as set up a pattern of learning that will stay with them forever. Primary grade teachers may be the most influential people in the child's educational career, and a strong beginning is most important to a strong education.

The process of learning in a classroom setting often begins in the primary grades (for children who have not previously participated in early childhood education). Arguably, first grade teachers have the toughest job. With that said, it may be the most rewarding as well. Few milestones are as memorable for student, parent, and teacher than learning to read. Watch a first grade teacher unravel the mystery of language with a class of children. One by one, students figure out the code, and the reading process begins. This is truly an exciting time in the classroom and a great moment for a teacher.

Teaching Practice

Once you have decided to become a teacher, get involved in activities with children. For example, you can

- volunteer at the local YMCA, YWCA, a Girls or Boys Club, or another community agency that provides after-school programs for children.
- intern in a nursery school or daycare center.
- tutor a child in your neighborhood.
- volunteer as a tutor at a local school.
- be a camp counselor for your community, church, or synagogue.
- babysit for your relatives.

Any of these activities will provide excellent experience by giving you a chance to put your learning into action while strengthening your skills (and your resume).

The early primary grades are also physically demanding on teachers. Ask physical education teachers, who are on their feet all day long, which classes are the most tiring. Most will say kindergarten. In the beginning, teachers have to do everything for the children, rendering educating secondary to the role of disciplinarian, babysitter, and nurse. Most primary grade teachers will tell you to save your best and most fragile clothing for the weekend; the hands-on teaching required often means getting your hands—and clothing—dirty.

Middle School or Junior High School

Traditionally, students entered the junior high school after grade six to complete grades seven and eight, and sometimes nine; the junior high school was a small version of the high school. Students followed a schedule and subject matter similar to those of the high school. The newer middle school concept has been adopted in many districts. Middle schools usually house grades 6–8 (and sometimes grade nine) and are organized on the belief that students in these grades are unique and need opportunities, beyond purely academic pursuits, to explore vocational and avocational interests. Students are offered exploratories that expose them to many interesting intellectual or social and emotional activities. Middle school schedules often are built on blocks of time that can be manipulated to provide longer periods for certain activities during the school day. Additionally, teachers are often organized into teams, so a group of students shares the same teachers in the core curriculum areas. The team teachers meet periodically to discuss the intellectual, emotional, and social needs of the students. For more information about middle schools, visit the National Middle School Association's website at www.nmsa.org.

High School

High schools house grades 9–12, or 10–12, depending on the district. A few districts group grade nine in the middle or junior high school, and some house the ninth grade separately. The schedule of the high school day may vary. Traditionally, the school day was divided into six or seven 45- to 60-minute teaching periods. Recently, high schools have been experimenting with block schedules that divide the school day into as few as four periods or as many as ten or more periods. Some schools, such as one in Reynoldsburg, Ohio, are adventurous enough to offer their students schedules in both traditional and block formats.

Middle, Junior, or High School Subject Specialties

If you love a particular subject, then you may want to choose a subject area to specialize in at the middle school, junior high school, or high school level. Are you a history buff who knows every battle from the Civil War? Do you love to read and find yourself trying to encourage others to read with you? Are you very good in math? Do you have a mechanical mind and love working on your car? Ron Brunner, who teaches at Pioneer High School in rural western New York, selected high school physical education and health because he could spend the day doing something he loved—playing sports. If you want to become an expert in one field and share your passion with your students, teaching at the secondary level may be for you. There are many different subject areas you can select, such as:

- ▶ English and language arts
- ▶ mathematics
- ▶ physical education
- ▶ health
- ▶ social studies
- ▶ music
- ▶ art
- ▶ drama
- ▶ sciences
- ▶ computers
- ▶ home economics
- ▶ technical and vocational education
- ▶ education media

Schools keep adding more departments, and each one has subspecialties within the broad scope of the curriculum. The license for many of the academic departments commonly found in middle school, junior high school, and high school is usually for grades 7–12. Licenses for music, art, and physical education are often K–12. Certification requirements vary by state, but each specialty requires a separate license.

With a subject-area specialization, you could teach five variations of a subject within a department or, if it is needed, you could repeat the same class four times to different groups of students. You may be asked to teach a class that is not in your subject area (and if you are new, you must say yes). Some teachers thrive in this kind of environment, rewarded by the opportunity to delve into a subject and to share their interest in that subject with many different students.

Special Education

Special education is a demanding, yet very satisfying, area of specialization that is growing by leaps and bounds. The Bureau of Labor and Statistics projects that by 2005, there will be a 53% increase in the need for special education teachers throughout the country. Indeed, many local school districts are offering special stipends or signing bonuses to attract new teachers to fill their critical shortages of special education teachers. So, if you have a soft spot in your heart for children with special needs, consider making this your specialty.

The range of possibilities in this area is vast. The special education license is usually very broad, covering grades K–12. If you have this certification, a school district can place you in any number of settings. You can even work in a residential setting if impaired students are too disabled to come to a general education building. Most public schools house their own special education classes, but this is not always the case.

There are, of course, many types of disabilities. Whenever possible, students with disabilities are mainstreamed into a regular classroom for all or part of their school day. Students with many kinds of physical disabilities, for instance, can learn right along with the "regularly abled" students of the same age. However, other kinds of disabilities may require that students get special support, either part-time out of the regular classroom or in a special class. Depending on your state, you may be able to get a special license to handle, for instance, students who are visually impaired, students with orthopedic disabilities, children with behavioral disorders, and many others.

Special education teachers may work alone or with others to create Individualized Education Programs (IEP) for each of their students. An IEP is a written agreement between the parents and the school about what each child needs and what will be done to address those needs; IEPs are mandated by a federal law called the Individuals with Disabilities Education Act (IDEA).

Children classified as "learning disabled" often have equal or better natural intelligence than other students in the school; they just have a problem in the processing. They fall under federal special education laws, and teachers must follow an Individual Education Program (IEP) for each one of them. While there is some room for creativity, the plan must be fully implemented.

Pat Petrone, a special education teacher in Long Island, New York, has worked in both state institutions and public schools. She would not change her job, even though she has other certifications that would allow her to work in high profile or more financially rewarding positions in education. The growth that she sees in children makes her more committed to the belief that "every child can learn something, even if it is a small task that others take for granted, such as feeding themselves." Pat feels that she has been rewarded personally by the role she has played in helping her students make progress.

Because truly gifted youngsters also need special services, some states classify these students under the federal laws for special education, which means that the license for teaching gifted students may be classified as a special education license. In other states, gifted education requires a separate license.

Special Education Categories

While the areas of specialization within the broad heading of special education vary significantly from state to state, here is a list of several categories of special needs:

- Attention Deficit Disorder
- At Risk
- Autism
- Blind
- Deaf
- Deaf Blind
- Developmentally Delayed
- Hard of Hearing
- Mental Retardation: Mild/Moderate
- Mental Retardation: Severe/Profound
- Multiple Disabled
- Orthopedic Impairments
- Other Health Impairments
- Serious Emotional Disturbance

- Specific Learning Disabilities
- Speech or Language Impairments
- Traumatic Brain Injury
- Visually Impaired
- Cross-categorical
- Non-categorical

A special education license allows you to teach children with varied needs. For a student with a serious disability, you may be the one person who helps integrate the special education student into society. Motivating children who have disabilities to succeed often requires tremendous patience and energy. These children may need more repetitive teaching strategies or more intensive assistance, such as being accompanied to the bathroom or physically moved from place to place. The degree of these challenges varies among the subspecialty areas. Special education requires a deep commitment. If you like to help others in addition to teaching them, this is an excellent area of education for you. For more information about issues in special education, contact the Council for Exceptional Children's website at www.cec.sped.org.

Concentrations in Special Education

Most teacher education programs prepare you for a special education license that allows you to work with many different disabilities. However, some teacher education programs offer *concentrations* of courses in one of the specialized areas below.

Resource Room
Students who need support in a particular deficit area may be taken out of their regular classroom for several hours a week to study with a small group. Teaching in a resource room, you work with children who spend most of their day in a regular classroom but require modified instruction. Resource room teachers sometimes work as consultants for the students in the regular classroom with another instructor.

Self-Contained Classroom

Every school district has a different method of assigning students to a self-contained classroom. The class may include children with different problems, only children with physical disabilities, or only children with emotional or learning disabilities. As teacher of a self-contained classroom, you probably spend most of the day with the same class. Classes are sometimes cross-graded, and you may have a teacher's aide assisting you. The class size may be up to, but cannot exceed, 15 students.

Visually Impaired

As a teacher of visually impaired students, you may work in a school that specializes in this area or within a regular education setting, one-on-one or with small groups. You would prepare special materials for the students, help other instructors modify programs, and you would probably need to know Braille. You may need a specialized license to work with visually impaired students in some states.

Hearing Impaired

Hearing impaired children who need special services may be in a regular classroom setting or in a school that specializes in this area. As a teacher of hearing impaired students, you probably would need to know sign language and would help full-time classroom teachers modify their programs for your students. Working with students who are hearing impaired requires a specialized license in some states.

Physically Disabled

Some students cannot do any physical tasks on their own; they must be fed, bathed, and tended to during the day by school staff. These children, from infants to age 21, may have full-time nurses and very serious physical limitations that make them unable to attend regular public schools. Their classes generally are held away from the regular classrooms because of the students' special physical needs.

Reading Specialist

To make yourself more marketable, you may want to obtain a license in reading in addition to either regular education or special education. This license offers flexibility in K–12 assignments. The job is varied and interesting. As a reading specialist, you may work with gifted students or with students who have fallen behind. Some reading teachers work as *teacher trainers*, helping other staff members. Other reading teachers work with the school's administration to develop standardized reading programs for that school. You may get the chance to organize reading clubs and contests, book fairs, or special visits from children's books authors.

Kathy Megali, a New York City reading teacher, was an English major in college and started her career at NBC. She was not satisfied; some of her friends were teaching and very happy, so she decided to give it a try. She started as a classroom teacher and then left the profession for several years. She wanted to return to teaching but wanted to work with her passion—literature and books. She returned to college for additional training and became a reading specialist. Now she loves what she does and feels great satisfaction when she teaches a student to read.

Each district has its own standards and regulations about how reading teachers are used. The bottom line is that this license can help you get a job, especially if you use it to support a regular education or special education license. For more information, contact the International Reading Association's website at www.reading.org.

Bilingual Education

This area of specialization requires that you be *fluent in a language in addition to English*. You teach limited-English proficient (LEP) students subject matter in their native tongue while they learn to speak English. In New York City, for example, there are bilingual classes in Russian, Farsi, Korean, Japanese, Chinese, Spanish, Creole, and other languages. Bilingual teachers mostly work in elementary schools and middle schools.

In the past, bilingual educators were needed mainly in large urban areas in California, Texas, Florida, and New York. However, limited-English proficient students are now entering school districts that have never had them before so opportunities for bilingual educators are increasing all across the nation. For example, in nine states (Alabama, Alaska, Idaho, Nebraska, Nevada, North Carolina, Oregon, Tennessee, and Virginia) the LEP population grew by more than 50% between 1993 and 1996. Nationwide, the number of LEP students increased between 1990 and 1997 from 2.1 million to 3.5 million, according to the Council of Chief State School Officers. Due to the severe lack of qualified bilingual teachers, several federal, state, and local programs have been created to help people obtain teacher training and certification in bilingual education—see Chapter 3 for information about how to find these types of programs. To get more information about bilingual education, visit the National Clearinghouse for Bilingual Education's website at www.ncbe.gwu.edu.

English as a Second Language

As an English as a Second Language (ESL) teacher, you *do not have to speak another language*. Using specialized techniques, you work with small groups of students—who may speak any number of foreign languages—to teach them English. Often, your students change throughout the day, coming to you from their regular or bilingual classrooms for a few hours of ESL work every day. You may have the help of one or more teacher aides who speak the language of the students you are teaching. However, this is not always the case.

ESL teachers are needed at all the levels: pre-kindergarten, elementary, middle school, junior high school, and high school. Many states require that this service be provided for several years. Children who are born in the United States but live in a house where English is not spoken can be eligible for this service. For more information, contact the Teachers of English to Speakers of Other Languages, Inc. (TESOL). Their web address is www.tesol.org.

Physical Education

If you love to play sports and take part in other physical activities, you may be interested in pursuing a career as a physical education teacher. Physical education teachers at the elementary and high school levels have very different roles to fulfill. For example, if you want to become a physical education teacher in an elementary school, you would focus on helping your students to develop motor skills and to play organized games together. Running games are popular at this level. You may need to teach at more than one elementary school if each school has limited physical education requirements for their students (some schools offer gym classes only once or twice a week).

If you choose to teach physical education at the middle school or junior high school level, you will probably teach six or seven different classes each day. You may specialize in one area, such as sports, health, or dance or rotate areas throughout the school year. In high schools, physical education teachers may teach students a variety of team and individual sports, including swimming, weight training, and gymnastics. You will most likely be encouraged to become a coach for one or more sports activities that take place after regular school hours—and you will get additional pay for each coaching assignment. If you get intensely involved in extracurricular team sports, you may spend a lot of time traveling to other schools and cities for games, competitions, and tournaments. For more information, contact the National Association for Sport and Physical Education's website at www.aahperd.org/naspe/naspemain.html.

Music Education

As a teacher specializing in music, several opportunities are available to you, including band teacher, choral teacher, and orchestra teacher. Your duties as an elementary school music teacher would include introducing young children to the history and rhythms of music and guiding children in singing activities. In older elementary grades, students are often encouraged to join choirs or begin playing a musical instrument. Similar to physical education teachers in elementary schools, you may need to teach music classes in more than one school per day. That is because students often attend music class only once or twice a week at this level.

If you choose to become a music teacher at the middle school level, you will probably spend time teaching students basic music appreciation, choral singing, and conducting bands or orchestras. You may sponsor or organize special concerts throughout the year in which your students perform for the public.

At the high school level, music teachers teach regular classes in different types of music, just like the other high school teachers teach classes in their subject area. However, many music teachers have duties after regular school hours, such as directing student bands, orchestras, and chorales for plays, sports events, and concerts. For more information on music education careers, visit the National Association for Music Education's website at www.menc.org.

Computers/Technology Education

Teachers who specialize in computers or technology education often manage a resource room that contains computers or some other type of computer lab in their school. They may focus on training both students and teachers in the use of computers—helping teachers to integrate the use of technology into their lessons and helping students to learn how to use computers. The level of expertise varies among teachers in the computer/technology area. Some have a background in computer hardware and software and do the actual maintenance and troubleshooting of the school's computers, while others may have a more managerial role, assigning repairs to someone else. Non-teaching duties for computer/technology specialists vary from school to school, but you may be expected to manage equipment budgets, design or update school Web pages, and develop new technology plans or programs. Teaching duties in a computer lab may include coaching small groups of students, leading a full class, or coteaching different subjects with another teacher. For more information, contact the International Technology Education Association at www.iteawww.org.

Choosing Your Area of Specialization

Which area of specialization is right for you? Keep in mind as you consider this question that you may want to achieve teacher certifications in more than one area. For instance, you could choose to specialize as an elementary teacher and a reading teacher. Indeed, having more than one area of specialization and becoming certified in each area can become a big plus when you begin looking for your first teaching job.

To help you choose your area(s) of specialization, take the time to evaluate your interests and abilities: Do you prefer working with small children or teenagers? Are you more of a generalist in your thinking, or are you more interested in a specific instructional area? In any case, investigate every possibility, and be honest with yourself.

If you are still undecided about your preferred level or area of specialization when you enroll in a teacher education program, don't panic. Not all of your choices will be obvious at the outset, and you don't have to decide right away. Most programs offer opportunities to observe or volunteer in classrooms early on, long before the student teaching assignment.

OTHER TEACHING OPPORTUNITIES

In addition to the areas of specialization discussed above, you can gain teaching experience as a substitute teacher. Or perhaps you would like to have the flexibility of teaching distance learning courses via the Internet or through some other format. Take a look at the two following teaching opportunities to see if one of them will work for you.

Substitute Teacher

If it fits into your schedule, spending time as a substitute teacher can help you to decide which teaching area to specialize in and which type of school district you'd like to work in. Not only that, but it can be a nice source of income. Indeed, some substitute teachers in a mid-size to large city can earn $100 a day. Most states will allow you to become a substitute teacher if you have a bachelor's degree in any subject and if you pass their hiring procedures (some districts will do a background check, take your fingerprints, and want medical information). Some states will allow you to substitute teach even if you do not have a college degree, while others have more stringent requirements including passing a national teachers exam, so be sure to check your state's requirements by contacting your state education department (see Chapter 4 for contact information).

Substitute teachers follow the school calendar, so you wouldn't work during school holidays and breaks, or during the summer. As a substitute, you get to choose which days you want to work and in which schools to take assignments. Once you are on a school district's list as an approved substitute teacher, you will get phone calls alerting you to an assignment—often early in the morning of the day they want you to teach. At the time of the phone call, you can say yes or no to the offer. However, if you say no more than yes, you may find that you will get fewer offers in the future. Some districts have automated calling systems in place, so you interact with a computer rather than a human.

It is not unusual for a beginning teacher to substitute at many grade levels and in various subject matters; such exposure can give you first-hand experience in the various options available. Sherrye Dotson, director of curriculum for secondary education in Jacksonville, Texas, clearly remembers how her substitute teaching experience influenced her career choice: "I was substituting in a second grade classroom. The children had just come into class, and one little girl began to take off her coat. As she removed her coat, a necklace she was wearing got caught on something. As she pulled the coat off, her necklace broke and beads went flying all over the floor. Everyone stopped to help her and just as the last bead was picked up, she dropped them again. I spent the entire day picking up beads. I knew then that *I did not want to be an elementary school teacher.*" Sherrye became a high school mathematics teacher. She was substituting when a position became available to teach algebra and geometry. Even though she was only a few years older than her students, high school was where she felt most comfortable.

Distance Learning Teacher

The growing popularity of distance learning as an alternative way to gain an education has opened up new and exciting teaching options at the high school level as well as in higher education. New virtual high schools are being created all the time. One example is the Florida Virtual School, which is an online high school that was begun in 1997. For this program, teachers from various districts around the state of Florida apply to become online distance learning teachers. If they are accepted, they remain employees of their local district, their salaries and benefits continue to be set by their home district, but they are assigned to the Florida Virtual School to teach. The Florida Virtual School funds the teachers salaries by reimbursing the home district that pays the teacher's salary. For this type of job, you need to be willing to work non-traditional teacher hours. To learn more about the Florida Virtual School, visit their website at www.flvs.net.

As a distance learning teacher, you strive to provide your students with close personal interaction through electronic means (perhaps in a chat room on the Internet), through regular mail correspondence, or on the telephone. You assess your students' knowledge, skills, and performance just as rigorously as teachers in classroom-based classes.

Distance education teachers often find their work interesting, varied, and rewarding. In 2001, the American Federation of Teachers (AFT) reported in their survey of distance learning practitioners that the overwhelming majority enjoyed teaching through distance learning. In fact, 84% of respondents indicated they would readily teach another distance education course.

In the past, online learning for high school and junior high school students focused mainly on students who lived in rural areas far from traditional classroom buildings, migrants, and American students living abroad. However, today's online learning is expanding and several states now have entire programs available for students who wants to obtain his or her high school diploma online.

Since this is such a fast growing area of education, new opportunities are opening up all the time for distance learning teachers. To find out more about virtual schools, visit one or more of the following websites.

Elearners.com	www.elearners.com
Apex Learning, Inc. (Includes information about Advanced Placement [AP] Courses)	www.apexlearning.com
Class.com	www.class.com
Virtual.net.uy (Includes lists of online high schools and how to create an online course)	http://virtual.net.uy/nethigh.html
VR Schoolhouse	www.vrschoolhouse.com

You can also request a list of accredited high schools that offer diplomas by distance study from the Distance Education and Training Council. Request a free copy of the *DETC Directory of Accredited Institutions* by calling 202-234-5100.

You can find information about obtaining specialized education in teaching online classes and other programs for teachers who wish to specialize in distance learning at the Geteducated.com website: www.geteducated.com/articles/teach2000.htm. For example, you could get a certificate and master's degree in online teaching from California State University–Hayward (www.online.csuhayward.edu). The Extended Education Division of California State University, Hayward offers a four-course graduate certificate program in online teaching as well as a master's degree. Education requirements for distance learning teachers differ dramatically from one program to the next because this is such a newly emerging area of specialization.

A LOOK AT DIFFERENT EDUCATIONAL SETTINGS

You may have decided which area of teaching to specialize in, but there are other options to consider. Where do you want to live and work, and where are the jobs?

Public Or Private School?

While the vast majority of teachers teach in public schools, you may also want to consider the possibility of teaching in a private school. A brief description of each setting will help you decide which one is more appropriate for you.

Consider several factors before deciding whether to apply to teach in a public or a private school. First, private school salaries may or may not be comparable to those in the public schools. Some private schools pay teachers more than public schools while others pay much less. Public school salaries are normally presented on a salary schedule that reflects length of service and advanced degrees. You should inquire into private school salaries so you can compare beginning salaries and increases over a period of time and find out how the school remunerates for advanced degrees.

Another issue is job security. Most state laws allow districts to grant teachers tenure, often after three to five continuous years of service. Barring a serious decline in student enrollment or a serious breach of contract, you may reasonably expect continuous employment in public schools. In a private school, you may have to renew and renegotiate your salary and benefits each year. Regardless of whether they provide expectations for long-term employment or have salary schedules comparable to those of the public schools, private schools have other desirable factors to consider, such as the size of your class and the kind of students you teach. Your talents and desires must match the education setting.

Traditional Public Schools

A public school system is open to all students who reside in a given community. Because the U.S. Constitution failed to mention education, the responsibility to provide a public education was established in state constitutions and defined by state laws. The money to run the schools comes from the local, state, and federal government. Therefore, the government supervises almost all functions of the school (curriculum, teacher certification, special education programs, vocational programs, test scores, school attendance, and teacher tenure).

Every state has established a department of education that supervises education within the state and serves as a liaison between the local district and the federal government. This department ensures that the school year has the required number of days in attendance (typically between 175 and 185 days). Each state has a recommended or required curriculum, and a statewide assessment is usually administered at several grade levels. Some states, including New York and Texas, require students to pass exit examinations in grade 12 before they can be awarded diplomas. Finally, the state department of education accredits a district's or a school's program so that teachers, parents, and students can rest assured that their school district or school meets certain quality standards.

Charter Schools

Charter schools are public schools that are freed from many state and local regulations and rules but are held accountable for improving student achievement. Thus far, over 2,100 charter schools have been formed in the 36 states that have passed charter school authorizing legislation. Many charter schools have atypical grade configurations (K–3, K–8). Some teachers choose to teach in charter schools because of the school's innovative approaches to education, their high academic standards, small class size, or because the charter school's educational philosophies are in line with their own.

Research reports released in 2001 from the U.S. Department of Education show that charter schools are actually helping other public schools and districts to improve. The reports are entitled *Challenge and Opportunity: The Impact of Charter Schools on Districts* and *A Study of Charter School Accountability*. Copies of these reports are available by calling 1-877-4ED-PUBS.

The first report shows that school districts are changing their educational services and operations in response to the creation of charter schools in those districts—suggesting that competition can play a positive role in helping to improve all public schools. The second report shows that strong accountability can lead to better instruction and improved schools. The report argues that traditional school districts can learn important lessons from the charter school experience about how to hold all public schools accountable for results.

Arizona leads the nation in its number of charter schools, with nearly 350 schools currently in operation, followed by California (234), Michigan (over 175), Texas (over 150), and Florida (112). Charter schools vary greatly from state to state and school to school, so if you are interested in teaching in a charter school, do some research on those that are available in your area. To find out more about charter schools and to find links to a list of charter schools in your state, visit the U.S. Charter Schools website at www.uscharterschools.org.

Private Schools

Private schools may be similar to public schools educationally, but one major difference exists: Private schools do not receive funding from state or federal sources. Therefore, they do not have to follow all the same rules and regulations as the public schools. Each private school operates independently, but its curriculum must be approved by the appropriate state department of education.

Private schools may be endowed or supported by a religious affiliation. They usually charge tuition, which may be substantial. Some schools offer student scholarships, and some have flexible tuition policies. A private school has a unique student population, because they can accept or refuse admission to students, whereas public schools must take in all residents within the district.

Many private schools' education programs prepare the students for college. Some offer a classical education, rather than the traditional liberal arts education offered in most public schools; these schools prepare students for elite U.S. colleges and universities. The pressure for students to achieve is intense. Military schools demand academic achievement along with physical training and strict discipline. Other schools may have an exploratory philosophy or specialize in a unique type of child, such as gifted youngsters. Teachers in these environments must follow the program set up by the school. Staff members may have special training or hold advanced degrees.

Religious Affiliation Schools

Private religious schools offer basic education in mathematics, science, communication arts, social studies, and all other subjects required by the state. Religious instruction and practice supplement this traditional program. Religious schools differ from other private schools because they attract students who usually, but not always, have a similar religious affiliation. Dr. Roger Callan, who has worked in both public high schools and high schools with religious affiliation, says, "I enjoyed the religious environment because there was a greater caring and a warmer atmosphere. There is a core set of values. If you subscribe to it, it's an accepting and comfortable place. Virtually everyone has had a core set of experiences too. They've gone through the same rituals."

The popularity of Catholic schools, especially in some regions of the country cannot be ignored. If you are of the Catholic faith, or just want to find out more about teaching in a Catholic private school, contact the National Catholic Education Association, which is the central clearinghouse for information for and about Catholic school teachers in America. Their members serve over 7.5 million students worldwide. You can visit their website at www. ncea.org. They publish an annual statistical report that presents information about Catholic school enrollment and staffing patterns for grades P-K–12. Statistics include enrollment by grade level, ethnicity, and religious affiliation, and ranking of dioceses with largest enrollments. The report is called *U.S. Catholic Elementary and Secondary Schools 2000–2001* and it costs $18 for non-members.

City, Town, or Country

Sharp differences exist among urban, suburban, and rural school districts. Your happiness in the teaching profession may be profoundly affected by where you decide to teach. In addition to the settings discussed below, keep in mind the option of becoming a distance learning teacher—you may find that your own home computer can become your setting for teaching.

Urban Schools

Urban schools have been adversely affected by the changing demographics in this country. Many urban schools have been able to maintain a high level of student achievement; however, as Jonathan Kozol's *Savage Inequalities* (HarperPerennial, 1992) revealed, many are in crisis. Middle-class flight from the city has decreased the tax base necessary to adequately pay teachers, maintain facilities, and provide appropriate and current resources.

Teaching in an urban school is a unique and demanding challenge. Students in urban schools tend to be more ethnically diverse and more likely to be affected by low socioeconomic factors than their rural and suburban counterparts. Also, many students in urban districts start school with fewer of the skills they need to be successful.

Urban districts tend to have a large bureaucracy and centralized control. This organizational structure decreases your flexibility as a teacher in the classroom. Teachers typically follow a district-adopted curriculum and use district-adopted materials in their classrooms. In addition, many inner-city parents feel disenfranchised from the school system and therefore do not actively participate in their children's education.

Despite these problems, many teachers in urban districts find their jobs very satisfying. Urban or inner-city schools often provide a wonderful opportunity for beginning teachers because more jobs are available in a large district. Lynda Sposato has been teaching in New York City schools for more than 25 years and wouldn't consider working in another environment. "It is a daily challenge. Each year is completely different because the children are different. There is no boredom. I get tremendous satisfaction working with these students. I always get students who come back and tell me how I affected them. That counts!"

Suburban Schools

Suburban school districts have boomed since the urban flight of the late 1950s and 1960s. These districts tend to have more money to spend on education than rural or urban districts and therefore have newer facilities, smaller class sizes, and more class resources and materials. Parents tend to be actively involved in the school and very demanding of both teachers and administrators. Traditionally, the suburban district had a rather homogeneous student body, but that population is changing as suburban communities become more racially and ethnically diverse.

Rural Schools

Rural school districts tend to have smaller student populations, fewer resources, and fewer opportunities than their urban and suburban counterparts. Reflections of rural America, they also tend to be more conservative (socially and politically) and more racially and ethnically homogeneous. Ron Brunner believes that rural schools are safer than urban or suburban districts: The community is very family-oriented; many students live on farms, which promotes a strong work ethic. Students are respectful toward the staff, and the community is relatively stable. Ron feels that he is a vital member of the community, and he writes a column for a local newspaper about the athletic teams he coaches. Generally, the school is the pride of the community and garners the support of not only parents but also the entire community. Rural teachers typically have more control over what is taught in the classroom and which materials are selected for their classes.

SALARIES—WHAT TEACHERS EARN

Although it is true that few people will say that they went into teaching for the salary, you can earn a decent living by becoming a teacher. Indeed, some teachers who have taught for many years and have achieved additional education and more than one certification, can earn quite a respectable salary ($60,000–$70,000 and above).

As of July 2001, Salary.com reports that an elementary school teacher in the United States with 15 years experience is expected to earn a median base salary of $41,489, while a high school teacher with 15 years experience is expected to earn a median base salary of $43,261.

Average Salaries

The American Federation of Teachers (AFT) studied U.S. teachers' salaries and published the results in *Survey and Analysis of Salary Trends 2000*. The study shows a wide range both within and among states, demonstrated by the figures in the following chart, which are arranged by rank within each region. Keep in mind that the salaries are as varied as the cost of living in each state. For example, it may cost you four times as much for housing in New York as it does in Alabama.

The national average teacher's salary during the 1999–2000 school year, as reported by the AFT, was $41,820. That figure represents the difference between the lowest average salary (South Dakota, at $29,072) and highest average salary (Connecticut, at $52,410). According to AFT figures, the average teacher's *starting* salary in the United States was $27,989.

The National Education Association (NEA) reports similar average salaries. They report that Connecticut has the second to highest average salary ($51,780), with New Jersey edging into the top spot for the 1999–2000 school year with an estimated average salary of $52,174. They also list South Dakota as having the lowest average teacher salary ($29,072).

Remember that these salaries are averages of *salary ranges*. Some teachers earn more, and some earn less. In addition to salary, most school districts pay into a retirement system and offer benefits such as medical insurance as part of the employment package.

SALARY TRENDS IN THE UNITED STATES
BEGINNING AND AVERAGE TEACHER SALARY IN 1999-2000
RANKED BY AVERAGE SALARY WITHIN REGION

State	Average Salary	Beginning Salary
NEW ENGLAND		
Connecticut	$52,410	$30,466
Rhode Island	48,138	27,286
Massachusetts	46,955	30,330
New Hampshire	37,734	24,650
Vermont	36,402	25,791
Maine	35,561	22,942
MIDEAST		
New York	$51,020	$31,910
New Jersey	50,878	30,480
Pennsylvania	48,321	30,185
District of Columbia	48,304	30,185
Delaware	44,435	30,945
Maryland	43,720	28,612
GREAT LAKES		
Michigan	$48,729	$28,545
Illinois	46,480	30,151
Indiana	41,855	26,553
Ohio	41,713	23,597
Minnesota	40,678	25,666
Wisconsin	39,897	25,344
PLAINS		
Kansas	$36,282	$25,252
Iowa	35,678	25,275
Missouri	35,660	25,977
Nebraska	33,237	22,923
North Dakota	29,863	20,422
South Dakota	29,072	21,889
SOUTHWEST		
Texas	$37,567	$28,400
Arizona	34,824	25,613
New Mexico	32,713	25,042
Oklahoma	29,525	24,025
SOUTHEAST		
North Carolina	39,404	27,968
Virginia	38,992	26,783
Florida	36,722	25,132
Alabama	36,689	29,790
Tennessee	36,328	27,228
Kentucky	36,255	24,753
South Carolina	36,081	25,215
West Virginia	35,011	23,829
Arkansas	33,691	22,599

Louisiana	33,109	25,738
Mississippi	31,897	23,040
ROCKY MOUNTAINS		
Colorado	$39,073	$24,875
Idaho	35,155	20,915
Utah	34,946	23,273
Wyoming	34,188	24,168
Montana	32,121	20,969
FAR WEST		
California	$47,680	$32,190
Alaska	46,481	33,676
Oregon	45,103	29,733
Nevada	43,083	28,734
Hawaii	41,292	29,204
Washington	41,047	26,514
OUTLYING AREAS		
Guam	$34,947	$26,917
Virgin Islands	34,784	22,751
Puerto Rico	24,980	18,700
U.S. AVERAGE	$41,820	$27,989

Source: American Federation of Teachers, annual survey of state departments of education.

How Your Salary Grows

Teachers employed in a public school setting are considered government employees. There are generally salary steps with yearly increments. In some districts, it may take 25 years to reach the top step. As you gain credit for each year, you move up the salary scale.

Most districts also give you credit for courses completed. This benefit varies from district to district, but the concept is the same. As you continue your education and earn more credits, you earn more money. Tom Shea, a principal by day and law student by night, earned more credits toward his teaching salary after he earned his degree.

There is more good news. Teachers can earn additional money by helping with extracurricular or co-curricular activities. Student council government needs supervision, teams need coaches, and plays need directors. If you have a hobby that you'd like to share with students, maybe you can sponsor an after-school club. Any of these activities add to your base salary.

HIRING TRENDS

The job market for teachers fluctuates by subject area, year, and geographical location. There are about 15,000 school districts nationwide, and each local school board can determine which teaching positions they want to add or delete. Sometimes, the size of a class is set by board policy or by contract. Therefore, as the community changes, so will the demographics of the school. Many suburban communities were developed as cities expanded. Young children needed schools, which were built to accommodate those needs. As the children grew and left home, the schools changed and, in many areas, were closed.

The Bureau of Labor Statistics' *Occupational Outlook Handbook* recently indicated that employment growth for secondary school teachers will be more rapid than for kindergarten and elementary school teachers due to student enrollments, but job outlook will vary by geographic area and subject specialty.

Indeed, particular areas of specialization are in very high demand. Several states offer free teacher education programs for people with education or experience in bilingual education, ESL, special education, math, or science. Yes, they will actually *pay tuition* for people who want to train for one of these jobs. In return, the teacher must guarantee one or more years of service to the school system. This is a good opportunity for someone entering the teaching profession for the first time, a teacher's aide who wants to advance, or a teacher who wants to become certified in a new area. See the state department of education's website (listed in Chapter 4) to find out about such programs if you are interested in teaching in one of these critical areas. If you are in school, your job placement office or career services department also may assist you in finding such programs.

On the next four pages, you will find a map and charts that illustrate the need for teachers in each area of specialization within eleven geographic regions of the United States. This information was provided by Dr. Charles A. Marshall, Executive Director of the American Association for Employment in Education (AAEE). The information was the most recent data available when this book was published. However, you should keep abreast of trends by staying in close touch with your college or university placement office.

1999 TEACHER SUPPLY AND

Region codes: 1—Northwest, 2—West, 3—Rocky Mountain, 4—Great Plains/Midwest, 5—South
Demand codes: 5.00 - 4.21 = Considerable shortage; 4.20 - 3.41 = Some Shortage; 3.40 - 2.61 =

TEACHING FIELD

	1	2	3	4	5
Agriculture	2.00	3.67	4.00	3.86	3.25
Art/Visual	2.45	2.55	2.40	2.96	2.80
Audiology	3.60	3.50	3.00	4.08	4.00
Bilingual Education	4.75	4.41	4.60	4.17	4.89
Business Education	3.60	3.13	3.33	3.28	2.63
Computer Science/Education	3.71	3.67	3.50	4.39	4.29
Counselor Education	3.25	2.96	3.00	4.14	3.56
Dance Education	2.00	3.00	—	2.40	2.67
Driver Education	2.00	3.00	—	3.44	2.11
Elementary—Pre-K	2.88	3.35	3.25	2.92	2.97
Elementa—Kindergarten	2.71	3.59	3.33	2.79	3.09
Elementa—Primary	2.81	3.81	3.22	2.69	2.97
Elementa—Intermediate	2.79	3.64	3.38	2.91	3.17
English/Language Arts	2.89	3.47	3.00	3.33	2.97
English as a Second Lang. (ESL)	3.77	4.23	4.20	4.17	4.16
Gifted/Talented Education	3.00	3.80	3.00	3.65	3.29
Health Education	2.50	3.07	3.25	2.51	2.27
Home Economics/Consumer Sci.	3.25	3.13	3.50	3.94	3.15
Journalism	2.80	3.13	—	2.84	2.73
Languages—Classics	2.40	2.71	3.67	3.31	3.13
Languages—French	2.44	2.92	3.60	3.45	4.43
Languages—German	2.41	3.00	3.25	3.44	3.11
Languages—Japanese	3.17	3.00	3.33	3.10	3.71
Languages—Spanish	3.94	3.96	4.20	4.05	4.00
Library—Science/Media Tech.	2.83	3.71	3.67	3.76	3.73
Mathematics	4.16	4.56	4.44	4.21	4.30
Music—Instrumental	3.61	3.54	3.60	3.75	3.29
Music—Vocal	3.50	3.20	3.60	3.77	4.23
Physical Education	2.50	3.00	2.67	2.55	2.35
Psychologist (School)	3.50	3.89	3.50	4.00	3.30
Reading	3.07	3.88	3.50	3.37	3.54
Science—Biology	3.42	4.28	3.86	3.94	4.03
Science—Chemistry	3.63	4.55	4.00	4.30	4.31
Science—Earth/Physical	3.25	4.41	3.75	3.91	4.03
Science—General	3.38	4.24	4.00	3.97	3.97
Science—Physics	3.67	4.59	3.80	4.32	4.48
Social—Sciences/Studies	2.35	2.25	2.56	2.44	2.36
Social Work (School)	3.25	3.38	2.00	3.43	2.67
Special Ed.—Behavioral Disorders	4.33	4.75	4.60	4.49	4.40
Special Ed.—Hearing Impaired	4.50	4.89	4.75	4.33	4.14
Special Ed.—Learning Disability	4.36	4.74	4.60	4.45	4.33
Special Ed.—Mentally Hand.	4.57	4.83	4.40	4.37	4.41
Special Ed.—Multiple Hand.	4.75	4.80	4.00	4.62	4.41
Special Ed.—Physically Impaired	4.57	5.00	4.00	4.26	4.50
Special Ed.—Visually Impaired	3.50	5.00	4.33	4.14	4.57
Speech/Drama/Theatre	2.53	2.77	2.00	3.04	2.77
Speech Pathology	4.57	4.46	4.00	4.67	4.06
Technology Education	4.25	3.91	3.00	4.61	3.78
COMPOSITE	**3.17**	**3.83**	**3.69**	**3.55**	**3.56**
Number of Participants	23	42	10	86	48

*Questionnaires returned without indication of region were computed in the national averages only. Total of

DEMAND BY FIELD AND REGION

Central, 6—Southeast, 7—Great Lakes, 8—Middle Atlantic, 9—Northeast, 10—Alaska; and 11—Hawaii.
Balanced; 2.60 - 1.81 = Some Surplus; 1.80 - 1.00 = Considerable Surplus

REGION						NATIONAL		CHANGE
6	7	8	9	10	11	1999	1998	
3.45	4.00	3.33	3.00	—	2.00	3.50	3.48	0.02
2.86	2.82	2.63	2.63	3.00	2.00	2.78	2.71	0.07
4.00	3.91	3.38	2.67	—	—	3.73	4.10	-0.37
4.30	4.12	3.27	4.25	—	—	4.32	4.48	-0.16
3.18	3.54	2.94	3.20	—	2.50	3.16	2.86	0.30
4.45	3.95	4.00	4.50	—	—	4.14	4.00	0.14
3.36	3.52	2.96	3.27	5.00	—	3.40	3.25	0.15
3.20	2.55	3.00	3.00	—	—	2.76	2.48	0.28
3.00	3.00	2.86	4.00	—	—	2.91	2.63	0.28
3.11	2.90	2.34	2.84	—	2.00	2.88	2.72	0.16
3.21	2.81	2.31	2.67	3.00	2.00	2.89	2.69	0.20
3.27	2.65	2.36	2.40	3.00	2.00	2.86	2.63	0.23
3.34	2.91	2.44	2.68	3.00	3.00	3.00	2.74	0.26
3.30	2.96	2.55	2.68	—	3.00	3.05	2.81	0.24
4.06	3.89	3.50	4.60	—	2.50	3.98	3.89	0.09
3.94	3.57	3.43	3.00	—	—	3.56	3.35	0.21
2.43	2.34	2.36	3.17	—	—	2.49	2.31	0.18
3.67	3.87	3.33	4.00	—	2.00	3.57	3.15	0.42
2.88	2.85	3.17	3.67	—	—	2.90	2.80	0.10
3.61	3.24	3.07	4.00	—	1.00	3.23	3.17	0.06
3.55	3.31	3.22	3.31	—	1.00	3.29	3.24	0.05
3.44	3.02	3.25	3.33	—	1.00	3.16	3.07	0.09
3.63	3.62	3.29	3.67	—	1.00	3.32	3.60	-0.28
4.24	4.16	3.73	4.00	—	—	4.04	3.86	0.18
3.86	3.67	3.83	3.40	—	—	3.69	3.61	0.08
4.33	4.13	3.85	4.08	—	2.50	4.18	4.00	0.18
3.29	3.21	2.82	3.27	—	2.00	3.35	3.25	0.10
3.18	3.30	2.84	3.36	—	1.00	3.31	3.19	0.12
2.68	2.47	2.24	2.27	—	1.50	2.54	2.32	0.22
3.41	3.76	2.77	3.40	—	—	3.51	3.58	-0.07
3.57	3.37	3.19	3.64	—	3.00	3.43	3.30	0.13
4.07	3.71	3.63	4.09	—	3.00	3.88	3.71	0.17
4.20	4.17	3.93	4.21	—	2.00	4.17	4.10	0.07
3.93	3.88	3.78	4.12	—	1.50	3.90	3.83	0.07
4.06	3.73	3.59	3.95	—	3.00	3.86	3.71	0.15
4.19	4.43	4.08	4.22	—	2.00	4.26	4.17	0.09
2.70	2.44	2.21	2.61	—	2.00	2.45	2.29	0.16
3.33	3.33	2.64	3.33	—	—	3.20	3.22	-0.02
4.66	4.23	4.10	4.29	—	2.50	4.39	4.39	0.00
4.55	3.73	4.05	4.00	—	2.00	4.25	4.27	-0.02
4.56	4.15	4.09	4.15	—	2.00	4.36	4.30	0.06
4.47	4.27	3.97	4.08	—	2.00	4.33	4.23	0.10
4.45	4.22	3.85	4.27	—	1.00	4.35	4.34	0.01
4.58	4.00	3.86	4.09	—	1.00	4.28	4.29	-0.01
4.54	4.25	3.82	3.86	—	1.00	4.18	4.10	0.08
2.85	2.80	2.67	4.00	—	—	2.84	2.74	0.10
4.00	4.38	3.76	3.67	—	—	4.18	4.37	-0.19
3.91	4.14	3.69	3.86	—	—	4.03	4.16	-0.13
3.62	**3.35**	**3.20**	**3.48**	**3.40**	**2.07**	**3.47**	**3.30**	**0.17**
114	115	85	33	1	2	559*	585*	

regional participants does not equal national total.

RELATIVE DEMAND BY TEACHING AREA—NATIONAL

	1999	+/- 0.1*	1998	1997	3-Year Trend
Teaching Fields with Considerable Shortage (5.00–4.21)					
Special Education—Behavioral Disorders	4.39		4.48	4.34	0
Special Education—Learning Disability	4.36		4.30	4.21	+
Special Education—Multiple Handicapped	4.35		4.34	4.25	+
Special Education—Mentally Handicapped	4.33	+.10	4.23	4.20	+
Bilingual Education	4.32	-.16	4.48	4.34	0
Special Education—Physically Impaired	4.28		4.29	4.23	0
Science—Physics	4.26		4.17	4.09	+
Special Education—Hearing Impaired	4.25		4.27	4.21	0
Teaching Fields with Some Shortage (4.20–3.41)					
Mathematics	4.18	+.18	4.00	3.81	+
Special Education—Visually Impaired	4.18		4.10	4.08	+
Speech Pathology	4.18	-.19	4.37	4.34	0
Science—Chemistry	4.17		4.10	4.04	+
Computer Science Education	4.14	+.14	4.00	3.70	+
Languages—Spanish	4.04	+.18	3.86	3.72	+
Technology Education	4.03	-.13	4.16	4.02	0
English as a Second Language (ESL)	3.98		3.89	4.01	0
Science—Earth/Physical	3.90		3.83	3.70	+
Science—Biology	3.88	+.17	3.71	3.62	+
Science—General	3.86	+.15	3.71	3.64	+
Audiology	3.73	-.37	4.10	4.06	0
Library Science/Media Technology	3.69		3.61	3.52	+
Home Economics/Family and Consumer Science	3.57	+.42	3.15	3.09	+
Gifted/Talented Education	3.56	+.21	3.35	3.36	0
Psychologist (School)	3.51		3.58	3.58	0
Agriculture	3.50		3.48	3.17	+
Reading	3.43	+.13	3.30	3.19	+
Teaching Fields with Balanced Supply and Demand (3.40–2.61)					
Counselor Education	3.40	+.15	3.25	3.25	0
Music—Instrumental	3.35	+.10	3.25	3.11	+
Languages—Japanese	3.32	-.28	3.60	3.54	0
Music—Vocal	3.31	+.12	3.19	3.02	+
Languages—French	3.29		3.24	3.08	+
Languages—Classics	3.23		3.17	3.14	+
Social Work (School)	3.20		3.22	3.13	0
Business Education	3.16	+.30	2.86	2.69	+
Languages—German	3.16		3.07	3.07	0
English/Language Arts	3.05	+.24	2.81	2.64	+
Elementary—Intermediate	3.00	+.26	2.74	2.54	+
Driver Education	2.91	+.28	2.63	2.59	+
Journalism	2.90	+.10	2.80	2.68	+
Elementary—Kindergarten	2.89	+.20	2.69	2.50	+
Elementary—Pre-Kindergarten	2.88	+.16	2.72	2.56	+
Elementary—Primary	2.86	+.23	2.63	2.44	+
Speech/Drama/Theatre	2.84	+.10	2.74	2.63	+
Art/Visual	2.78		2.71	2.53	+
Dance Education	2.76	+.38	2.48	2.45	+
Teaching Fields with Some Surplus (2.60–1.81)					
Physical Education	2.54	+.22	2.32	2.11	+
Health Education	2.49	+.18	2.31	2.31	0
Social Sciences/Studies	2.45	+.16	2.29	2.05	+
Teaching Fields with Considerable Surplus (1.80–1.00)					
None					
Composite	**3.47**	**+.17**	**3.30**	**3.19**	**+**

*One-year change (1998–1999) with difference values of .10 or greater.

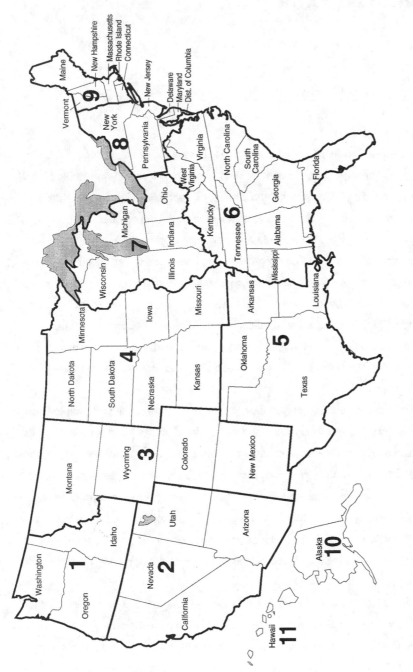

1=*Northwest;* **2**=*West;* **3**=*Rocky Mountain;* **4**=*Great Plains/Midwest;*
5=*South Central;* **6**=*Southeast;* **7**=*Great Lakes;* **8**=*Middle Atlantic;*
9=*Northeast;* **10**=*Alaska;* **11**=*Hawaii*

Source: American Association for Employment in Education. Reprinted with permission from
AAEE, 1998 Report, *Teacher Supply and Demand.*

THE INSIDE TRACK

Who: Joellen Piskitel

What: Music Teacher

Where: Oakland, California

INSIDER'S STORY

I have always loved music, so when it came time to pursue a career, I decided that teaching music would be a great way to use my skills while being involved with students and learning. I received both a bachelor's and a master's degree in music, plus a certificate that licenses me to teach music for kindergarten through twelfth grade.

In 40 years of teaching, I have taught many different students at a variety of levels. I have taught several courses at the college level, and I have also taught private music lessons in piano, organ, and voice. The most challenging experience I had was as music specialist in a private school where I taught music classes from kindergarten through eighth grade. The job required me to adjust rapidly to different age groups, which was sometimes difficult when an eighth grade class followed a kindergarten. The subject matter and level of proficiency of the two age groups are so different that it was sometimes hard to switch gears.

Teaching a secondary subject is challenging because it takes longer to get to know the students since you only teach them for about an hour, once or twice a week. Also, it's harder to establish yourself as an authority figure while establishing a fun rapport with the kids at the same time. But, after learning some strategies to deal with this challenge, I realized that I was lucky to be able to follow the students along from year to year and to get to know them as they grew, matured, and became more accomplished. I got to keep in contact with many of my students for longer than most classroom teachers, and I found that I really enjoyed hearing from students who had graduated then returned to share their lives with me.

I discovered that, in many ways, I needed to be even more thoroughly prepared than a classroom teacher. It's important to understand how to plan short, fun, and challenging lessons that last just the right amount of time. In addition, interacting with classroom teachers can take some practice. Sharing lessons and ideas, especially when other teachers see your class as secondary to the core subjects (reading, writing, math, and so on) that they teach can be a challenge. I found that the best way to manage this relationship is to include them. I followed what the classroom teachers were teaching and adapted the music lessons to fit in with their subject matter. For example, if the students were studying antebellum history, I would teach folk ballads, spirituals, and patriotic songs from that period. This strategy also helped engage the students as they began to make connections between the classroom materials and the music as primary resources.

This is one reason why it's so important for a specialist, whether she is teaching art, health, or computers, to make sure that she communicates clearly what the value of the secondary subject is to students, to other teachers, and particularly to the administration. This communication is especially important in the arts because they often get neglected in curriculum and budget planning. To help myself in this area, I quickly learned how to write grants to supplement the meager budgets provided to me for music.

All these challenges, however, are well worth it. It's wonderful to see the excitement in a child, or even an adult's face when he "gets" something I'm teaching. It's also really interesting to present a rather complex musical idea to a child and find that it is not so complex to a child, with a young, absorbent mind, ready to soak up the world. I learned that children can do so much more than we think they are capable of; you simply have to work hard to find out the best way for you to impart your knowledge so that they can absorb it and take it with them.

CHAPTER two

ALL ABOUT TEACHER EDUCATION PROGRAMS

Many steps are involved in becoming a teacher. One of the most basic steps is to find out which type of teacher education programs are available to you. Then, you need to select the program that will meet the future demands of your profession. This chapter explains the requirements common to most teacher education programs in the United States, offers tips on how to select the one that's right for you, and presents one undergraduate and one graduate sample program.

BEFORE YOU can begin your career as a teacher, you must acquire the necessary education. The good news is that many routes exist for you to get the teaching education you need. Depending on your current educational background, this could mean obtaining a four-year college degree from an accredited teacher education program. If you already hold a college degree but it isn't in the education field, you can enroll in a teacher education graduate program or may only need to take a few specific education courses at a institution approved by your state department of education. Another option available to you is distance learning, which enables you to learn in your own home at your own pace.

While you have to complete a certain amount of teacher education in order to become a certified teacher, you don't always need to obtain your full certification in order to land your first full-time teaching job. This is especially true in urban areas where there is often a high demand for teachers. See the section entitled "Alternative Teacher Education Programs" that appears in this chapter, as well as the alternative education and certification sections in Chapters 3 and 4 for more information about these options.

If you are in high school and are debating which route to take to become a teacher, keep in mind that you can choose a bachelor's degree teacher education program in your area of interest or you can select a more specialized major in science or math, for example, and then go on for a graduate degree with a concentration in education. Either way, you get *specialized training in education* that will serve you well once you become a teacher.

Choosing a teacher education program is not an easy task, because education is in the midst of systemic reform; some experts and practitioners predict that schools will change radically in the near future. Some predict the demise of the four-year high school, and some believe education will completely break out of the traditional classroom. So, when you are looking for a teacher education program, factor in how much each program is focused on the needs of the future.

CHANGES IN TEACHER EDUCATION

Several major changes in both theory and practice are turning the traditional classroom into a more exciting learning environment. These changes include new instructional materials, technology, and understanding of how children learn. These elements have changed the way teachers instruct students, and the training program you select should provide you with information and opportunities to learn about and experience these changes.

Instructional Materials

Just a few years ago, every student had a textbook, and every teacher had a teacher's edition of that book and possibly a workbook for reinforcement of key concepts. Using a formal lesson plan, teachers would assign a chapter to read on Monday, provide several worksheets to complete and grade in class during the week, and then give a chapter test on Friday.

Today, teachers still use textbooks, but the books come with kits containing multiple resources such as videos, CD-ROMs, and software to use in their classrooms. Teachers are expected to incorporate these materials into their lessons, selecting the most appropriate ones for each specific group of students. Planning lessons to meet the needs of every student is more complicated and time-consuming than ever before.

It is essential that you begin your teaching career with an understanding of the kinds of materials that are available and how they should be used. You will most likely be exposed to a variety of these resources in your teacher education program. In fact, your practical classroom experience (known as student teaching, directed teaching, or practicum) should provide you with ample opportunities to use a variety of modern resources and materials.

Technology

Technology is changing all aspects of society, including education. The Internet has completely transformed how people gain information, perform research, interact with others (via e-mail and chat rooms) and purchase goods and services.

Students today can receive and transmit assignments to their teachers using e-mail. The research capabilities of today's students (and teachers) appear limitless because the knowledge of the world sits at their fingertips in the form of a personal computer, a modem, and an Internet connection. Take a close look at how technology is integrated into the teacher education programs you are considering. You must be prepared to use this medium in your classroom.

In some locations, the classroom of tomorrow is already here today, and that virtual classroom is transforming the way children learn. David Howe, an environmental educator, teaches students through a distance learning program from Spokane, Washington. From his home base in Spokane, he can provide interactive instruction for students at many different locations. In fact, his courses are broadcast to students from a dozen different cultural backgrounds in an area encompassing half the northern hemisphere. With the flick of a switch, he is able to show them the latest shuttle launch or Mars landing, many times when it is actually happening. However, technology is not without its drawbacks. David says, "I do miss the teacher-student relationship—the personal touch of being in the classroom with the students."

Students' Learning Process

Researchers are discovering new ways that students learn and process information. Theories among educators about how students retain information—learning styles, multiple intelligences, and brain-based learning—help teachers better respond to individual students' needs. This means that preparing to teach is now more complicated than it used to be. A teacher can no longer expect to lecture for 40 or 50 minutes, because research suggests that most students do not learn effectively using that method; many students do not have an auditory strength. Learning is now viewed as a more active process that requires the teacher to facilitate learning rather than be a source of all knowledge.

Education often addresses the needs of the business world, where individuals are required to work together as a team. Teachers are now using more team-building strategies, such as cooperative learning, which allows students to work together in the learning process while being held responsible for their individual achievement. The courses you complete in a teacher education program should teach you these methods and allow you to put some of this theory into practice during your student teaching assignment.

How These Changes Affect Teacher Education

Teacher education programs are in transition, reflecting the changes taking place in elementary and secondary schools across the country. The factory method of preparing teachers for schools that were bound by the same factory-oriented philosophy of educating children is disappearing. Because this is a time of transition, some education programs still produce teachers in a traditional manner, whereas other teacher education programs are on the cutting edge. At minimum, you should at least be exposed to all of the modern materials, technology, and methods.

ALTERNATIVE TEACHER CERTIFICATION PROGRAMS

If you already have a bachelor's degree, you may be eligible for alternative teacher certification if your degree is in the subject area you want to teach. Generally, state certification boards require you to pass approved teacher examinations such as Praxis I and II, complete professional education courses, and, if appropriate, complete a student teaching requirement. However, states vary in their requirements for alternative teacher education programs; some will allow you to begin teaching right away as long as you enroll in teacher education courses and complete a certain number of courses within a specified time frame.

For example, a college graduate with a degree in English can begin teaching high school English immediately in Pinellas County, Florida. As long as her bachelor's degree is from an accredited college, she is eligible to apply for an initial two-year nonrenewable temporary Florida Educator's Certificate. This certificate enables her to begin a teaching career immediately as long as she enrolls in and completes 14 credit hours of teacher education courses during the first two years she is teaching. Here's a look at the type of courses that make up the 14 credit hours:

Number of Semester Hours	Type of Course	Names of Specific Courses
3	Sociological Foundations of Education	School and Society
		Introduction to Education
		History of Education
		Principles and Philosophy of Education
3	Psychological Foundations of Education	Educational Psychology
		Child Psychology
		Adolescent Psychology
		Psychology of Learning
		Growth and Development of the Individual
6	General Methods of Teaching and Curriculum in the Secondary School	Principles of Teaching in Secondary Schools
		General Curriculum in Secondary Schools
		Instructional Design
		Testing and Measurement
		Evaluation of School Programs

		General Teaching Methods
		School Organization in Secondary Schools
2	Specialized Methods	Methods of Teaching English in Secondary Schools

If you are contemplating changing careers to become a teacher, and you are a four-year college graduate, find out the specific requirements of the state department of education and school district where you want to teach (see Chapter 4 for contact information for each state department of education).

You may also be able to enter the teaching profession through one of these alternative routes: Teach for America, Troops to Teachers, or Americorps. Each of these programs is discussed in Chapter 4 in the section entitled "Alternative Teacher Certification Programs."

BACHELOR OF SCIENCE DEGREE EDUCATION PROGRAMS

If you are in high school or are a career changer who doesn't hold a bachelor's degree, you will want to investigate bachelor's degree education programs. Finding the right teacher education program can be a challenging task, particularly in this time of educational reform and change. Regardless of your present situation, you should investigate your options carefully. Here are a few questions to consider as you investigate bachelor's degree education programs:

▶ Can I major in another subject, minor in education, and meet the certification standards of my state?
▶ Can I have a dual major?
▶ How many credits are required for my major, and will room remain to take elective courses?
▶ What are the courses like?
▶ Can I see a description of the prerequisite, required, and elective courses? Some schools may limit your choices and others may have more variety. The larger schools may offer more options because they have more faculty members to run the courses.

The following sections provide information common to most undergraduate teacher education programs as well as actual program requirements from an exemplary undergraduate teacher education program.

Mission of the Program

Every teacher education program has a stated mission or overall focus that defines it. This mission should match your desired career goal as closely as possible because the program's mission will affect every aspect of your educational experience, particularly the curriculum you will study and the kinds of student teaching you can expect. The School of Education at the State University of New York at Geneseo, for example, has this general mission: Preparation of individuals who demonstrate the abilities, values, aesthetic responsiveness, commitment, and leadership for excellence in teaching and for honorable and responsible membership in society. By contrast, the mission of the Graduate School of Education and Information Studies at the University of California–Los Angeles is more specific: To prepare teachers to work with low-income students in urban schools.

Admission Requirements

Admission requirements at colleges and universities vary; however, most teacher education programs have some basic requirements in common. These requirements act as filters to ensure that only the best candidates become teachers. Certain requirements based on your high school career must be met to be accepted by a college or university. Likewise, another set of requirements must be met to be accepted into a teacher education program. How important are these admission requirements? Some schools limit or control the number of students entering the teacher education program. Typically you would apply for admission to the teaching program as a junior, so a large part of what determines if you will be allowed to enter the teacher education program will be your performance as a college freshman and sophomore. Thus, if you apply to an institution that has enrollment controls, such as Penn State

University or the University of Wisconsin–Madison, your academic performance from your first day on campus is extremely important.

Most teacher education programs have the following basic admission requirements:

▶ minimum coursework in a general degree and/or major area (usually 50–60 hours)

▶ minimum cumulative grade point average (GPA) in the first two years of college (usually 2.50; however, some programs may require a 3.00 or higher GPA)

▶ score at or above required levels on a state or national teacher's examination (some candidates also may be required to pass a content area examination)

▶ core of education courses specified by the certification program (typically, introductory and methods education courses)

▶ early field experience approved by the teacher education program (for example, tutoring at-risk students or working as a volunteer teacher aide)

▶ essays and/or interviews (faculties at some colleges evaluate how applicants write and interact with others before granting admission to the degree program)

▶ reference letters regarding your character and your ability to teach

Keep Your Standards High

The first two years of college are the most difficult for many students because they must adjust to the rigors of college. Your performance during this period, however, could determine whether or not you gain admission to a teacher education degree program in your junior year.

In some colleges, you must apply for admission to a specific department after successfully completing two years of required courses. Find out whether this policy applies at the school that you are considering. What would happen if your grades did not meet the criteria for admission—or are you certain that you can make the grade?

Bachelor's Degree Requirements

Most universities have general requirements you must meet before you can get your degree. However, like the admission requirements, they vary from institution to institution. Some of the more common degree requirements you will have to meet to get your teacher education degree are listed here:

- ▶ minimum number of credit hours (usually 120–130 hours for a bachelor's degree)
- ▶ minimum overall GPA in your major and minor fields of study and in your professional education courses
- ▶ residency requirement (that is, a certain number of courses or credit hours must be completed at the campus of the school awarding the degree; some schools require that *all* courses be taken in residence)
- ▶ coursework for teacher certification, including education courses
- ▶ general studies coursework (sometimes referred to as the liberal arts requirements, or courses of study required of all degree candidates) that provides the foundation for more advanced study
- ▶ major and minor courses of study in specific academic areas (which normally require 30+ and 20+ hours, respectively)
- ▶ directed teaching or student teaching experience

SAMPLE UNDERGRADUATE TEACHER EDUCATION PROGRAM

To get an idea of the type of courses and requirements of a typical undergraduate teacher education program, take a look at the following sample program from State University of New York at Geneseo. If you are considering attending this program, obtain the latest information from the school by contacting it directly. Requirements may change from year to year as schools continue to modify, update, and improve their programs. This sample program is for illustrative purposes only, and is not intended as a recommendation. Equally wonderful schools of education, both undergraduate and graduate, are located throughout the country.

B.S. in Education—Elementary Education
Sample Program Outline/Advising Guide

FIRST YEAR

Fall	Hours	Spring	Hours
English Elective	3	Math. 140 Math Concepts for Elem. Ed. I	3
N/ Core	4	S/ Core	3
F/ Core	3	M/ Requirement	3
INTD 105	3	F/ Core	3
		N/ Core	4
Total	13	Total	16

SECOND YEAR

	Hours		Hours
Intd. 203 Soc. Foundations of American Education	3	Educ. 213 Rdg. Process	3
R/Math. 141 Math Concepts for Elem. Educ.II	3	Educ. 214 Dim. of Teaching	3
Concentration Course	3	Humn. 221 Humanities II	4
Concentration Course	3	Concentration Course	3
Humn. 220 Humanities I	4	S/Psyc. 215 Child Development	3
Total	16	Total	16

THIRD YEAR

	Hours		Hours
Educ. 313 Classroom Reading. Program	3	Concentration Course	3
Educ. 316 Teaching Strategies: Science/Math	3	Concentration Course	3
Educ. 351 Teaching Young Children	3	Educ. 353 Curriculum Dev. Yng. Chld.	3
Concentration Course	3		
Educ. 352 Intro. ECE	3	Educ. 354 Family & Comm. Elective	1
Total	15	Total	13

FOURTH YEAR

Concentration Course	3	Educ. 331 Elem. St. Teaching	7.5
Concentration Course	3	Educ. 333 EC St. Tchg.	7.5
		(Student Teaching Semester)	
Educ. 317 Teaching Stratgs:	3		
Soc. St./Lang. Arts			
Educ. 355 Mainstrmg. in Preprim.	3		
and Prim. Grades			
H&PE. 350 Drugs, Alcohol,	1		
and Tobacco			
Concentration Course or Elective	3		
Total	16	Total	15

Total Semester Hours—120

MASTER OF ARTS AND MASTER OF SCIENCE DEGREE EDUCATION PROGRAMS

There are approximately 800 graduate schools of education in the United States today. These graduate schools offer one or more of these master's degrees for teachers:

▶ Master of Arts (M.A.)
▶ Master of Education (Ed.M.)
▶ Master of Teaching (M.A.T.)
▶ Master of Science in Education (MS.Ed.)

Some graduate teacher education programs are meant for people who hold a bachelor's degree with a major outside of teaching—sometimes these programs are called *preservice teacher* programs. That is, the person who is enrolling in the graduate program has little or no teaching experience.

Other graduate teacher education programs focus on the needs of full-time teachers who are obtaining a master's degree to meet permanent state certification requirements. In some states, you need to obtain a master's degree within a certain number of years after you begin teaching in order to meet the permanent certification requirements of that state. Graduate programs that are geared toward teachers who are already in the field are often called *inservice teacher* programs. Inservice teacher programs may include teachers who do not need to obtain a master's degree to meet certification requirements but who want to further their education for their own professional development or to receive a higher salary. Still other programs include both preservice students and students who are teaching full-time in the same program. This can be an advantage to you if you don't have much teaching experience—you will get to hear opinions, viewpoints, and anecdotes in your classes from teachers who are already in the profession. Programs offered in graduate schools of education include:

▶ elementary teacher education
▶ secondary teacher education
▶ special education
▶ educational psychology
▶ curriculum and instruction
▶ education administration/supervision
▶ education policy
▶ student counseling and personnel services

You will find that some graduate programs offer their students more flexibility than others. In fact, some programs enable you to tailor-make your own area of concentration within a general field of education. For example, at the Teachers College at Columbia University, you can enroll in an Ed.M. or a M.A. program called Interdisciplinary Studies in Education. In this program, you are allowed to pursue a specialized interdisciplinary program of your choosing if you can obtain the support of at least two faculty advisors from the relevant disciplines.

Many education departments have added programs that integrate technology into an educational context. For example, Teachers College recently initiated a few different programs that encompass a range of technology interests. They offer three different interdisciplinary programs focusing on technology: Communication and Technology, Computing and Education, and Instructional Technology and Media. As technology becomes more and more ubiquitous in the classroom setting, the demand for such programs is dramatically increasing, as is the demand for integrating these concepts and ideas into other, more traditional education programs.

If you attend a master's degree program full-time, you can normally expect to complete all requirements in two semesters and two summer sessions. Of course some master's degree programs are shorter and others are longer. But for the majority of programs, if you start school at the beginning of the summer, also attend the fall and spring semesters, and then the following summer semester, you should be able to graduate from the program by the end of the second summer.

Master's Degree Admission Requirements

While graduate programs have varying entrance requirements, here are a few basic requirements that are common to most programs:

- ▶ bachelor's degree from an accredited college or university
- ▶ minimum cumulative grade point average (GPA) in your undergraduate coursework
- ▶ for secondary teaching: a certain number of undergraduate or graduate credits in the subject area you are specializing in, or equivalencies, prior to entering the program (usually about 24 credits).
- ▶ score at or above required levels on a state or national teachers' examination
- ▶ obtain certain minimum scores on the Graduate Record Examination (GRE)
- ▶ written personal statement or academic essay
- ▶ letters of recommendation regarding your academic skills and/or character

Some programs are much more competitive than others, as you will see once you begin investigating the schools that appeal to you. For example, the graduate students who enrolled in the Teachers College at Columbia University in the fall of 2000 had these average GRE scores:

▶ average GRE verbal: 548
▶ average GRE quantitative: 618
▶ average GRE analytical: 609

On the other hand, graduate students who enrolled in the school of education at San Diego State University in the fall of 2000 had these average GRE scores:

▶ average GRE verbal: 447
▶ average GRE quantitative: 481
▶ average GRE analytical: 490

You may want to take the GRE before you pick out your desired graduate schools to ensure that you are aiming at the schools where you have a strong chance for being admitted.

Master's Degree General Requirements

Most universities have general degree requirements. However, like the admissions requirements, they often vary from institution to institution. Here are some of the more common requirements you will have to meet before being awarded your master's degree:

▶ minimum number of credit hours (can range from less than 30 to over 60, but most programs require around 32 hours)
▶ minimum overall GPA in your graduate coursework (often, a 3.0 GPA is required)
▶ special project, thesis, research report, teaching portfolio, or other written work
▶ student teaching experience
▶ comprehensive written and/or oral examinations
▶ complete all requirements for graduation within a specified time frame (usually five to seven years)

Sample Graduate Degree Teacher Education Program

The University of California–Los Angeles (UCLA) has a teacher education program that is ranked as one of the best in the United States. This program, called Center X, is based in the Graduate School of Education and Information Studies (GSE&IS), so that students graduate with a master's degree in education. A master's degree is one criterion for permanent certification in California (and many other states—you can check with your state's department of education to find out if you need to meet this requirement).

The School's Mission

The Center X program has a unique focus: You are prepared to instruct low-income students in underserved urban schools where student populations are racially, culturally, and/or linguistically diverse. The mission of the program is to give you the understanding and skills to promote social justice through caring and instructional equity.

UCLA offers a two-year graduate program, so the candidate must have already completed a bachelor's degree. The first year consists primarily of coursework, accentuated by a novice or student teaching experience in an urban school. During the second year, students complete coursework and their portfolio while doing practical field experience. Dr. Eloise Metcalf, head of the Teacher Education Department, describes the portfolio as a compilation of papers completed during coursework that presents the student's philosophy of education and demonstrates what he or she has learned; it should include an understanding of theory and practice. The portfolio is required of all candidates. Another unique feature of this program occurs during the second year: Each candidate must complete a paid residency at an urban school.

Another strong feature of this program is the integration of technology. You are taught innovative ways to integrate technology into the classroom and to use technology to develop and complete assignments. In fact, incoming students are required to have a computer system with a modem so they can communicate electronically with other students and their professors.

Admission Requirements

Applicants to the Teacher Education Program Master in Education and Credential Program offered at Center X must submit applications to two divisions: the Graduate Admissions Division and the Graduate School of Education and Information Studies (GSE&IS). The GSE&IS application is reviewed by the Department of Education admissions committee, who evaluate the applicant's qualifications and interest in teaching in a multicultural, urban school environment in addition to the more commonly expected criteria:

- ▶ GPA (3.0 in the junior and senior years)
- ▶ academic preparation
- ▶ Graduate Record Examination (GRE) Score (recommended 1,000 total for the verbal and quantitative sections)
- ▶ California Basic Educational Skills Test (CBEST) Score
- ▶ subject matter competence
- ▶ reference letters
- ▶ essay questions
- ▶ second language requirements, which are unique to this program and prepare candidates for the California CLAD or BCLAD certificate (described below)

The highly selective application review process is very intense and indicates that *only highly qualified individuals* who can fulfill the challenging mission of the program are accepted. In addition to California certification requirements (discussed in Chapter 4), all UCLA teacher education graduates complete a supplemental certificate in either Cross-Cultural Language and Academic Development (CLAD) or Bilingual Cross-Cultural Language and Academic Development (BCLAD). CLAD is for candidates *exposed to another language*. They may complete this requirement in several ways. In fact, the language courses you completed in high school can count towards this requirement. You should be familiar with a language other than English, and three years of high school foreign language may be sufficient. BCLAD requires candidates to be *fluent in another language*. Spanish, the predominant language at UCLA for these credentials, reflects the needs of the local urban setting.

TEACHING SKILLS FOR THE FUTURE

Whether you pursue a graduate or undergraduate teacher education program, the main thing you expect your program to do is prepare you to succeed as a teacher. The criteria listed below, from the American Association of School Personnel Administrators (AASPA) publication *Teacher of the Future: A Continuous Cycle of Improvement*, will help you evaluate teacher education programs, whether they are graduate or undergraduate. AASPA identifies the critical knowledge and skill levels a teacher will need to be successful today and in the future. Look for a teacher education program that promises to provide them.

Knowledge

In addition to knowing the subjects you teach and how those subjects are related to other subjects, you should know how to

- ▶ teach your subjects to students
- ▶ assess student progress on a regular basis
- ▶ plan lessons in a logical sequence
- ▶ reflect on your own teaching and devise ongoing improvement
- ▶ collaborate with educators to create a complete educational environment
- ▶ use technology, at least at an intermediate level
- ▶ appreciate various cultures and establish rapport with a diverse population
- ▶ get information and educate students to seek and evaluate information

Skills

Besides the knowledge that teachers are required to have, they also should be able to

- ▶ recognize and respond to individual differences in students
- ▶ implement a variety of teaching methods that result in higher student achievement

- ▶ work cooperatively with parents, colleagues, and others
- ▶ display a genuine love of teaching
- ▶ implement full-inclusion techniques for special education students
- ▶ differentiate instruction for development and ability levels
- ▶ write, speak, and present information well
- ▶ help students develop critical thinking skills
- ▶ relate well to parents and community members
- ▶ apply technology
- ▶ implement conflict resolution strategies

Quality Field Education

To gain the knowledge and develop the skills you need, choose a teacher education program that is field-based. In other words, it should offer many opportunities to practice with children in actual classroom settings throughout the program—not only in your student teaching experience. The theory of teaching is important; however, the practice is crucial in preparing you to meet the challenges you will face in your future classrooms.

Getting the Most from Student Teaching

The best preparation for the classroom is *experience in the classroom.* Your student teaching, directed teaching, or field experience is the crucial component before taking over your own classroom. Teacher training is an ongoing process, and experienced teachers will tell you they continue to learn new methods and technology (especially technology) every year. But you must begin somewhere, and that first experience—student teaching—is vitally important.

Dr. Dale Allee, professor emeritus in the Department of Curriculum and Instruction at Southwest Missouri State University in Springfield, Missouri, has been preparing teachers for more than 30 years. He also continues to work with school-aged children. Dale believes that to have a successful student teaching experience, you should keep several points in mind:

▪ Establish a good rapport with all those around you, including your cooperating teacher, other teachers, your students, the principal, and support staff.

▪ Do not be afraid to ask for help.

- Take criticism as it is given—constructively.

- Be prompt, conscientious, and tactful.

- Be willing to do more than is asked of you.

- Accept that you cannot totally be your own person or do your own thing.

- Remember, it is not your classroom. The professional and legal obligation for what happens still rests with the cooperating teacher.

- Make a concerted effort to learn to plan, organize, and manage.

- Do not be afraid to use some of the materials and activities of your cooperating teacher, but develop and use some of your own, too.

- Although it may sometimes feel as if your primary objective is to "just survive," remember that student teaching is designed to allow you to grow and develop as a teacher.

- Do not be consumed by the deadlines, pressures, and rigors of student teaching—try to find ways to get away from it (both literally and figuratively). You will need to start fresh and renewed every day and every week.

MEETING STATE CERTIFICATION REQUIREMENTS

In most cases, you are not automatically certified as a teacher upon graduation from an accredited teacher education program. You must file an application for a license (certification) with the state department of education in the state where you will be working and meet all of their requirements. Every state requires a bachelor's degree, but requirements that vary include the kinds of courses taken and the exams that are required. The course of study in most teacher education programs matches the exact requirements for teacher certification *in that state*.

However, if you plan to teach in another state, you may have to add a course or specialized requirement to your studies. It is worthwhile to choose a teacher education program in the state where you ultimately want to teach—or at least to know the certification requirements for that state when you start school—so you can fulfill them as you study. See Chapter 4 for a list of state departments of education and contact the ones where you may want to teach or study to request information about specific requirements. Chapter 4 also lists the basic certification requirements for each state along with contact information for all of the state certification boards.

CHOOSING YOUR PROGRAM

When you consider different programs, reflect on the kind of environment that suits your personality, budget, and family needs. Evaluate each factor separately, first, and then put them together. There may be numerous schools for you to consider, or you may be limited by circumstances such as commuting distance, cost of the program, and personal situations. If possible, apply to several different colleges or universities because there is no guarantee of gaining admission to the college of your choice.

Applying to a college can be a lengthy process that costs both time and money. For each application—which may be quite lengthy—you must write an essay, pay an application fee, enclose letters of recommendation and copies of transcripts, and take and sometimes achieve a certain score on one or more entrance exams.

Before you send in any applications, however, check to see that the college or university you are planning to attend has an *accredited* teacher education program. A mish-mash of courses taken at different colleges may not meet the requirements necessary for state certification. Most states require that the school you attend sign off on your credentials and grades.

What to Look for in a Program

Selecting a teacher education program that matches your personality and career goals is critical to your success as a teacher. According to Dr. Dale Allee, professor emeritus in the Department of Curriculum and Instruction at Southwest Missouri State University, a good teacher education program should:

▶ offer courses that ensure your preparation to teach in your chosen field or specialization
▶ have admission criteria that examines your personality traits
▶ require practicum experiences connected with your college coursework
▶ provide opportunities for you to work in community schools as a teacher's aide

► offer a broad range of courses that allows you to study teaching and learning theories that have been validated by examined practice, research, and conventional wisdom

► provide opportunities through coursework, seminars, observations, and interviews for you to examine and reflect on your beliefs and values about teaching and schooling

► provide opportunities to become inducted into the teaching profession by offering a variety of organizations for students in the program

► recognize that there is not one best way to teach and that your teaching style will be a function of many things, including your personality traits, beliefs, and learning style

► provide a variety of feedback mechanisms that serve as markers to measure your growth as a teacher

► avoid "trial-by-fire" approaches that induct you into the rigors of teaching before you are ready

► avoid "ivory tower" approaches that totally isolate you from the real life of classrooms and the joys of teaching

Focus on Academic Quality

There are many factors to consider in selecting a school, but the quality of professional training it provides must be your primary concern. First, make sure that the school's teacher education program is accredited. Then, look for the specific concentrations or specializations you are interested in—the right academic fit. Finally, evaluate the overall quality of the program.

Accreditation

Each state department of education allows you to take the certification exams and apply for a provisional license immediately upon graduation from an accredited program. A school that is accredited has been positively evaluated based on the essential courses needed to prepare teachers to begin their careers. Ensure that the accreditation is specifically for the undergraduate or graduate department you are planning to apply to.

For undergraduate degrees, if you want to major in a curriculum such as psychology or political science *and* want to teach, find out whether you can have a dual major or whether you can minor in education and still meet the requirements for certification. If not, you can meet all of your education requirements in a graduate teacher education degree program and have the benefit of studying another area as an undergraduate. Some states are changing their certification requirements, expecting teachers to have a curriculum concentration in addition to teaching methods coursework.

Is This a Quality Program?

There are many ways of evaluating the quality of a teacher education program besides its accreditation. Several questions can help you determine the quality of a program. Each consideration will vary in importance from person to person, and of course the best quality elementary education program in the world will do you no good if you want to specialize in high school math. Consider the quality of the program when choosing your school—it could make the difference between success and failure in your first year of teaching.

- **Can I sit in on a course?** It is important to see how small or large the classes are and how they are conducted.
- **Can I speak to someone in the program?** Speaking with a current student gives you the "inside scoop" about life in that college and will help you determine whether you will feel comfortable in that environment.
- **What methodology does the program promote: traditional, experience based, or both?** It is *essential* that you leave college with a variety of methods to use in the classroom. Students learn in very different ways, and you must understand which teaching techniques work best with each learning style. If the college you are considering does not have a hands-on approach to instruction, they probably have not updated their curriculum. You should be able to use and understand cooperative learning, whole language, theories of multiple intelligences, the discovery or museum approach, process writing, portfolio assessment, and all other kinds of interactive methodology *in addition to* direct traditional instruction.
- **Is the career planning and placement office helpful?** The career counselors should be able to help you secure a job after graduation.
- **What is the attrition rate in the program?** Students who start the program should be able to finish it. The higher the percentage of students who stay, the stronger the department.

▓ **What kind of fieldwork will I do?** The college should place you in a school *early* in the program. Experience as a student observer, student participant, or student teacher may help you decide what level or what area you want to specialize in. Doing fieldwork strongly reinforces your credentials, and the more experience you have, the more attractive a candidate you will be to potential employers.

▓ **Will I be prepared to take the certification exams?** Many states allow you to begin teaching before you complete the licensing exams. Eventually, however, you must take them. Although the exams vary from state to state, the school should help you with the certification process.

Nonacademic Concerns

Once you have a sense of what you want from your teacher education program, consider nonacademic concerns. These concerns apply to all prospective students.

Admissions Standards

Take a realistic look at your grades and other credentials. What kind of student are you? Admission standards vary, and colleges are classified by their degree of competitiveness and the relative importance of grades on your application. Top-ranked schools attract students with the highest grades and strongest academic portfolios. Other schools have easier admission policies, which means that your chances of being admitted are better. Select one school you would ideally *like* to attend (sometimes called your "reach") and some schools that are less competitive (often referred to as "safe" because they have less strict admission standards).

Cost of Tuition and Fees

There was a time that a higher education was very inexpensive, but those days seem to be gone for good in the United States. A four-year college degree from a private college or university can cost more than $100,000, but state school tuition can be less expensive. You are literally shopping for a school, and it should fit both your pocketbook and your resources.

Graduate programs also have a wide range of costs. For example, you can expect to spend $1,854 per year for full-time enrollment at San Diego State University if you are a resident of California. If you are not a state resident, the same program will cost you $4,914. In stark contrast to these somewhat affordable figures, consider the annual costs of attending a graduate program full-time at New York University: $17,640 or Harvard: $22,600. Considering that none of these prices include room and board, you will probably want to check out Chapter 3, which discusses financial aid opportunities you can take advantage of to help fund your education. While college costs are an important factor when considering teacher education programs, they shouldn't keep you from attending the college of your choice.

Every state has a system of state colleges and universities. Generally, tuition is considerably lower for state residents at a state college or university than at a private one. Residents of a given state normally pay less tuition to attend an in-state college or university than students from other states. In fact, the total non-resident fees are often comparable to private school tuition. Some states are more generous than others to out-of-state students, so investigate all costs carefully.

Public or Private?

One of the ways public universities keep costs down is by holding large classes. Courses during the first few years are often given in large lecture halls and are attended by hundreds of students at the same time. Occasionally, a course is given at one location and broadcast by satellite to other schools. Can you learn under these circumstances? Private schools also have some large lecture classes and satellite broadcasts, but such programs are usually kept to a minimum.

Private universities may be geared to a specific population. Some are supported by a religious organization, and the values and culture of that belief system may permeate the entire environment. It can be very comforting to know you have a shared experience, prior to college, with your new friends and classmates. At a small school, you may feel uncomfortable if you are not part of the religious majority. However, many fine colleges run by religious organizations attract a large population of students who do not adhere to that religion and it would be difficult to identify that school's religious affiliation by talking to students or sitting in on classes.

Size and Culture

Colleges come in all sizes, and the size of the college or university you choose can have a major effect on your comfort and happiness. If you grew up in a small town or city, you may think a small rural college is the place for you. Such schools offer a secure environment, where everyone eventually gets to know each other; they may even enroll as few as several hundred students. Often, small schools have a limited variety of courses. There may be a very homogeneous student population.

On the other hand, you may be looking for a school that has a large and diverse student body, a busy social atmosphere, various athletic programs, and opportunities to meet people from many different backgrounds. A university usually has many colleges (e.g., liberal arts, engineering, sciences) on its campus as well as several graduate programs. Both part-time and full-time students attend classes; some students live on campus, and others commute. Because people are constantly coming and going, you can be more anonymous on a large campus. It is possible to feel a bit isolated, but you can make friends with students who have similar interests.

Make an effort to find the right-sized school, because being happy will enhance your college experience. Ask yourself, *What kind of student life do I want?* A small rural school might eventually bore you, or a large university with a great football team might be overwhelming.

Location Matters

Schools are located in every part of the country, and your ability to find true happiness may depend on where you settle for the years it will take to complete your program.

Small rural and suburban colleges and universities are often enclosed units. There may literally be a wall surrounding the entire campus, providing a feeling of security. All of the buildings are located on the grounds, including classrooms, dormitories, dining halls, recreation centers, and the library.

In contrast, a college or university in a large city usually encompasses many city blocks. Although the buildings are within a given area, the streets are open to pedestrian and vehicular traffic. Business establishments, bookstores, dormitories, art galleries, food stores, restaurants, banks, clothing stores, museums, and movie theaters may be mixed in with the classroom buildings. It can be a very exciting environment for one person but very difficult for another person to adjust to.

Climate Control

If you live in Florida or southern California, can you adjust to the cold weather of Maine or Michigan? There are excellent schools all over the northern United States, but winter brings cold and snow—and the difficulties associated with such a climate. The University of Wisconsin–Madison, for example, is an excellent university with a wonderful education program and a beautiful campus, but winter temperatures can drop below zero! People who live in temperate climates often love the change of seasons. Attending school in southern Florida or California will provide opportunities for sun and fun, but can you live with one season year round?

The Distance Factor

If you are a working adult with a family of your own, you may not have much of a choice in the location of your school if your spouse needs to be near work and your children want to stay in their schools.

If you are single, how far away from your parents and friends do you really want to be? Many students initially think that the distance away from home doesn't matter, only to find that it does. No matter how involved you are on campus, there always comes a point when you will want to go home or to be visited by family and friends.

One consideration in distance is whether you can make the trip back and forth in one day. Costs increase if your parents have to stay in a motel when they come to visit. If you are invited home for a special occasion, could you complete travel in time to be back for classes? If the school is close enough to drive to in a short period of time, you will be able to come and go more easily.

If you are considering going further away, is the plane ride an easy one? Do you have to make many connections, or can you do it without great complications? How much is the plane fare? If the school is so far from your home that you cannot travel, be aware that you may be shut out of your dorm during some breaks.

Housing Options

Many colleges and universities that have dorms insist that freshmen live on campus because it helps them form a community of friends who will become a support system. Some schools have wonderful educational programs but no dormitories; therefore, you must rent a room or an apartment on your own. This can be difficult to do as a freshman if you don't know many people. Many colleges have special apartments available for married students with or without children, either on campus or in a nearby community.

Take a Tour

You really must visit a campus before you accept an offer of admission, because a mismatch can affect your happiness, your grades, and, ultimately, your future career. Many colleges give guided tours for prospective students and their families during the application period. Most have a counselor available to speak to you about the coursework and other concerns. Some colleges even have special weekends where prospective students can spend time in the dorms with students who have similar interests and career aspirations.

DISTANCE LEARNING TEACHER EDUCATION PROGRAMS

If, after reading all about traditional education programs, it just doesn't seem feasible for you to physically attend classes on a campus, you can opt for a distance learning teacher education program. These days, it's possible to earn an entire college degree or graduate degree by participating in a distance learning program. This means you learn the same material as you would by participating in traditional classes; however, your education is done at home, at your own pace, through reading, participating in online courses, and taking exams.

Depending on the course of study, students may not need to be enrolled full-time, and they usually have more flexible schedules for finishing their work. Taking courses by distance study is often more challenging and time consuming than attending classes—especially for adults who have other obligations. Success depends on an individual student's motivation. Students usually do reading assignments on their own. Written exercises, which they complete and send to an instructor for grading, supplement their reading material.

Assuming you pass the exams associated with the distance learning program, the end result and the degree or certification you earn is identical to what someone who attended a traditional educational institution would earn.

Distance learning programs may or may not have a residency requirement. Be sure to investigate carefully each program you are considering. For example, Goddard College (www.goddard.edu) offers a B.A. and a M.A. in education via distance learning. Both of these programs have a residency requirement—you must physically attend workshops on the Goddard campus at least once a year. Other schools offer programs with no residency requirement. For example, Saint Joseph College (www.sjcme.edu/cps) offers a B.S. degree in professional arts with a concentration in education via distance learning with no residency requirement.

Some schools offer only one or more education courses via distance learning, while others offer entire degrees. For example, you can obtain a Master of Arts degree in education with a curriculum and technology specialty from the University of Phoenix entirely online, without having to physically go to any campus. This specialization covers how to integrate technology into K–12 curriculum, accommodate diverse learners with assistive technology, explore ethical issues pertaining to the use of technology in schools, and learn how to plan for implementation.

On the other hand, the University of Iowa doesn't offer an entire education degree through distance learning, but you can take individual undergraduate education courses. One example is the course entitled *Introduction to Education*, which gives you a basic orientation to the field of education: consideration of administrative organization, instructional procedures, and contemporary problems at both elementary and secondary levels. This course satisfies the basic foundation requirement for most teacher preparation programs across the nation and would be a good way to find out more about the education field without having to attend a traditional program at a nearby campus.

To learn more about how to evaluate distance education programs, you may want to read the report entitled *Distance Education Guidelines for Good Practice* published in 2001 by the American Federation of Teachers. This entire report is available online at www.aft.org/higher_ed/technology. To get more information about specific distance learning programs in teacher education, see Chapter 3.

THE INSIDE TRACK

Who: Noah Kravitz

What: Computer Teacher

Where: New York, New York

INSIDER'S STORY

After college, I worked for a few years in New York City doing freelance writing and computer-related consulting work. Then, I decided to go back to school to combine my interest in technology with my interest in education. I started teaching in 1997, when the Web was just about to take off (in a business sense). My master's program in Communication and Technology at Teachers College, Columbia University didn't involve student teaching, so I figured that teaching part-time would be a good practical compliment to my studies. While I earned my M.A., I taught computers for two years at a private school in Brooklyn, New York. At that time, there was no state certification for teaching any sort of computer technology.

When I started teaching full time, I already had a little experience working as a teacher—I had taught summer school writing classes to middle schoolers, I had worked as a teacher's aide in college, and I also had the technical expertise to teach computer classes. The hardest part of teaching was discipline. The second Friday of school, I was teaching my last-period class, a particularly rowdy group of beginning programmers. That afternoon, absolutely *everything* went wrong: my lesson plan collapsed, the computer network crashed, and I had to get my department head to fix the network. I felt totally lost and I had to ask for help, which was awful because the students thought I was even more incompetent. While I was struggling to fix the computers, I overheard some students talking about how I was a horrible teacher and how they wished that another teacher was teaching the class. After school I went home feeling awful.

Luckily I had the weekend to cool down and I thought a lot about what I could do to gain control of the classroom. On Monday, I talked to another, more experienced teacher about effective strategies for dealing with difficult middle schoolers. Once they settled down and I got control of them, we had a lot of fun in class. By the end of the year, due to the guidance of more experienced teachers, and also due to changes I made in my own behavior, the class was still rowdy, but they had all learned a lot about programming. I certainly know that I had learned a lot from them.

In my two years of teaching, I discovered that there's a fine line between being a teacher and being a friend in the classroom. There's a way to walk that line effectively and still have control of your classroom. At first I tended to act a little too much like a friend and therefore I lost control of the classroom sometimes. It's so important to establish authority and discipline and to gain the students' respect first, and then slowly show your friendly side as the year goes on.

I learned that as a teacher, you have to be prepared for everything, especially if you're working with kids. You have to be an adult authority figure, but also be open and flexible. It really helps to keep up to date with what the kids who you're working with are into so you can relate to them. You might even find yourself learning to enjoy the finer points of Pokemon, video games, or first-date dramas. Be prepared to feel like one of the gang sometimes and a totally unwelcome outsider at other times. The hardest thing for me to remember was that it's your job to be the authority figure—remember, you're the adult and you're in charge. I think that for young teachers it can sometimes be hard to act like that adult, but you still have to remember to have fun—if you're not having fun, at least sometimes, it's probably not the job for you.

The beginning will probably be rough, no matter what; teaching is both emotionally and physically draining. I'm a pretty emotional person, so that first year was a roller coaster—

I had real high points and real low points, but you get through it and you figure out if you want to come back. After you adjust, it starts to become like any other job in that you learn how to do it. You find other colleagues to share with, to help you brainstorm new, creative ideas, and to help you think of ways to deal with troublesome children or classes.

CHAPTER three

HOW TO FIND TEACHER EDUCATION PROGRAMS AND FINANCIAL AID

This chapter gives you the tools you need to find specific teacher education programs and many different kinds of financial aid to help you finance that education.

NO MATTER what your situation is—a high school student getting ready for college, a community college student who wants to transfer to an education program at a four-year college, a career-changer who wants to become a teacher, or anyone else—you can find out which teacher education programs are available to you and where you can find the money to pay for them by reading this chapter. Here are the four main categories of teacher education programs discussed in this chapter:

▶ bachelor's degree programs
▶ graduate degree programs
▶ alternative education programs
▶ distance learning programs

What Type of Teacher Education Do I Need?

To find out what type of teacher education options are available to you, take a look at the following three scenarios:

1. **If you've graduated from high school but haven't yet been to college**

   This is considered the traditional route to becoming a teacher. After graduating from high school, you enroll in an accredited college or university that offers B.S. and/or B.A. degrees in teacher education.

2. **If you have a four-year college degree, but it's not in teacher education**

   Perhaps you are in a different career but want to make the switch to becoming a teacher. Or perhaps you just graduated from college but don't intend to go into the field in which you hold a major. In either of these cases, you could pursue one of the following paths to becoming a teacher:

   A. Enroll in a teacher education graduate program and obtain a master's degree.

   B. Seek an alternative path to certification, and enroll in the specific education courses required by your state department of education—note that not all districts allow this option. However, this scenario is becoming more and more common as school districts across the nation scramble to fill severe teaching shortages.

3. **If you are in any of the above categories, you may be able to obtain some or all of your education through distance learning.**

   If you have time or location constraints, you may not be able to enroll in traditional college courses. If so, distance learning may be for you.

BACHELOR'S DEGREE PROGRAMS IN TEACHER EDUCATION

If you want to get a bachelor's degree in a teacher education program, but you aren't sure how to begin the whole process of selecting an appropriate school, you've come to the right place. Now that you're armed with all the tips and techniques from Chapter 2 about how to evaluate different teacher education programs, you need to find out how to locate specific programs near you. You can find this information from high school or college guidance offices, in published books at your local library or bookstore, or you can surf the Internet.

School Guidance Offices

If possible, begin your search for a teacher education program at your high school or college guidance office. Even if you are not currently enrolled, you might be able to use the resources of the high school, community college, or university guidance office nearest you. A trained career counselor can provide a list of teacher education programs for you to consider and visit. Many career counselors have access to *The Guidance Information System*, published by Riverside Publishing, which is a computer program that will take into account your preferences (course of study, school size, location, and cost) and provide a list of colleges that meet these criteria. It also can supply you with a complete profile of each school, including all the majors, the number of students who attend full-time or part-time, and the grades needed to gain admission. Many other Internet-based computer programs are also now available to guidance and career counselors, so their office is a good place to start your search.

The Internet

If you have access to the Internet, conducting research on the Web is an excellent way of discovering teacher education programs in your city or target geographic area. Remember that each state has its own requirements and guidelines regarding teacher education and certification, so planning ahead is vital. You should make every attempt to attend a college or university in the state in which you want to teach, so you can begin fulfilling that state's certification requirements while still in school. See Chapter 4 for the website address of your state's department of education. Then go visit that website as your first step in the process. You may find out that your state is one that offers links to all the teacher education programs available in that state.

For example, if you visit this web page on California's State Department of Education's Commission on Teacher Credentialing website: www.ctc.ca.gov/credentialinfo/leaflets/cl402/cl402.html, you'll find the names, addresses, and phone numbers to the over 75 colleges and universities located in California that offer teacher education programs. You can also go to this page of their website: www.ctc.ca.gov/othersites.html#PROGRAMS if you want to find online links to these same schools—just click on the name of the school, and off you go to that school's website. Having all those links available on one site can save you considerable time in finding out which schools have teacher education programs in your state.

If your state department of education's website does not have such a list of links on it, you'll need to do a little more digging to come up with names of appropriate schools. Here are some websites that you can visit to search for schools of education in your targeted geographic region and area of specialty.

www.Petersons.com

Thomson Learning's Peterson's website has a database of thousands of colleges and universities and gives you the opportunity to personalize your search. After selecting "education" as your major, you can further narrow the search by choosing other criteria such as location, size, cost, etc. It displays detailed information about schools that meet your criteria, including links to their websites. The site offers much information about the selection process, financial aid, and other topics of interest to the college applicant.

www.collegeview.com

At Hobson's College View, you can search over 3,000 colleges and take a virtual tour of hundreds of featured campuses. Includes indexes for locating particular types of schools, for example: You can select "Study at a Historically Black College or University," or "Discover the Benefits of a Christian College." You can search for colleges by selecting "education" in the section entitled "major" and narrow your search by location, type of school, student size, city size, and other criteria.

This is a free version of the more extensive and full-featured site that is available in many high school guidance offices called the *CollegeView Internet Edition*. It provides many things you can't get on the free site, including scholarship searches, the ability to save searches and bookmark schools, and much more information on financial aid, careers and career planning, and thousands of college applications. If you can't get *CollegeView Internet Edition* at your school but would like to, you can complete a form at this website to request it.

www.special-ed-careers.org

The National Clearinghouse for Professions in Special Education) website includes information on more than 700 colleges and universities with programs in special education, including institution name, address, contact person, telephone, fax, Internet, accreditation status, size of faculty, level of program, and areas of specialty.

www.ncate.org

National Council for Accreditation of Teacher Education provides a directory of all their accredited colleges and universities. Click on "Find Accredited Schools"; it will lead you to the list, which is arranged in order of states and has direct links to each school's website.

www.collegeboard.com

Collegeboard.com, the site of the creators of the SAT, allows you to search through a database of 3,500 schools according to your personal criteria. It also contains information about testing and other subjects of interest to those choosing a college.

www.collegecenter.com

This site is hosted by Thomas C. Hayden, author of *Handbook for College Admissions: A Family Guide*. It offers advice to students and parents about selecting appropriate colleges and universities, financing college costs, and choosing the school that is most suitable to the student's academic and career interests and family finances. The site provides some free information about the college admissions process; however, it charges fees for specific guidance services.

www.usnews.com

At U.S. News and World Report, you can perform a customized search of a database of 1,400 schools.

www.nces.ed.gov/nceskids/college

The National Center for Education Statistics (NCES) supplies a listing of colleges and universities. You can select by location, major and other criteria and get basic information about the schools, as well as a direct link to their websites.

Other websites that offer similar customized college and university searches including links to school websites:

www.anycollege.net
www.collegenet.com
www.embark.com
www.gocollege.com
www.xap.com

Print Directories

If you do not have access to the Internet, or you would rather work with books that you can hold in your hand and page through, you may want to search for the perfect teacher education program by using printed directories. These directories should be available at your local library (in the reference section to get the most up-to-date edition) or at your local bookstore. Here's a list of several books that have the information you need:

Peterson's Guide to Colleges for Careers in Teaching **(Princeton, NJ: Peterson's Guides, Inc., 1996).** Although this book has not been updated since 1996, it does include helpful information on close to 1,300 teacher education programs and the specific education majors offered. This book could be used along with another more current guide. It also includes a CD-ROM containing all the school information.

National Council for Accreditation of Teacher Education. *A Guide to College Programs in Teacher Preparation* **(San Francisco, CA: Jossey-Bass Inc., 1999).** This book is a valuable resource containing information on each NCATE-accredited college and university teacher education program, including tuition, enrollment, degree data and other program features.

Peterson's 4-Year Colleges 2002 **(Princeton, NJ: Peterson's Guides, Inc., 2001).** Published by Peterson's Guides, this directory provides detailed information on over 2,100 undergraduate institutions in the United States and

Canada. The indexes help you search by major, school name, or geographic location.

Guide to Undergraduate and Graduate Teaching and Education Programs in the USA **(Cincinnati, OH: Seven Hills Book Distributors, 1999).** A comprehensive guide to accredited education programs in the United States. Provides a two-page profile on each program plus articles on trends and careers in education.

College Handbook 2002, 39th Edition **(New York: The College Board, 2001).** A guide providing in-depth information about 3,600 four-year and two-year colleges in the U.S. It also includes a CD-ROM giving college, scholarship and test preparation information.

America's Best Colleges 2001 **(New York: U.S. News and World Report, 2000).** This guide has a directory of over 1,400 schools, as well as U.S. News college rankings and many articles containing advice on navigating the college admissions process.

College Catalog 2002 **(New York: Simon & Schuster, 2001).** Edited by Kaplan, this guide gives detailed information on 1,000 colleges and universities, with in-depth profile of top colleges.

Barron's Profiles of American Colleges 2001 **(Hauppage, NY: Barron's Educational Series Inc., 2000).** Provides a detailed profile of more than 1,650 schools and includes a CD-ROM.

GRADUATE DEGREE PROGRAMS IN TEACHER EDUCATION

To find graduate teacher education programs, you can use some of the same resources that are listed above under the heading "Bachelor's Degree Programs in Teacher Education," so you may want to browse through that section first. In this section, you'll find additional tools that are specifically geared for locating graduate programs.

The Internet

You can use the Internet to find graduate teacher education programs in your desired location if you already have a bachelor's degree. Again, as with the bachelor's degree programs, the first step is to locate the website of your state's department of education—you can look up this website in Chapter 4. When you go to your state's website, look for a list of links to all the teacher education programs in that state. If there is such a list, you may find that the list of schools is not broken down into graduate and undergraduate; however, you could still use this list as a source of schools. After selecting a few specific schools, you can then investigate several of these schools to find out if they offer a graduate degree in education.

Two other helpful tools you might want to use in your search for the perfect graduate degree program are listed below.

U.S. News and World Report
www.usnews.com/usnews/edu/eduhome.htm
You can access the 2002 rankings of graduate schools of education at this website. The 2002 rankings focus on doctoral graduate programs, but you can still use the ratings and the links to the schools to find out more about master's degree programs if that is what you're interested in. Most of the schools that offer doctoral degrees in education also offer a master's degree in education.

For each school listed in the *U.S. News & World Report* ratings, you'll find a snapshot of that school when you click on the school name. This snapshot includes the school name, a website address link, tuition and fees costs, average GRE scores, and the number of students enrolled. You can also perform a search of all the graduate schools of education listed on the *U.S. News'* website by entering data such as the geographic location of the schools, the GRE scores, or the top 50 education schools in the nation.

Educational Directories Unlimited, Inc.
www.gradschools.com
This website offers an extensive database of grad schools that you can search by major—just click on "Education." Then, you can select areas of specialization within the field of education, such as "Elementary Education," "Physical Education," "Gifted Education," and many more. Then, you can further

narrow your search by selecting a geographic region. For each grad school that meets your search criteria, you'll see the school's name, contact information, program description, and degree(s) it offers. Distance learning programs in teacher education are also included at this site.

Print Directories

Graduate Programs in Education 2002 **(Princeton, NJ: Peterson's Guides, Inc., 2001).** This book gives detailed descriptions of accredited masters and doctoral programs in education.

Graduate Schools in the United States 2001 **(Princeton, NJ: Peterson's Guides, Inc., 2000).** Provides an in-depth introduction to selected graduate schools.

Directory of Graduate Programs in Social Sciences and Education **(Princeton, NJ: Educational Testing Services, 2000).** Contains detailed information on over 850 institutions.

ALTERNATIVE TEACHER EDUCATION PROGRAMS

If you are a career-changer who is interested in becoming a teacher, you may want to investigate the alternative education options available to you. Just as if you were searching for undergraduate or graduate programs, one of the best places to begin a search for alternative education programs is by contacting your state's department of education (see Chapter 4 for contact information). For example, if you go to a portion of the state department of education's website for Texas (www.sbec.state.tx.us/edprep/region.htm), you will find a list of approved educator preparation programs within the state. These teacher-training programs are organized into three categories:

Alternative/Accelerated Programs
University-based Undergraduate Programs
Post-Baccalaureate Programs

The Alternative/Accelerated programs offer teacher training from education service centers, school districts, and other entities, as well as colleges and universities to individuals who already hold a baccalaureate degree.

You'll find out that many career-changers in Texas who want to become teachers can begin teaching immediately if they already hold a four-year degree from an accredited college. They can attend specified teacher education courses at various locations in the state while they are full-time teachers.

Although the most common source of teacher education is a four-year college or university, for specific areas, you could attend a local community college or other education service center in the state of Texas. For example, Laredo Community College in Laredo, Texas, provides training for those who want to teach Technology Education in grades 8–12. You can enroll in the program if you hold a bachelor's degree in any subject. The program ranges from one semester to two years depending on your qualifications.

For more information about how to find alternative certification and education programs, see the section entitled "Alternative Certification Programs" in Chapter 4.

The Internet

You can check out alternative education programs by visiting the website of the National Association for Alternative Certification (NAAC) at www.alt-teachercert.org/index.asp. The NAAC seeks to expand the options available to individuals who are seeking to achieve certification for the elementary or secondary level.

Print Directory

Another way to find alternative teacher education programs is to consult the book entitled *Alternative Paths to Teaching: A Directory of Post-Baccalaureate Programs, Third Edition* published by the American Association of Colleges for Teacher Education, 2000. This directory provides information on 290 college and university programs of alternative routes for post-baccalaureate students to earn a teaching license. Each entry in the directory describes the program, the approximate time needed to complete it, the type of license that can be earned, and a contact person at the college or university. You can order it online from the publisher's website at www.aacte.org. Just click on "Publications," and then search for it by title. The directory is 164 pages long and costs $20.

DISTANCE LEARNING TEACHER EDUCATION PROGRAMS

There are many reasons why you might want or need to pursue your education through a distance learning program, and with recent advances in Internet technology, distance learning has been brought to an whole new level, making it easier to obtain a complete education from any desktop computer that's connected to the Internet. In addition to Web-based programs, you'll find distance learning programs that use audiocassettes, videotapes, and regular mail correspondence as a part of their programs. Distance learning is an extremely viable option if you are currently holding down a full-time job, have limited time in your daily schedule, or have financial limitations.

Many well-known and accredited colleges and universities now offer distance learning programs in the education field. You can find a wealth of information on distance learning programs on the Internet or from print directories.

The Internet

Here are several websites that offer helpful information about distance learning programs and give you access to many different specific teacher education programs.

www.petersons.com/dlearn
Thomson Learning's Peterson's website offers a searchable database of distance learning programs and courses. This site includes name and contact information of the school, cost, and description of courses.

It offers links to view a virtual tour of the school and provides direct links to the schools' websites. It also contains articles on subjects of interest to the distance learning student.

www.edsurf.net
The Online Distance Education Learning Resource for Adult Students. While this site lists only a few specific education-related distance learning courses, it does offer a wealth of general information about distance education, and includes a free subscription to a newsletter.

www.gnacademy.org
Global Network Academy. This nonprofit website's distance learning catalog has 28,212 courses in 3,357 programs offered by schools worldwide. It supplies detailed information about each school, including a link to the school's website. It also provides additional information and resources helpful to distance learners.

www.newpromise.com
MindEdge, Inc. At this site you can search an extensive database of education courses and programs. For each program, the site provides the school name, course description, cost, textbook(s) required, delivery format, and website link.

www.distancelearn.about.com
Distance Learning with Kristen Hirst is an information-packed site about distance learning. Also provides details about numerous schools that offer distance learning, and includes links to their websites.

www.geteducated.com
Geteducated.com is a distance learning consulting firm. Their site has listings of undergraduate and graduate distance learning programs, with direct links to the schools. Additional services include online articles and a monthly newsletter.

www.detc.org
The Distance Education and Training Council (formerly the National Home Study Council) is a non-profit educational association located in Washington,

DC. DETC serves as a clearinghouse of information about the distance study/correspondence field and sponsors a nationally recognized accrediting agency called the Accrediting Commission of the Distance Education and Training Council.

Print Directories

To find out more about distance learning programs in teacher education from printed resources, check out one or more of the following books at your local library reference section or at your local bookstore.

Bear, John and Mariah P. Bear. *Bear's Guide to Earning Degrees by Distance Learning* **(Berkeley: Ten Speed Press, 2001).** Covers alternative methods of earning a degree such as night and weekend colleges, Internet, and others.

Bear, John and Mariah P. Bear. *College Degrees by Mail & Internet: 100 Accredited Schools That Offer Bachelor's, Master's, Doctorates, and Law Degrees by Home Study* **(Berkeley: Ten Speed Press, 2001).** The information on 100 distance learning schools worldwide includes contact names, e-mail addresses, and websites.

Criscito, Pat. *Barron's Guide to Distance Learning Degrees: Degrees, Certificates, Courses* **(Hauppauge, NY: Barron's Educational Series, Inc., 1999).** A catalog of accredited colleges and universities that offer degrees and certificates via distance learning.

Kaplan, Jeremy Schlosberg, Adele Scheele, and Inabeth Miller. *Kaplan Guide to Distance Learning* **(New York: Kaplan, 1997).** Information on 100 distance learning schools as well as a discussion of distance learning.

Peterson's Guides. *Peterson's Guides to Distance Learning Programs, 6th Edition* **(Princeton, NJ: Peterson's Guides, 2001).** Contains a comprehensive list of schools with distance learning courses and programs. Provides details on 1,000 degree and certificate programs available from nearly 900 institutions and includes subjects, requirements, tuition and financial aid information.

Princeton Review Publishing Staff. *Complete Book of Distance Learning Schools* **(Princeton, NJ: Princeton Review Publishing Corp., 2001).** Profiles over 1,000 accredited distance learning schools in the U.S., both under-graduate and graduate.

Thorson, Marie K. *Thorson's Guide to Accredited Campus Degrees Through Distance Learning* **(Tulsa, OK: Thorson Guides, 2000).** A guide to accredited college degree programs which can be pursued from a distance.

Yager, Cindy. *The Best Distance Learning Graduate Schools: Earning Your Degree Without Leaving Home* **(Princeton, NJ: Princeton Review Publishing Corp, 1998).** Provides information about distance learning and includes a directory of 195 accredited institutions that offer graduate degrees via distance learning.

TAKING THE NEXT STEP—HOW TO FIND FINANCIAL AID AND SCHOLARSHIPS

Once you find the best teacher education program for you, the next step is to determine how to pay for it. The rest of this chapter explains how you can use financial aid and scholarships to help you save hundreds and even thousands of dollars over the course of your education program. You'll find out how to determine your eligibility for financial aid, and where you can get specific loans, grants, and scholarships.

There are many different types of financial aid available, plus an even larger selection of scholarships for which you may be eligible. Chances are, you can qualify even if you're attending only part-time. The financial aid you'll get may be less than that for longer, full-time programs, but it still can help you pay for a portion of your teacher education program. Also, if you're currently employed, be sure to contact your employer to determine if it will cover any part of your education. Even if you can't get tuition assistance for all your required courses, perhaps you can at least take some electives or general education classes under an employer-based tuition assistance or reimbursement plan.

Getting Started

The first step in the financial aid process is to get a form that is called the *Free Application for Federal Student Aid* (FAFSA). You need to get this form, fill it out, and file it because it is the foundation of so many different types of financial aid. In fact, most schools will not process your request for loans, work-study programs, or any other financial assistance until you file this form. Because the FAFSA, as it is commonly referred to, is such an integral part of the financial aid process, it is the best place to start. You can get this important form from your public library, your school's financial aid office, or by calling 1-800-4-FED-AID. Be aware that photocopies of federal forms are not acceptable. If you want to use the Internet, you can access the FAFSA online at www.fafsa.ed.gov. At this site, you can fill out and submit the FAFSA online. You can request a PIN, which allows you to complete the entire process online without having to print any signature forms. Otherwise, you can print out, sign, and send in the signature pages.

You can also complete the FAFSA online using a program called FAFSA Express; go to: www.sfadownload.ed.gov/fafsa/fexpress.html. FAFSA Express makes applying online for financial aid faster and easier. The process automatically checks electronic FAFSA data, resulting in fewer rejected applications.

According to the federal government, anyone in the process of applying to school should complete the FAFSA form. "Many families mistakenly think they don't qualify for aid and prevent themselves from receiving financial aid by failing to apply for it. In addition, there are a few sources of aid, such as unsubsidized Stafford and PLUS Loans, that are available regardless of need. The FAFSA form is free. There is no good excuse for not applying," explains one FAFSA brochure.

For more information, contact the Federal Student Aid Information Center (FSAIC) and ask for a free copy of *The Student Guide: Financial Aid from the U.S. Department of Education*. The toll free hotline (1-800-4-FED-AID) is run by the U.S. Department of Education and can answer questions about federal and state student aid programs and applications. You can also write to: Federal Student Aid Information Center, P.O. Box 84, Washington, DC 20044.

Are You Considered Dependent or Independent?

When you apply for financial aid, your answers to certain questions will determine whether you're considered dependent on your parents and must report their income and assets as well as your own, or whether you're independent and must report only your own income and assets (and those of your spouse if you're married).

If you are a dependent student, you will need financial information from your parents to fill out the FAFSA. Read the following list to determine if you are dependent or independent according to financial aid rules set by the U.S. Department of Education. You are considered an independent student if you meet any one of the following criteria:

1. You are at least 24 years old.
2. You are married.
3. You have a dependent other than a spouse.
4. You are a graduate student or professional student.
5. You are a ward of the court or an orphan.
6. You are a veteran of the U.S. Armed Forces.

The need analysis service or federal processor looks at the following if you are a dependent student:

▶ family assets, including savings, stocks and bonds, real estate investments, business/farm ownership, and trusts
▶ parents' age and need for retirement income
▶ number of children and other dependents in the family household
▶ number of family members in college
▶ cost of attendance, also called student expense budget, which includes tuition/fees, books and supplies, room and board (living with parents, on campus, or off campus), transportation, and personal expenses

Gathering Your Records

To complete the FAFSA, you'll need to gather the following records:

- ▶ records for income earned in the year prior to when you will start school. (You may also need records of your parent's income information.) For the 2002–2003 school year, you will need 2001 information.
- ▶ your Social Security card and driver's license
- ▶ W-2 Forms or other records of income earned
- ▶ your (and your spouse's, if you are married) federal income tax return
- ▶ your parent's federal income tax return if you are considered dependent
- ▶ records of other untaxed income received such as welfare benefits, Social Security benefits, TANF, veteran's benefits, or military or clergy allowances
- ▶ current bank statements and records of stocks, bonds, and other investments
- ▶ business or farm records, if applicable
- ▶ your alien registration card (if you are not a U.S. citizen)

Determining Your Eligibility

To receive financial aid from an accredited college or institution's student aid program, you must be a U.S. citizen or an eligible non-citizen with a Social Security number. Check with the Immigration and Naturalization Service (INS) if you are not a U.S. citizen and are unsure of your eligibility (800-375-5283/www.ins.usdoj.gov/graphics/index.htm).

Eligibility is a very complicated matter, but it can be simplified to the following two equations.

Your contribution + Your parents' contribution = Expected family contribution

Cost of attendance – Expected family contribution = Your financial need

TYPES OF FINANCIAL AID

There are many different types of financial aid available to help with school expenses. Here are three general categories for financial aid:

- ▶ grants and scholarships—aid that you don't have to pay back
- ▶ work/study—aid that you earn by working
- ▶ loans—aid that you have to pay back

Grants and Scholarships

Grants are an advantageous form of financial aid because they do not need to be paid back. Two of the most common forms of grants for undergraduate students from the federal government are the Pell Grant and the Federal Supplemental Educational Opportunity Grant (FSEOG). They are normally awarded based on financial need. In some cases, you may receive a Pell Grant for attending a post baccalaureate teacher certificate program. Awards for the award year July 1, 2001 to June 30, 2002 will depend on program funding. The maximum award for the 2000–2001 award year was $3,300 for Pell Grants and $4,000 for the FSEOG. To find out more about federal, state, school, and private grants, visit the website www.finaid.org/otheraid/grants.phtml.

In addition to grants, you can get scholarships from federal, state, school, and private sources. Of course, as with grants, you do not need to repay the money you get from a scholarship. You can search online for scholarships by visiting these websites:

www.fastweb.com
If you answer a series of questions about yourself and your education interests and goals, you will receive a list of scholarships for which you may qualify. Their database is updated regularly, and your list will be updated when new scholarships are added that fit your profile.

www.collegenet.com
At this site, you can click on "Scholarships" to search a database that contains over 600,000 awards totaling over $1.6 billion. You can narrow your search by entering your gender and age, and then you can search by major. Just type in "education."

You can also browse through scholarship and fellowship books at your local library or bookstore. See the section entitled "Financial Aid" in Appendix B to find relevant scholarship book titles. If you're currently employed, check to see if your employer has scholarship funds or tuition reimbursement programs available. If you're a dependent student, ask your parents, aunts, uncles, and cousins to check with their employers or organizations they belong to for possible aid sources. You never know what type of scholarships you might dig up. For example, any of the following groups may know of money that could be yours:

- professional teacher associations
- religious organizations
- fraternal organizations
- clubs, such as the Boy and Girl Scouts, Rotary, Kiwanis, American Legion, or 4-H
- athletic clubs
- veterans groups
- ethnic group associations
- unions

As you look for sources of scholarships, continue to enhance your chances of winning one by participating in extracurricular events and volunteer activities. You should also obtain letters of reference from people who know you well and are leaders in the community, so you can submit their names or letters of recommendation with your scholarship applications. Make a list of any awards you've received or other special honors that you could list on your scholarship application.

Most of the scholarships that are available to people who are planning to become teachers are offered by individual states and are only good for education students in that state. Check with your school's financial aid office for more information about these scholarships. You may be able to find a scholarship in the particular area of specialization you are planning to major in at school. Try searching the Internet and financial aid guides for more information about these types of scholarships.

Phi Delta Kappa is an international association of professional educators that offers national teacher scholarships. To obtain more information about the organization and the scholarships it offers, visit www.pdkintl.org. The following is an outline of scholarships offered by the association.

Scholarship Grants for Prospective Educators

This program is for current high school seniors whose intended college major is education. Applications may be requested each year between October 15 and January 15; the deadline for completed applications to be returned is January 31. Available are 30 $1,000 scholarships; one $2,000 scholarship, one $4,000 scholarship, and one $5,000 scholarship.

Excellence in Student Teaching Awards

Applicants for this program must be members of Phi Delta Kappa International. The scholarship is for undergraduate and graduate students student teaching in the summer, fall, and spring of the current year. The deadline for applications is June 30. Among other rewards, scholarship winners will receive $1,000 cash; a scholarship to attend a PDK-sponsored Professional Development Institute, and recognition in PDK publications and through press releases to local newspapers and alumni magazines.

Phi Delta Kappa International Graduate Fellowships in Educational Leadership

This program is for Phi Delta Kappa members only. Applicants for this scholarship must be pursuing a graduate or doctoral degree program in educational leadership and must be full-time students during the year of tuition and fee awards. Applications are available between January 15 and May 15 each year. Two fellowships of $1,500, one fellowship of $1,000, one fellowship of $750, and three fellowships of $500 are awarded annually.

WORK-STUDY PROGRAMS

A variety of work-study programs are available as a form of financial aid. If you already know what school you want to attend, you can find out about its school-based work-study options from the student employment office. Job possibilities may include on- or off-campus jobs. Another type of work-study program is called the Federal Work-Study (FWS) program, and it can be applied for on the FAFSA.

The federal work-study program provides jobs for undergraduate and graduate students *with financial need* allowing them to earn money to help pay education expenses. The program encourages community service work and provides hands-on experience related to a student's course of study, when available. The amount of the FWS award depends on:

- ▶ when you apply (the earlier you apply, the better)
- ▶ your level of financial need
- ▶ the funds that are available at your particular school

Your FWS salary will be at least the current federal minimum wage or higher depending on the type of work you do and the skills required. As an undergraduate, you'll be paid by the hour (a graduate student may receive a salary), and you will receive the money directly from your school at least monthly. The awards are not transferable from year to year. Not all schools participate in the FWS program.

You will be assigned a job on campus, in a private non-profit organization, or a public agency that offers a public service. The total hourly wages you earn in each year cannot exceed your total FWS award for that year, and you cannot work more than 20 hours per week.

LOAN PROGRAMS

If you cannot finance your entire training program through scholarships, grants, or work-study exclusively, the next step is to consider taking out a loan. The first step in finding a student loan is to learn the basics of loan programs. You may want to begin by browsing the website: www.finaid.org/loans; it discusses many options available to you, such as student loans, parent loans, private loans, and loan consolidation. Another good source of loan information online is www.educaid.com. You can also call them at 1-800-EDUCAID to get loan information. At the Educaid website, you can narrow your search for loans to these categories: undergraduate, graduate, foreign study, and consolidated loans.

You can also visit the Federal College Student Loans Directory website at www.college-student-loans.com. This site is a free online service put together with the assistance of former financial aid counselors. They index the websites college students need to learn about and begin the student loan borrowing process. They include a "Lenders" section that features accredited student loan lenders and they provide free loan counseling via e-mail, answering most questions the same day.

SPECIAL LOAN PROGRAMS FOR TEACHERS

As you investigate loan options for your teacher education program, be on the lookout for special loan forgiveness programs for teachers. Thirty-one states currently offer some form of a loan forgiveness program for students who will make a commitment to teach in that state for a certain number of years. Contact your state department of education for details.

In some states, you are eligible for the loan forgiveness program only if you are planning to enter a critical shortage area, such as special education, math, or science. For example, if you plan to attend school in the state of Florida, you may be eligible for the Critical Teacher Shortage Student Loan Forgiveness program. This program awards up to $5,000 in the form of a loan that does not need to be paid back if you become certified to teach a critical shortage area subject as designated by the State Board of Education and agree to teach for a specified length of time in the state of Florida.

Federal Perkins Loans

A Federal Perkins Loan has the lowest interest rate (approximately 5%) of any loan available, and it is offered to students with exceptional financial need. You repay your school, who lends the money to you with government funds.

Depending on when you apply, your level of need, and the funding level of the school, you can borrow up to $3,000 for each year of undergraduate study for up to five years. Graduate students can borrow up to $5,000 per year, or $30,000 for the entire time enrolled—including Federal Perkins Loans you borrowed as an undergraduate.

The school pays you directly by check or credits your tuition account. You have nine months after you graduate (provided you were continuously enrolled at least half-time) to begin repayment, with up to ten years to pay off the entire loan.

Federal Stafford Loans

Federal Stafford Loans are low interest loans, and you must attend school at least half-time to be eligible. The lender is usually a bank or credit union if the school does not participate in direct lending. Stafford Loans are either subsidized or unsubsidized.

Subsidized loans are awarded on the basis of financial need. You will not be charged any interest before you begin repayment or during authorized periods of deferment. The federal government "subsidizes" the interest during these periods.

Unsubsidized loans are not awarded on the basis of financial need. You'll be charged interest from the time the loan is disbursed until it is paid in full. If you allow the interest to accumulate, it will be capitalized—that is, the interest will be added to the principal amount of your loan, and additional interest will be based upon the higher amount. This will increase the total amount you have to repay.

There are many borrowing limit categories to these loans, depending on whether you get an unsubsidized or subsidized loan, which year in school you're enrolled, how long your program of study is, and if you're independent or dependent. You can have both kinds of Stafford Loans at the same time, but the total amount of money loaned at any given time cannot exceed $23,000. The interest rate varies, but as of July 1, 2001, it will be at the lowest level ever, 5.99%. Previously, the interest rate was 8.19%. (The in-school interest rate will be 5.39%.)

An origination fee for a Stafford Loan is approximately three or four percent of the loan, and the fee will be deducted from each loan disbursement you receive. There is a six-month grace period after graduation before you must start repaying the loan.

Federal Direct Student Loans

Federal Direct Student Loans have basically the same terms as the Federal Stafford Loans and PLUS Loans for parents. The main difference is that the U.S. Department of Education is the lender instead of a bank. One advantage of federal direct student loans is that they offer a variety of repayment terms, such as a fixed monthly payment for ten years or a variable monthly payment for up to 25 years that is based on a percentage of income. This is a relatively new program, so not all colleges participate.

Parent Loans for Undergraduate Students (PLUS)

PLUS Loans enable parents with good credit histories to borrow money to pay education expenses of a child who is a dependent undergraduate student enrolled at least half-time. To be eligible, your parents must meet citizenship requirements and pass a credit check. If they don't pass the credit check, they might still be able to receive a loan if they can show that extenuating circumstances exist or if someone who is able to pass the credit check agrees to co-sign the loan.

The annual limit on a PLUS Loan is equal to your cost of attendance minus any other financial aid you receive. For instance, if your cost of attendance is $6,000 and you receive $2,000 in other financial aid, your parents could borrow up to, but no more than, $4,000. The interest rate varies, but cannot exceed 9% over the life of the loan. The interest rate is adjusted each year on July 1. As of July 1, 2001, the interest rate for PLUS Loans was 6.79%, down from the previous 8.99%. Your parents must begin repayment while you're still in school—there is no grace period.

MAXIMIZE YOUR ELIGIBILITY FOR LOANS AND SCHOLARSHIPS

Loans and scholarships are often awarded based on your eligibility. Depending on the type of loan or scholarship you pursue, the eligibility requirements will be different. eStudentLoan.com (www.estudentloan.com/workshop.asp) offers the following tips and strategies for improving your eligibility when applying for loans and/or scholarships:

▶ Save money in the parent's name, not the student's name.
▶ Pay off consumer debt, such as credit card and auto loan balances.
▶ Parents considering going back to school should do so at the same time as their children. The more family members in school simultaneously, the more aid may be available to each.
▶ Spend student assets and income first, before other assets and income.
▶ If you believe that your family's financial circumstances are unusual, make an appointment with the financial aid administrator at your school to review your case. Sometimes the school will be able to adjust your financial aid package to compensate.
▶ Minimize capital gains.
▶ Do not withdraw money from your retirement fund to pay for school. If you must use this money, *borrow* from your retirement fund.
▶ Minimize educational debt.
▶ Ask grandparents to wait until the grandchild graduates before giving them money to help with their education.
▶ Trust funds are generally ineffective at sheltering money from the need analysis process, and can backfire on you.

▶ If you have a second home, and you need a home equity loan, take the equity loan on the second home and pay off the mortgage on the primary home.

FINANCIAL AID RESOURCES

Here are several resources that you can use to obtain more information about financial aid.

Telephone Numbers

One or more of these phone numbers may prove helpful during the financial aid process.

Federal Student Aid Information Center (U.S. Department of Education)
  Hotline 800-4-FED-AID or 800-433-3243
  TDD Number for Hearing-Impaired 800-730-8913
  For suspicion of fraud or abuse of federal aid call 800-MIS-USED
    800-647-8733
Selective Service 847-688-6888
Immigration and Naturalization Service (INS) 415-705-4205
Internal Revenue Service (IRS) 800-829-1040
Social Security Administration 800-772-1213
National Merit Scholarship Corporation 708-866-5100
Sallie Mae's College AnswerSM Service 800-222-7183
Need Access/Need Analysis Service 800-282-1550
FAFSA on the WEB Processing/Software Problems 800-801-0576

Websites

Check out these websites for financial information.

www.ed.gov/prog_info/SFA/StudentGuide

The Student Guide is a free informative brochure about financial aid and is available online at the Department of Education's website listed above.

www.fafsa.ed.gov

This site enables you to fill out and submit the FAFSA online.

www.ed.gov/offices/OSFAP/Students/apply/dwnload01-2.html

Another way to send your FAFSA electronically is by downloading *FAFSA Express* software to your computer. You'll need a PC equipped with Windows® and a modem to complete this electronic form and send your completed FAFSA to the Department. *FAFSA Express* instructions are provided to help walk you through the application process.

www.finaid.org

This comprehensive site has a wealth of information on financial aid, including special situations, such as divorced parents, financially unsupportive parents, bankruptcy, defaulting on student loans, international students, and myths about financial aid.

www.fastweb.com

This site is called FastWEB.com. If you answer a few simple questions for them (such as name and address, geographic location, organizations that you are affiliated with, age and so on), they will give you a free list of scholarships you might qualify for. Their database is updated regularly, and your list gets updated when new scholarships are added that fit your profile. FastWEB boasts that their database includes more than 400,000 awards.

www.college-student-loans.com

This site, Federal College Student Loans Directory, is a free online service put together with the assistance of former financial aid counselors. They index the websites college students need to learn about and begin the student loan borrowing process. They include a "Lenders" section that features accredited student loan lenders and they provide free loan counseling via e-mail, answering most questions the same day.

www.advocacy-net.com/scholarmks.htm

Many helpful financial aid web sites have links from this page, including the ever-popular ones mentioned above: "fastweb" and "finaid." You can select a link to view a different financial aid website while the original page is still loading.

www.students.gov

This site is sponsored by the U.S. Department of Education, and it offers a variety of information about financial aid. You will find general information about the major federal student aid programs (who is eligible and how to apply), tax credits for education expenses, and other federal, state, and private sources of information.

www.educaid.com

Educaid's web site offers significant information about student loans and other forms of financial aid. They are student loan specialists.

Pamphlets

These two pamphlets are provided free of charge and offer a good overview of the financial aid process. You can order them by calling the toll free numbers listed.

> *The Student Guide* is published by the U.S. Department of Education and is *the* handbook about federal aid programs. To get a printed copy, call 1-800-4-FED-AID.
> *Looking for Student Aid* is also published by the U.S. Department of Education and is an overview of sources of information about financial aid. To get a printed copy, call 1-800-4-FED-AID.

THE INSIDE TRACK

Who: Colleen Schultz

What: Math Teacher

Where: Vestal, New York

INSIDER'S STORY

Being a middle school math teacher is more work than I ever could have imagined, but it is also more rewarding than I could have imagined. Ten years ago I would have never thought I would wake up in the middle of the night thinking of new ways to teach math concepts!

One of my biggest challenges as a teacher is feeling that I am keeping up with all of the changes in curriculum and instruction, especially with the advent of all the new classroom technology that is out there. You need to be flexible and keep an open mind, but you also need to develop your own philosophy of teaching and learning—and stick with it. I subscribe to and access trade journals (*Mathematics Teacher, Mathematics Teaching in the Middle School*) that are put out by professional organizations to give me new ideas. Then I try to imagine how I can fit those ideas into my curriculum to engage my middle school students—it is harder than ever to engage middle schoolers in the math classroom. That is why I continue to pursue my own education as a teacher. I have completed over 300 hours of staff development in addition to my Bachelor and Masters Degrees, and I have even been trained by Texas Instruments on the graphing calculator.

I knew that my educational investment was well worth the extra time when I was contacted by the Harvard-Smithsonian Center for Astrophysics to be taped for an appearance in a series they were presenting on PBS for teachers. I was both excited and extremely flattered that such a distinguished institution was recognizing my teaching strategies.

I have also become actively involved in my district's staff development program. I teach a variety of classes to other teachers in the district and the local area, mainly on using technology in the classroom. I enjoy sharing my knowledge with anyone willing to learn, both students and teachers.

My advice to new teachers is to keep up with the latest innovations in teaching in your area, and in education in general. It will help make you a stronger and successful teacher, and greater certification and credentials add up to a larger salary.

CHAPTER four

TEACHER CERTIFICATION

The teacher certification process is complex. This chapter guides you through the general requirements. It also includes a state-by-state directory of certification requirements and contact information for your department of education, so you can verify specific requirements.

EVERY PROFESSION has a way of guaranteeing that the people delivering a specialized service have the qualifications to perform that duty well. A license or certification provides that assurance—a means of quality control for professions like medicine, law, accounting . . . and education. Because teachers mold the lives of children and have a tremendous impact on their students' future success in school and in real life, ensuring that teachers are qualified is essential. Every state has a department of education that oversees the education and preparation of the teachers who work in that state. By providing this service, the state government assists local school districts in their search for qualified staff and sets minimum standards for all teachers across the state. Each state education department also guarantees, to its constituents, that equally qualified teachers provide education for all of the students throughout the state.

THE TRADITIONAL ROUTE TO CERTIFICATION

Completing a teacher education program is only the first step in becoming a teacher. Then, you must fulfill all the requirements for the state in which you wish to teach, take the exam or exams required by the state, and officially apply for certification. Traditionally, to become a certified teacher, each person must have to complete the following steps. However, if you are a career-changer or someone else who wants to find out about alternative routes to teacher certification, you may want to skip this section and go directly to the next section, which is entitled, "Alternative Routes to Certification."

Step One: Obtain Your Degree

Traditionally, the first step in meeting the certification requirements of any state is to complete a program of study at an accredited college or university, with an accredited department of education. To graduate, you are required to complete a series of required courses, including practicums such as student teaching, and a series of elective courses that enrich your experience. If you pass these courses, then you can graduate and go on to take required tests and secure a teaching position. Regulations vary across the country, but all have the same purpose of guaranteeing uniformity of knowledge and preparation.

Step Two: Meet Department of Education Requirements

Each state has its own department of education, which is responsible for verifying teachers' qualifications for certification. Each state requires that you complete a set of forms, pay application fees, and have background checks done. Listed below are some of the requirements you may have to meet when completing the application for certification.

Citizenship
Many states require that applicants for teacher certification be United States citizens, eligible for citizenship, or in the process of becoming a citizen. It is important for you to find this out before applying for a position. Of course,

if you are a foreign exchange teacher (from a program abroad), this does not apply to you.

No Criminal Record

Most states require fingerprinting, which is used to check for a criminal record. Some colleges and universities require this as part of their matriculation process. If you have had a problem that is believed to be in conflict with a teaching position, you *will not* be able to receive a teaching certificate. If you have had a problem, you should be honest about it. Have your college or university check this out for you—it is very possible that the situation can be straightened out before you apply for certification.

Moral Character Reference

Some states require several letters of reference regarding your moral character. As a teacher, you will deal with children and young adults, so it is essential that you have high standards in your personal life.

Recency Requirement

Some people do not begin to teach immediately after completing their teacher education program. If you were trained as a teacher but went into a different career before going into teaching, you may have to provide evidence of taking education courses within a specified period of time. The state wants to ensure that your teaching knowledge is up-to-date. If you are a teacher returning from a leave of absence or transferring to another state and requesting certification, you may also be required to show evidence that you have completed recent education courses or other professional development courses related to teaching.

Step Three: Written Tests

Many states require that you pass one or more competency tests, which are standardized exams that test your academic proficiency. Many states accept the Praxis series of exams, while others have their own tests, which are similar, but may focus on the specific needs of the state. Later in this chapter, you will find out more about the testing process and examples of test questions from the Praxis series.

Step Four: Apply for Certification

This chapter provides a brief list of certification requirements in each state. Once you have met all the certification requirements for the state in which you want to teach, you can formally apply for certification. This normally means filling out an application and paying an application fee. In some states, the first certificate that is issued is provisional and you have to complete additional requirements before getting permanent certification.

ALTERNATIVE ROUTES TO CERTIFICATION

In many cases, you don't actually have to be certified to be hired as a teacher. When the demand for teachers in a specific area is greater than the availability of licensed personnel, you can be hired through what is often called an *alternate route*. This means the state will allow you to begin teaching immediately as long as you demonstrate competency in your subject area. Sometimes you have to be enrolled in an approved teacher education program and/or be under the mentorship of a master teacher. Requirements vary from state to state and sometimes even within a state if there are extreme needs in one area. Check with your state's department of education to see if they offer an alternative route to certification and to find out if you are eligible for one or more of their alternative programs. As a general rule, southern and western states tend to have more teacher shortages than the Northeast and Midwest, although inner city areas in the Northeast and Midwest often are in need of teachers, too.

Texas is one of the southern states that offers alternative routes to certification if you hold a bachelor's degree from an accredited institution. For example, you could begin teaching secondary school immediately if you achieved a 2.5 GPA or above on a four-point scale in all your college courses taken, if you have at least 24 semester hours in the subject to be taught, and can pass the Texas standardized test for teachers (TASP) that tests your math, reading, and writing skills. Secondary certification areas available include: art, biology, chemistry, computer information systems, dance, earth science, English, foreign languages, geography, government, history, journalism, mathematics, music, physics, reading, and theater arts. If you are accepted into the program and hired by a school district, you are eligible for first-year teacher's pay. You are considered the teacher of record and an employee of that school district.

Another state-specific program that offers an alternative route to certification can be found in New York City. This program is for Peace Corps volunteers who are returning to America from their international tour of duty. Selected participants are placed in full-time, salaried positions in the public schools of New York City and attend Teachers College part-time at Columbia University. The program, the first of its kind in the United States and now in its second decade, carries a two-year commitment with at least an additional two years of teaching in the city strongly encouraged. The program is for master's degree candidates only in the following teacher shortage areas: bilingual (English/Spanish) education (pre-K–6), math or science (grades 7–12), special education, and ESOL (pre-K–12). Anticipated scholarships (partial tuition remission) are competitive. For more information you can contact the Peace Corps Fellows Program, Box 90, Teachers College, Columbia University, 525 West 120th Street, New York, NY 10027 or telephone 212-678-4080. The program's website can be accessed at www.tc.columbia.edu/pcfellows.

In addition to alternative routes to teacher certification offered by specific states, you may be eligible for one of these national programs.

Teach for America

A national program recognized by most states, Teach for America is designed for college graduates who have not majored in education. If you are chosen for this program, you must commit to teach for two years in underserved urban and rural public schools. Once you are selected, you will attend a five-week training session that offers you an introduction to education methodology, and then you will be placed in one of Teach for America's fifteen urban or rural sites to become a full-time teacher, earning the same salary as the other beginning teachers in that area. Once you are employed as a teacher, you will get additional professional support to help you as you teach. The hope for the program is ultimately to recruit and change the career paths of participants who would be headed into other fields.

You have the best chances to enter this program if you have a major or minor in math, science, or engineering or if you are a bilingual Spanish speaker. You must have a cumulative undergraduate GPA of 2.50 to take part in this program. The application process is rigorous and highly selective—just last year over 4,000 people applied for only 900 spots. To learn more about the background of Teach for America, check out the book entitled *One Day, All Children . . . The Unlikely Triumph of Teach for America and What I Learned Along the Way* (Public Affairs, 2001) written by Teach for America's founder, Wendy Kopp. The book details the challenges her organization faced in trying to model itself after the Peace Corps. To apply for the Teach for America program or to obtain more information, contact them at:

Teach for America, Inc.
315 West 36th Street, 6th Floor
New York, NY 10018
www.teachforamerica.org
1-800-832-1230, extension 225

Troops to Teachers

A federally funded program, Troops to Teachers is designed to assist outgoing military personnel who want to work in the field of education as a teacher or teacher's aide. It provides counseling and assistance to help participants identify employment opportunities and teacher certification programs. Participants choose the area in which they want to teach. State support offices have been established in 24 states to assist participants with both certification requirements and employment leads. The Troops to Teachers program can help you to find employment after completing the appropriate training.

You may apply for this program if you were a part of the military or Coast Guard, including the Reserve component and you were discharged after

October 1, 1990. Those interested in "academic" teaching positions must have a bachelor's degree from an accredited college. If you want to teach one or more vocational subjects, such as electronics, computers, and construction trades, you are not required to have a college degree to apply, but you must be able to document your skill level or expertise.

You can visit their website at www.voled.doded.mil/dantes/ttt/index.htm or view the listing of job postings they offer at www.jobs2teach.doded.mil. To apply for the Troops to Teachers program or to obtain more information, contact them at:

DANTES Troops-to-Teachers
6490 Saufley Field Road
Pensacola, FL 32509-5243
1-800-231-6242

STATE LICENSING INFORMATION

Because the state—not federal—government regulates education, there are 50 versions of licensing requirements. You must find out what these requirements are for the state(s) in which you wish to teach so you can ensure that you are properly qualified. The directory of state departments of education, at the end of this chapter, provides contact information for all states.

Categories of Licenses

The licensing systems of most states are divided into elementary, secondary specialty subjects, and K–12 specialty areas, including areas such as art, music, physical education, and sometimes special education. Often they are further divided into primary and middle school levels. For special education, some states have only one license for K–12, but others break special education down into specific disability categories.

Dual Licenses

Each area of instruction requires a different course of study. To obtain dual licenses, you may have to take almost twice the number of courses, but it is usually worth the effort. Dual certification is a great benefit when you start to interview for a job. A secondary teacher who is able to teach both social studies and English may be more desirable than one who can teach only one subject area. As enrollment increases, for example, class sections that do not require a full-time position may be added to a school schedule. A teacher with more than one specialty can sometimes fill two part-time positions.

At the elementary level, it is a bonus for a district to hire a teacher who has elementary certification and also is trained in reading and/or special education. In fact, any additional license often supports the first one. In addition, the person reviewing the hundreds of resumes submitted for consideration will look for something to differentiate candidates. Multiple certifications indicate that you can work with students who have disabilities (special education) or with students who are struggling to understand the required textbooks (reading specialist). In any case, it is something to consider either at the beginning or later in your teaching career. Sometimes there is an overlap in requirements, and one teacher education course can count for two or three different certifications, which is a time and money saver for you as a student.

The Final Phase—Obtaining a "Full" License

When you start teaching, you probably will not be fully licensed as a teacher. You will hold a nonrenewable, temporary, provisional, or limited certificate—the name and category depend on the state. The point is that some kind of initial license is granted to anyone who has a bachelor's degree and meets that state's other requirements, but there are usually several more steps you must fulfill before you obtain a *full* (also known as a permanent or renewable) license. Most states require beginning teachers to demonstrate proficiency in the classroom over a period of three to five years. You must also demonstrate professional growth and development through the completion of additional education courses; in fact, most states require you to complete a master's degree before you can be permanently certified. Some states even require that you take continuing education courses to maintain your license. Indeed, each state has its own unique system of certification requirements for you to unravel.

Reciprocity

Many states have reciprocal agreements for certification; that is, if you have attended school at an accredited college with an approved program in one state, you can probably use your transcripts to apply for a license in another state without taking all of the professional courses over. States with reciprocal agreements will accept your teaching credentials from another state and allow you to seek employment without additional schooling. However, sometimes a state will require one or more specialized courses or a qualifying exam before you can begin to teach in their state. Other states will allow you to begin to work but will require you to be enrolled in an appropriate course. Requirements vary, and it is up to you to find out exactly what you need to begin your first job.

TESTING

Each state has a unique list of requirements for certification. Forty-three states require some form of testing. Thirty-five of the forty-three states that require testing use the Praxis series of tests, which are developed nationally by the Educational Testing Service (ETS). Several other states have their own tests, which are used only in their state. Some of these states are Colorado, California, Florida, Texas, and New York.

Some states (and even some teacher education programs) require standardized exams that test your academic proficiency, such as the Praxis I: Academic Skills Assessments, which evaluates general knowledge in reading, writing, and mathematics. Similar state-specific tests are required in California and Texas. Instead of, or in addition to, these basic skills tests, many states test your professional knowledge using a test such as Praxis II: Subject

Assessments, specific to your area of licensing. Some states also require Praxis III: Classroom Performance Assessments.

The Praxis series, like its predecessor test, the National Teacher Exam (NTE), was designed to develop a national minimum standard for all teachers who participate in this program. It is in your best interest to do as well as you can on these tests, because *interviewers will look at your scores*, and if they are forced to choose between equally dynamic candidates, the scale may tip toward the one with the higher scores.

The information about the Praxis series that follows will be helpful to you not only if you have to take Praxis exams but also if you have to take a state-specific test, because most of the states tests have similarities to the Praxis tests.

Use Study Groups

You may have to take some of your required tests before you graduate from your teacher education program. If so, you will have some support from your education department to help you pass your exam. In fact, you will also have quite a bit of company. You may want to take advantage of this fact and join a test preparation study group. Select people who are serious about studying and who also want to spend considerable time preparing for the exam(s).

Praxis I: Academic Skills Assessments

The first test in the Praxis series measures basic reading, writing, and mathematics and can be taken in one of two formats, either CBT or PPST. You can take the Computer-Based Test (CBT), administered by computer, whenever you can schedule an appointment. It is given throughout the year at many sites. You usually do not have to register in advance, and results for the reading and math sections are given immediately. The Pre-Professional Skills Test (PPST), the old-fashioned paper version, is given six times per year. Each subtest of the PPST is a one-hour multiple-choice test; however, the writing component also contains an essay, which you must complete in 30 minutes. The CBT also has these subtests, though the timing differs. In January 2002, the CBT was renamed as the Computerized PPST.

During the 2000–2001 school year, the PPST began to include a Listening Skills test. This test is only available as a paper-based test and will be offered on all six national test dates.

Reading

The first part of the Praxis I assessment measures your ability to read a passage and to demonstrate comprehension skills—identifying the main idea, finding specific information, and understanding the organization of the passage. It also measures your ability to analyze the passage, apply information, make inferences, and use words in context.

You are given a passage to read with specific questions to answer. The passages and questions vary in difficulty. For example, a nonfiction 100- or 200-word selection might be presented with many kinds of multiple-choice questions. The following examples of multiple-choice questions are taken directly from the *Praxis Tests at a Glance* booklets and are reprinted by permission of Educational Testing Service, the copyright owner.

In this passage the author is primarily concerned with
- (A) explaining an event
- (B) making a comparison
- (C) listing facts
- (D) retelling a story
- (E) refuting an argument

Which of the following words, if substituted for the word "occult" in line five would introduce the LEAST change in the meaning of the sentence?
- (A) legendary
- (B) subtle
- (C) invisible
- (D) persuasive
- (E) supernatural

Other multiple-choice questions include:

> ▶ Which of the following is an unstated assumption of the author?
>
> ▶ Which of the following statements best expresses the author's main point of the passage?
>
> ▶ Which of the following best describes the organization of the passage?

Writing

Another component of the Praxis I series is a writing test. It is divided into two parts: a multiple-choice segment and a writing sample. You are allowed 30 minutes for the multiple-choice segment and another 30 minutes for the writing sample segment for a total of one hour.

One kind of multiple-choice question is Error Recognition; you are asked to identify incorrect punctuation and word usage. You read a sentence or paragraph in which portions are underlined and lettered and then fill in the corresponding lettered space on the answer sheet to identify errors in grammatical relationships, mechanics, and idiom or word choice. You also may be asked to select a better way to state the given phrase or statement.

One such example, taken from the Praxis I, is

The club members <u>agreed</u> that <u>each would contribute</u> ten days of
                A   B
volunteer work <u>annually each year</u> <u>at the local hospital</u>. <u>No error</u>.
               C   D   E

There also is a series of multiple-choice questions called Sentence Corrections, which require you to determine whether the underlined portion of the sentence or one of the other options is the best way to express the author's thought. The following example is offered by ETS:

Martin Luther King, Jr. <u>spoke out passionately</u> for the poor of all races.
    (A) spoke out passionately
    (B) spoke out passionate
    (C) did spoke out passionately
    (D) has spoke out passionately
    (E) had spoken out passionate

The second part of the Praxis I writing component is a writing sample. You must select one of two topics and write an essay on that topic. The essay portion of the writing component makes up 50% of your score on this section. The examiners are looking for your ability to "take a position on an issue" and support your point of view with solid reasoning and concrete examples. The writing component is scored holistically, from one to six, where one is completely unacceptable and six is excellent. A school district might have a hard time justifying the hiring of a teacher with a score lower than four. ETS lists 72 *Topics in Advance* for applicants of the Computer-Based Test: Writing Component. You can do well on the test because you can plan ahead, write or think about the various topics, and then gather your supporting information or documentation. One example of a question posed in this part of the test is, "Which of your possessions would be the most difficult for you to give up or lose? Discuss why." ETS offers free copies of *Tests at a Glance*, which gives examples of excellent and poorly written writing samples.

Mathematics

The mathematics component of the Praxis I series covers basic mathematical information that a student would learn by middle or junior high school. However, many people forget some of these common equations—do you readily remember how to multiply fractions or reduce to the lowest common denominator? If not, you should spend extra time preparing for this part of the exam.

Math concepts tested include place value, equivalent forms, sequence of operations, square roots, prime numbers, problem solving, algorithms, ratio, proportion, interpretation of data on charts and tables, measurement, geometry, systems, and logic.

Examples of mathematical questions posed include the following:

Some values of x are less than 100. Which of the following is NOT consistent with the sentence above?
(A)   5 is not a value of x
(B)   95 is a value of x
(C)   Some values of x are greater than 100
(D)   All values of x are greater than 100
(E)   No numbers less than 100 are values of x

If $P \div 5 = Q$, then $P \div 10 =$
  (A) $10Q$
  (B) $2Q$
  (C) $Q \div 2$
  (D) $Q \div 10$
  (E) $Q \div 20$

Listening

The new Listening Skills component of the Praxis I measures your ability to retain and interpret spoken messages. You listen to questions that have been previously recorded. These questions do not appear in the test book for you to read; however, the answer choices are printed in the book for you to refer to. You are allowed one hour to take this test, which contains 55 multiple-choice questions based on recorded segments. The test is divided into three parts. In the first portion, you listen to short questions or statements and then either select the best answer to the question or select a sentence that is best supported by the statement you heard. In the second part, you listen to short dialogues between two speakers and then answer multiple-choice questions based on those dialogues. In the last part, you listen to short talks given by individual speakers and then answer multiple-choice questions based on those speeches.

Praxis II: Subject Assessments

Completely separate from Praxis I, the Praxis II: Subject Assessments are tests that measure your content area knowledge. There are over 140 different content tests available. If you want to become certified in only one area, you may have to take only one test; however, to become dually certified, you may have to take two or more.

One version of Praxis II is the Principles of Learning and Teaching tests. There are three of these tests, broken down by grade level: K–6, 5–9, or 7–12. Each of these three tests offers a case study approach that "measures a candidate's pedagogical knowledge" in the grade level tested. Another version of the Praxis II is the Multiple Subjects Assessment for Teachers (MSAT):

Content Knowledge and MSAT: Content Area Exercises. These are geared to elementary school teachers.

The third version of the Praxis II is the individual subject exams geared to the secondary school level. There are subject exams in the Praxis II series to certify every specialty you can think of—agriculture, driver education, early childhood education, health, every category of special education, English, reading, foreign language, music, mathematics, various levels of science instruction, and social studies, to name a few. These tests often are required for certification in middle and high school curriculum areas.

Many of the Praxis II exams have more than 100 multiple-choice questions. The English Language, Literature, and Composition assessment, for example, has a content knowledge component with 120 multiple-choice questions and an essay component that requires two hours of writing. Other exams incorporate newly constructed-response modules in addition to multiple-choice questions. Each test is unique, so if your state requires one or more of these subject tests, be sure to investigate each test's specific format and requirements.

How to Pass

Test taking is a skill, and the better prepared you are, the better your chances of achieving a high score. Use whatever materials you can find to help you study for the tests you need to take. The first step is to find out which tests are required in your state, then request any literature or sample study questions that are provided by the testing agency (ETS or the state). ETS offers study guides, study tips, and free practice materials for their tests. Begin by ordering their free *Tests at a Glance* booklets for a preview of the types of questions you will be asked and the format of the assessments. You may be able to obtain *Tests at a Glance* from your school, or you can download the booklet from www.ets.org.

Books by commercial publishers are available for both ETS and state-administered tests. If you want extra practice and instruction in the test areas, purchase one of these books or find them at your local library. If you have a choice of several books, choose one that has as many sample exams as possible and offers concrete advice for all of the kinds of questions on the test.

Test-Taking Tips

ETS offers some tips on how to pass its exams that will work equally well for *any exam* you have to take.

- Familiarize yourself with the test.
- Read the directions thoroughly and carefully.
- Try to understand the entire question before you respond.
- Pace yourself.
- Answer the easy questions first.
- Do not leave blank spaces; guess if you are not sure of an answer.
- Mark the answer sheet carefully.
- If it is a writing task, take notes and organize them before you begin the task.
- Review your responses for errors.

Remember that it is important to do well on standardized exams because they are part of the package that a prospective employer will review when you apply for a job.

Praxis III: Classroom Performance Assessments

The final test in the Praxis series, the Praxis III: Classroom Performance Assessment can be replaced by having your principal or other administrator observe you while teaching classes. No matter how much you would like to avoid this kind of evaluation, it is used throughout your teaching career when contracts are renewed, instructors are rehired, and teachers are granted tenure—so you may as well get used to the idea of classroom observations. (See Chapter 7 for information about being observed in the classroom.) The Praxis III is used for beginning teachers to assess various aspects of the new teacher's job performance. It is only used in some states.

STATE DEPARTMENTS OF EDUCATION

The following pages list every state department of education, with a brief rundown of certification requirements for each. The descriptions of the licensing areas and testing requirements are somewhat general, but the specific requirements for most states are quite complex and change from time to time. Also, many states provide more than one route to meeting the requirements and will accept a teacher from out of state, particularly if that teacher has several years of full-time experience. You should be able to fine tune the details needed for your particular license by contacting the department of education in your state for additional information.

Alabama Teacher Education and Certification Office

State Department of Education

P.O. Box 302101

Montgomery, AL 36130-2101

334-242-9935; FAX: 334-242-0498

www.alsde.edu

Licenses include early childhood, elementary, middle level, high school, elementary, secondary, and special education. All licenses for high school and some for middle school are based on competency in a specific teaching curriculum area. Alabama has a Department of Teacher Placement and Recruitment at the State Education Department, which has information regarding job opportunities in the state.

Alaska Department of Education

801 W. 10th Street, Suite 200

Juneau, AK 99801

907-465-2800; FAX: 907-465-4156

www.eed.state.ak.us

To secure a teaching certificate, the State Department of Education recommends that every candidate have taken six semester hours (or nine quarter hours) of credit within the five years prior to the application and *must have* three semester hours of "approved Alaska studies" and three semester hours of "approved multicultural education/cross-cultural communications." Alaska has a teacher placement clearinghouse at the University of Alaska–Fairbanks where you can register for jobs, although the jobs are located mainly in rural areas of the state.

Arizona Department of Education—Certification Unit

Phoenix Office

P.O. Box 6490

Phoenix, AZ 85005-6490

602-542-4367; FAX: 602-542-1141

www.ade.state.az.us

Arizona offers several kinds of certificates in the following categories: substitute teacher, elementary teacher (K–8), secondary education (7–12), alternative education (7–12), special education (K–12), and vocational education (K–12). In addition, you can add an *endorsement* for a specialty to the teaching certificate, which includes nine areas of special education. Candidates must pass the Arizona Teacher Proficiency Exam (ATPE).

In addition, to teach in Arizona applicants must take a course on the Arizona constitution (or pass an appropriate test) and the United States Constitution (or pass an appropriate test).

Arkansas Department of Education

General Education Division

Four State Capitol Mall, Room 304A

Little Rock, AR 72201-1071

501-682-4344

www.arkedu.state.ar.us

The levels and areas of licensure are early childhood (Pre-K–3), preschool/early adolescence (Pre-K–8), preschool/young adulthood (Pre-K–12), middle school/early adolescence (4–8), early adolescence/young adulthood (7–12). Within each of these levels there are varied specialties, including some that are integrated in grades 4–12. There are three categories of special education licenses. Arkansas requires the Praxis Exam in your area of specialty.

California Commission on Teacher Credentialing

P.O. Box 944270

1900 Capitol Avenue

Sacramento, CA 94244-2700

916-445-7254

www.ctc.ca.gov

There are multiple-subject licenses for elementary and self-contained classrooms and single-subject licenses for secondary education. All candidates must pass the California Basic Educational Skills Test (CBEST) and a district proficiency exam. Everyone must have a fifth year of training that includes courses in mainstreaming, use of computers, and health education. All candidates must know the U.S. Constitution, how to teach reading, and demonstrate subject matter proficiency.

Colorado Department of Education

201 E. Colfax Avenue

Denver, CO 80203

303-866-6628; FAX: 303-866-6866

www.cde.state.co.us/index_home.htm

Licenses are available in early childhood education, elementary education, middle school education, and secondary education, with specialties in specific subjects. There also are several K–12 special education licenses. Every candidate must pass the appropriate Program for Licensing Assessments for Colorado Educators (PLACE) assessments and must demonstrate proficiency in oral English.

Connecticut Department of Education

State Office Building

165 Capital Ave., Room 305

Hartford, CT 06106-1630

860-566-5061; FAX: 860-566-8890

www.state.ct.us

Certification is offered in early childhood education, elementary education, middle grades, Pre-K–8, and secondary academic areas. There are also Pre-K–12 certifications that include several special education licenses. Teachers are expected to pass the Praxis I Computer-Based Tests or Praxis II Subject Assessments and complete a teacher training program, Beginning Educator Support and Training (BEST).

Delaware Department of Public Instruction

401 Federal Street

P.O. Box 1402

Townsend Building, Room 279

Dover, DE 19903

302-739-4601; FAX: 302-739-4654

www.doe.state.de.us

Delaware offers certificates for early childhood (K–3), early childhood with nursery and kindergarten (N–3), elementary teacher (1–8), and secondary teacher (7–12) in specific subjects. Several specialties are K–12, and several special education licenses are available. Delaware requires testing such as the Pre-Professional Skills Test/Praxis I.

District of Columbia

Teacher Education and Licensure Branch

215 G Street NE, Suite 101A

Washington, DC 20002

202-724-4246; FAX: 202-724-88784

www.k12.dc.us

The District of Columbia offers licenses in early childhood (Pre-K–3), elementary (1–6), and middle school and secondary education (7–12). There are also noncategorical licenses in special education (K–12) and several specialty licenses that are K–12. All applicants must submit results from the Praxis I: Pre-Professional Skills Test.

Florida Department of Education

Bureau of Educator Certification

325 W. Gaines Street

Turlington Building, Suite 201

Tallahassee, FL 32399-0400

In state: 850-488-2317; out of state: 800-445-6739

www.firn.edu/doe

Florida offers many licenses: preschool (birth to age four), Pre-K–primary (age three to grade three), elementary grades (1–6), specialties in the middle grades (5–9), and secondary specialties (6–12). There also are K–12 specialties in addition to eight separate special education licenses. Candidates must complete the Florida Professional Orientation Program and demonstrate a passing score on the Florida Professional Education Test, the College Level Academic Skills Test (CLAST), and the subject area tests for that certificate.

Georgia Professional Standards Commission

Certification Section

1452 Twin Towers East

Atlanta, GA 30334

404-657-9000; FAX: 404-651-9185

www.doe.k12.ga.us

Georgia offers certificates in early childhood education (Pre-K–5), middle grades (4–8), and secondary education subject areas (7–12). K–12 certification is also offered in many areas, and there are seven special education licenses. All applicants must pass the Praxis exams in their field or meet requirements for exemption.

Hawaii Department of Education

Office of Personnel Certification and Development

P.O. Box 2360

Honolulu, HI 96804

808-586-3230; FAX: 808-586-3234

www.k12.hi.us

Hawaii has several areas of certification: elementary (K–6), subject areas specialties (7–12), and some K–12 specialties. Special education has seven categories of licenses. Hawaii has a unique feature of requiring an interview with authorized staff to become certified. The appropriate Praxis tests are required to demonstrate proficiency.

Idaho Department of Education

Len B. Jordan Office Building

650 W. State Street

P.O. Box 8370

Boise, ID 83720

208-332-6800

www.sde.state.id.us/Dept

Idaho has an elementary license (K–8), a general license (7–9), secondary subject licenses (7–9), and complete secondary certification (6–12). Each candidate must complete courses in reading, which is expected, but they also require reading in the content area for secondary subject certification. There is one special education license with eight separate endorsements.

Illinois Board of Education

Division of Professional Preparation

100 N. First Street

Springfield, IL 62777

217-782-4321

www.isbe.state.il.us

Illinois offers several licenses: early childhood (birth to grade three), elementary grades (K–9), and secondary grades in area of specialization (6–12). Several special education licenses and some specialty certifications are K–12. All applicants must pass the Illinois Certification Tests.

Indiana Department of Education

Professional Standards Board

101 W. Ohio Street, Suite 300

Indianapolis, IN 46204

317-232-9010; FAX: 317-232-9023

www.doe.state.in.us

Indiana has licenses in early childhood, kindergarten/primary (up to grade 3), elementary (1–6), middle school (5–9), secondary (9–12), and middle senior combined (5–12). In addition, there are several K–12 specialty licenses and several special education categories of certification. All applicants must submit verification of passing Praxis exam scores.

Iowa Department of Education

Grimes State Office Building

E. 14th and Grand Streets

Des Moines, IA 50319-0146

515-281-5294; FAX: 515-242-5988

www.state.ia.us/educatel

Iowa lists a Pre-K and kindergarten license, Pre-K to grade 3, elementary (K–6), and grades 7–12 specialties licenses. There are several special education categories and several K–12 licenses (such as reading). All candidates must complete a human relations component in their education program.

Kansas Department of Education

120 SE 10th Avenue

Topeka, KS 66612-1182

785-296-3201; FAX: 785-296-7933

www.ksbe.state.ks.us

Kansas offers licenses in early childhood, preschool, elementary school (K–9), middle school (5–9), junior high school (7-9), and secondary school (7–12). Special education endorsements are available in the various categories of disabilities; gifted education also falls under this heading. K–12 licenses are granted for reading specialists. Two test scores are required: the Praxis I: Pre-Professional Skills Test and the Professional Knowledge section of Praxis II.

Kentucky Department of Education

Capital Plaza Tower

500 Metro Street

Frankfort, KY 40601

502-573-4606; FAX: 502-573-1610

www.kde.state.ky.us

Kentucky offers teacher certification for three grade categories: K–4, 5–8, and 9–12. K–12 licenses are offered for some specialties, and there are several special education categories of certification. Every teacher seeking initial certification must pass the Praxis I and the Praxis II Subject Assessment appropriate for each certificate.

Louisiana Higher Education and Teaching

P.O. Box 94064

Baton Rouge, LA 70804

225-342-3790; FAX: 225-342-3499

www.doe.state.la.us

Louisiana offers certificates in Pre-K, kindergarten, elementary grades (1–8), and secondary grades (7–12). In addition, there are some K–12 licenses and special endorsements in specialty areas. There are several classifications of special education licenses. Praxis test scores are required.

Maine Department of Education

Certification Office

23 State House Station

Augusta, ME 04333

207-627-6603

www.state.me.us/education/homepage.htm

Maine classifies licenses into two main categories: elementary (K–8) and secondary (7–12). K–12 endorsements can be added in some areas. Special education licenses are also K–8 or 7–12, with specialty certifications available. A passing score on the Praxis exam is required.

Maryland State Department of Education

Certification Branch

200 W. Baltimore Street

Baltimore, MD 21201

410-767-0100

www.msde.state.md.us

Certificates are offered in elementary education (1–6), middle school (7–8), and single subject specialties (N–12 or 7–12). Special education is K–12, and there are several special education concentrations. Scores from the appropriate Praxis II test are required.

Massachusetts Department of Education

Office of Certification and Credentialing

350 Main Street

Malden, MA 02148

781-338-3000, ext 6600

www.doe.mass.edu

Massachusetts offers certificates in early childhood (Pre-K–3), elementary (1–6), middle school (5–9), and specialty subjects, both academic and nonacademic (5–9 and 9–12) in some areas. There are many special education categories issued at various levels. Candidates must pass a two-part exam demonstrating communication and literacy skills in addition to subject matter knowledge.

Michigan Department of Education

608 W. Allegan Street

Hannah Building

Lansing, MI 48933

517-373-3310

www.mde.state.mi.us

Michigan has two levels of certificates: elementary (all subjects in K–5 and a subject area in 6–8) and secondary (a subject area in 7–12). There are K–12 licenses in several areas and multiple certifications for special education. Teachers must demonstrate competency by taking the Michigan Test for Teacher Certification.

Minnesota Department of Children, Families, and Learning

1500 Hwy. 36 West

Roseville, MN 55113

651-582-8833

www.educ.state.mn.us

Minnesota offers an elementary license (1–6) and a secondary license (7–12). A candidate can obtain a middle school license as an endorsement to either the elementary or the secondary license after completing an additional 18 semester hours. Special education licenses are K–12 and are divided into many subcategories. Completion of the Minnesota Human Relations program and passing scores on the Praxis I exam are required.

Mississippi Department of Education

P.O. Box 771

359 North West Street

Jackson, MS 39205-0771

601-359-3483

www.mde.k12.ms.us

Mississippi issues a standard license for everyone. Special endorsements must be added and include nursery, kindergarten, several elementary groupings, reading, special education concentrations, gifted education, and some academic subcategories. Supplemental endorsements are granted in other areas after a candidate completes an additional 18 semester hours. The Praxis II Principles of Learning and Teaching and the Praxis II Specialty Area Test are required.

Missouri Department of Elementary and Secondary Education

Division of Urban and Teacher Education—Teacher Certification

P.O. Box 480

Jefferson City, MO 65102-0480

573-751-0051

www.dese.state.mo.us

Missouri offers licenses in early education (Pre-K–3), elementary (1–6), middle school (5–9), and secondary education in specific subjects (7–12). There are K–12 licenses for some specialties and several categories of certification for special education. A minimum GPA of 2.5 (out of 4.0) in your degree program and a minimum qualifying score on the Praxis exam are required.

Montana Office of Public Instruction

Certification Services

Box 202501

Helena, MT 59620-2501

406-444-3150; FAX: 406-444-2893

www.metnet.state.mt.us

Several categories of licenses are available: elementary (K–8), secondary (5–12 or 7–12), and K–12 areas, including special education. A qualifying test (such as the Praxis I: Pre-Professional Skills Test or the Computer-Based Test) is required.

Nebraska Department of Education

301 Centennial Mall South

P.O. Box 94987

Lincoln, NE 68509-4987

402-471-2295

www.nde.state.ne.us

Licenses are available in early childhood (birth to grade three), elementary (K–3), middle grades (4–9), secondary (7–12), or preschool disabled (birth to kindergarten). Candidates must demonstrate basic skills competency on the Praxis I, have human relations training, and demonstrate special education competencies.

Nevada Department of Education

1820 E. Sahara, Suite 205

Las Vegas, NV 89104-3746

702-486-6458; FAX: 702-486-6450

www.nde.state.nv.us

Nevada offers licenses in elementary education (K–8) for specialized areas or self-contained classes, and secondary education (7–12) in specialized areas. There are several K–12 specialty areas and 14 special education licenses, which are also K–12; this includes gifted education. Competency tests such as the Praxis I and special-area subject assessments on the Praxis II are required. Candidates must complete courses in Nevada School Law, the Nevada Constitution, and the U.S. Constitution.

New Hampshire Department of Education

Bureau of Credentialing

101 Pleasant Street

Concord, NH 03301

603-271-2407; FAX: 603-271-3494

www.state.he.us/doel

New Hampshire offers licenses in N–K, elementary education, specialized content areas, and several special education areas. New Hampshire requires a passing score on Praxis I, and Praxis II where applicable.

New Jersey Department of Education

Office of Licensing

P.O. Box 500

100 Riverview

Trenton, NJ 08625

609-292-2070

www.state.nj.us/education

Elementary licenses are granted for N–8, and there are N–12 specialty licenses. There are separate K–12 licenses for several categories in special education and separate K–12 licenses in other specialties such as bilingual education and English as a Second Language. A passing score on the Praxis II Specialty Area Test for the subject teaching field, and the Elementary Education Content Knowledge Test for elementary school is required.

New Mexico Department of Education

Licensure Unit

Education Building

300 Don Gaspar

Santa Fe, NM 87501-2786

505-827-6587

www.sde.state.nm.us

New Mexico offers licenses in elementary education (K–8), middle school (5–9), and secondary education (7–12). Special education is K–12. Endorsements to these licenses are available after completing an additional 24–36 credits in the subject area. Candidates must demonstrate proficiency by taking a Praxis II exam.

New York State Education Department

Office of Teaching

Cultural Education Center, Room 5A 11

Nelson A. Rockefeller Empire State Plaza

Albany, NY 12230

518-474-3901; FAX: 518-473-0271

www.nysed.gov/cert

New York offers an elementary certificate that is subdivided into Pre-K–3 and 4–6, secondary specialty teaching certificates (7–12), and K–12 licenses in some areas. Special education teachers are licensed K–12, with some special certificates required. There is a four-part assessment system: the New York State Teacher Certification Exam (NYSTCE), which includes a liberal arts and science test (LAST); an elementary and secondary assessment of teaching skills-written (ATS-W); a content specialty test (CST); and a language proficiency assessment (LPA). Additional exams are required for some specialty licenses.

North Carolina

State Department of Public Instruction

Licensure Section

301 North Wilmington Street

Raleigh, NC 27601

919-807-3300

www.dpi.state.nc.us

Licenses are issued for birth through kindergarten, elementary education (K–6), middle school (6–9), and secondary education (9–12). Special education licenses are K–12 for "exceptional children" and have several categories. Other K–12 licenses are issued in several areas, including Junior ROTC. Candidates must pass the Praxis I and a specialty or subject area exam.

North Dakota Education Standards and Practices Board

600 E. Boulevard Ave.

Bismark, ND 58505-0440

701-328-2264

www.dpi.state.nd.us

Available licenses are elementary (K–8, 1–8, or 5–8) and specialty licenses for secondary education, which are classified K–12. Special education teachers require either elementary or secondary training, and restricted categories require specialized training. Reading specialists must have either elementary or secondary classroom experience and advanced courses from an accredited program beyond the bachelor's degree. A minimum GPA of 2.5 from an accredited program is required.

Ohio Department of Education

Teacher Education and Certification and Professional Development

Ohio Departments Building

65 Front Street, Room 412

Columbus, OH 43215-4183

614-466-3593; FAX: 614-466-1999

www.state.oh.us

Ohio offers licenses in Pre-K, elementary education (K–3 and 1–8), and secondary education up to grade twelve. K–12 licenses are granted for some specialty areas, including special education, which has a variety of subcategories. All teachers must pass the appropriate Praxis exams.

Oklahoma State Department of Education

Hodge Education Building

2500 N. Lincoln Boulevard

Oklahoma City, OK 73105-4599

405-521-3301; FAX: 405-521-6205

www.sde.state.ok.us

Licenses are given in elementary education (1–8), elementary and secondary (1–8), and secondary education (7–12). Teachers who wish to teach in grades six, seven, or eight must hold a special subject area endorsement for middle schools. There also are early childhood licenses (Pre-K–3 and N–K). K–12 licenses are issued in several areas, including special education, which is subdivided into six additional categories.

Oregon Department of Education

Teacher Standards and Practices

255 Capitol Street NE

Salem, OR 97310-1332

503-378-3586; FAX: 503-378-4448

www.ode.state.or.us

Licenses are issued for elementary education (Pre-K–9), which is combined with early childhood education. Subject area licenses are issued for middle and high school (5–12), and there are K–12 specialties. Special education licenses (pre-primary through grade twelve) are issued in several categories, with one special license for early intervention birth to preschool. Candidates must demonstrate knowledge of discrimination laws and pass standardized tests such as the CBEST, the Praxis I: Pre-Professional Skills Test (PPST), or the CBT.

Pennsylvania Department of Education

Bureau of Teacher Preparation and Certification

333 Market Street

Harrisburg, PA 17126-0333

717-783-6788; FAX: 717-783-6736

www.pde.psu.edu

Licenses are issued for elementary education (K–6), early childhood education (N–3), and secondary subject areas (7–12). Many licenses are K–12, including special education, which has several categories of certification. Praxis I and II assessments are required.

Rhode Island Department of Education

Certification and Placement

255 Westminster Street

Providence, RI 02903

401-277-4600

www.ridoe.net

Certificates are available in early childhood education (Pre-K–2), elementary education (1–6), and secondary education (7–12). There are K–12 licenses in several specialty areas and six categories of special education licenses. Bilingual education is an endorsement to the elementary and secondary certificates, and English as a Second Language is an endorsement to elementary, secondary, and foreign language certificates. Candidates must submit scores from the Praxis II: Principles of Learning and Teaching exam.

South Carolina Department of Education

1006 Rutledge Building

1429 Senate St.

Columbia, SC 29201

803-734-8466

www.sde.state.sc.us

South Carolina offers teaching endorsements in early childhood education (K–4), elementary education (1–8), middle school (7–8) in some areas, and secondary education (7–12) in specific subject areas. Special education is K–12 and is divided in different areas for licensing. Candidates must present appropriate scores on the Praxis II Professional Knowledge Examination and the appropriate Praxis II Subject Assessment and Specialty Area Tests.

South Dakota Department of Education and Cultural Affairs

700 Governors Drive

Pierre, SD 57501-2291

605-773-3553; FAX: 605-773-6139

www.state.sd.us/state/executive/deca

South Dakota offers one license to all teachers; various endorsements are added. Endorsements are issued based on the configuration of the school setting: K–8, 5–8, 6–8, 7–8, 7–9, or 9–12. Separate certifications are offered for gifted education and special education, which is subdivided into several K–12 areas. Reading certificates are offered after three years of classroom experience in the elementary or secondary area and specified courses are completed on the graduate level.

Tennessee State Department of Education

Andrew Johnson Tower, 6th Floor

710 James Robertson Parkway

Nashville, TN 37243-0375

615-741-2731; FAX: 615-741-6236

www.state.tn.us/education

Tennessee issues licenses Pre-K–3, elementary education (1–8), secondary education (7–12), and K–12 for several specialties, including special education. Special endorsements are needed to teach some specialties. To gain certification, a candidate must have a letter of intent to hire from the superintendent of a school district and documentation of appropriate scores on the Praxis II Specialty Area tests.

Texas Education Agency

William B. Travis Building

1701 N. Congress Avenue

Austin, TX 78701-1494

512-463-9734; FAX: 512-463-9008

www.tea.state.tx.us

Certificates are issued in elementary education (Pre-K–6, 1–6, 1–8), secondary education (6–12), and all levels (K–12) for some specialties. Special endorsements are granted for early childhood education, bilingual education, English as a Second Language, technology, and special education. Special education is further divided into other categories. Candidates must pass state assessment tests in reading, mathematics, and writing and pass exit level tests designed by the state, the Examination for the Certification of Educators in Texas (ExCET) in the specific teaching field.

Utah State Office of Education

250 East 500 South

Salt Lake City, UT 84111

801-538-7510; FAX: 801-538-7521

www.usoe.k12.ut.us

Certificates are available for early childhood education (K–3), elementary education (1–8), and secondary education (6–12). Special education certificates are separate and available in several categories.

Vermont Department of Education

120 State Street

Montpelier, VT 05620-2501

802-828-2445

www.state.vt.us

Licenses are issued for early childhood (birth through grade eight), elementary education (K–6), middle school (5–8), and secondary education (7–12). There are also seven special education certifications. Applicants must pass the appropriate Praxis I or II exam.

Virginia Department of Education

P.O. Box 2120

101 N. 14th Street

Richmond, VA 23218

804-225-2020; FAX: 804-371-2455

www.pen.k12.va.us

Virginia offers licenses in early childhood (N, K–3), elementary (3–6), middle school (6–8), and secondary education (8–12). There are several Pre-K–12 specialty areas and several endorsements for special education, which is generally N–12, except for an early childhood specialty. Reading teachers are considered support personnel and require a master's degree. Candidates are required to take the Praxis I and Praxis II: Specialty Area tests.

Washington Professional Education and Certification

Old Capitol Building

P.O. Box 47200

Olympia, WA 98504-7200

360-753-6773; FAX: 360-586-0145

www.k12.wa.us

Teaching certificates are granted with one or more of the 44 available endorsements. There are very specific courses required to earn a teaching license and appropriate endorsements. Specialty endorsements include early childhood education (N–3), elementary education (K–8), and academic areas. Some of these academic endorsements are 4–12 and others are K–12, such as bilingual education and English as a Second Language. Special education is also K–12, except for a specialty in early childhood education.

West Virginia Office of Professional Preparation

1900 Kanawha Boulevard E

Charleston, WV 25305

304-558-7011

www.wvde.state.wv.us

Certificates are available in early childhood education (Pre-K–K), multi-subjects (K–8), middle school (5–8), middle and adolescent (5–12), or adolescent (9–12) for specific subjects. Gifted education is either K–8 or 5–12. K–12 licenses are issued in some specialties and special education is K–12, with endorsements in seven areas. Appropriate scores from the Praxis I: Pre-Professional Skills Test or the Computer-Based Test and the Praxis II (the subject area competency tests in a candidate's specialty area) are required. If a candidate can demonstrate high scores on college entrance tests such as the ACT or SAT, then the Praxis I test can be waived.

Wisconsin Department of Public Instruction

125 S. Webster Street

P.O. Box 7841

Madison, WI 53707

608-266-1027; FAX: 608-267-2920

www.dpi.state.wi.us

Licenses are available in early childhood (Pre-K–3), elementary (1–6), elementary and middle (1–9), middle (5–9), middle and secondary (5–12), and secondary (9–12). Some specialty areas, such as reading, are K–12. Special education is K–12, except for early childhood, with many specialty endorsements. The Praxis I test is necessary for certification.

Wyoming Department of Education

Hathaway Building, 2nd Floor

2300 Capitol Avenue

Cheyenne, WY 82002-0050

307-777-7291; FAX: 307-777-6234

www.k12.wy.us

Standard teaching certificates are offered, with endorsements in some areas. Teachers can be certified in early childhood education (birth to age eight), elementary education (K–8), middle school (5–8), and secondary education (7–12). There are K–12 endorsements in some areas, and reading teachers must hold a standard certificate with an advanced degree in reading. Candidates must demonstrate knowledge of the U.S. Constitution and the Wyoming Constitution. The superintendent of schools in each district administers these exams.

INSIDE TRACK

Who:	Lily Harding
What:	ESL Teacher
Where:	Boulder, Colorado

INSIDER'S STORY

I have been an adult educator for four years, but I've really been teaching for the past ten years. I graduated from college with a degree in art history; no longer interested in the art world, I decided to apply to the Peace Corps to get some real world experience. The next thing I knew, I was embarking as an education volunteer on a trip to the South Pacific that would forever change my life—everything from opinions to ideals, from perceptions to aspirations, from personal style to career ambitions.

My experience in Kiribati exposed me to some harsh realities as I struggled to teach English to adolescents—many of whom had little formal education. As I learned how to communicate to the class I surprised myself by realizing that I didn't need a lot of fancy classroom supplies or computers to get the principles of language across to my students. My students were eager to learn English, and I soon discovered that a rapt audience is always a strong learning tool.

After two years on the island, I came back to the states excited about teaching. I went back to college to earn a teaching certificate, and to support myself, I taught English as a Second Language to the families of foreign students enrolled at the Wharton School of Business at the University of Pennsylvania. I taught a group of young children in one group and their mothers in another. Both groups needed different types of instruction, neither of which I was provided with by my program. The resourcefulness I learned working Kiribati came in handy—I used familiar items from around my students' apartments to help me with my spontaneous lesson plans.

Two years later, I had my Master's in English along with my teaching certificate. It's very difficult to find a job as a high school English teacher, so I found my first job as a middle school art teacher in a private school in the suburbs of Philadelphia. It was exciting at first to combine my artistic side with my newly acquired teaching credentials. However, I soon realized that this limited role in education was not satisfying. While I think that teaching secondary subjects is a very important part of education, I felt that it wasn't enough for me—I wanted to be more involved and to help students on a deeper level.

My next position was in an inner-city school teaching 7th grade English. It was very demanding, and although I really felt needed by the school, I didn't enjoy teaching in front of a classroom of disinterested students. I wanted the enchanted faces from Kiribati, eager to learn.

I thought long and hard about my next move. I needed a change professionally and personally, so when the school year ended, I picked up and moved to one of my very favorite places: Boulder, Colorado. I looked into programs at the local university and in the Denver area. I ended up customizing my current position, which is perfect for me in every way.

Three days a week, I commute to Denver and teach ESL to adults, mostly immigrants from Mexico. Talk about a captive audience! They are so warm and receptive that I sometimes feel as though I'm not working, simply communicating and connecting. My other job is as a creative writing instructor at the continuing education department at my local community college two nights per week. Next semester, I'm adding an art class to my teaching assignments, and I can't wait!

My advice for new teachers is to honor your inspiration. Take the time to evaluate the reasons why you became interested in education, especially when the going gets tough. And it does get tough—ask any teacher. Education encompasses so many different jobs. If you're passionate about education, keep trying out different levels and classes until you strike the right chord. Maybe your first job is not right for you, as mine wasn't. It's OK to figure your career out through process of elimination, as very few people know exactly what they want to be when they grow up, even when they have spent years being properly trained, certified, and employed.

CHAPTER five

FINDING JOB OPENINGS AND CREATING YOUR RESUME

In this chapter, you will find a wealth of tools for landing a great teaching job. First, you will get the inside scoop on conducting your job search—from networking and using online career resources to attending job fairs and answering classified ads. Then, you will find the tools you need to create a great resume.

FINDING the right job requires intensive effort. Many positions may be available in your area of certification, so during the job search, application, and interview process, you must provide the proper information about yourself to ensure that you land in a school that is a good match for your specific talents and interests. This includes thoroughly researching the schools for which you are applying to work, so that you can determine whether you are a good match for the job.

HOW TO FIND JOB OPENINGS

There are many ways to conduct a job search, but the most productive method is to combine the resources discussed in this section. Using several different methods of searching for a job will increase your chances for success. One excellent resource if you are in or recently graduated from college is the career placement office. Another good resource is the education department at your college.

College Placement Office and Education Department

The career placement office at your college or university is an excellent job-hunting resource. The placement office has brochures, books, and other data that can help direct your job search. In many placement offices, you can create a file containing your unofficial transcripts and letters of recommendation to send to prospective employers. Often, these services are also available to alumni, so if you've already graduated, consider calling the placement office to see if you can use their placement file service.

In addition, many teacher education departments receive job postings directly from school districts and provide a list of job openings at the local, regional, and state level to their students. Sometimes these listings will be posted on a bulletin board in plain view, in other schools you may need to ask the department secretary where to find them.

Sample Resources for Job-Hunting Teachers

You might be surprised at the wealth of material available from your own teacher education program that will help you conduct your job search. For instance, Southwest Missouri State University, a major teacher preparation institution, issues an annual report on teacher supply and demand and average starting salary in Missouri. Issued by the Career Planning and Placement Center, the report is a compilation of data from a survey of public school administrators from ten regions of the state. This format also is used to report teacher supply and demand nationally. Because this report is issued annually, a beginning teacher or teacher candidate can use the most current information to see which trends have developed in particular areas of certification.

Student Teaching or Substitute Experience

While you are student teaching or substitute teaching, be on the lookout for job vacancies that may open up in the school you are in. This is a great way to get hired full-time because the school administrators and other teachers can become familiar with your teaching skills and style. Try to develop good working relationships with everyone you meet during your student or substitute teaching experiences. You may be able to land a permanent position right at that very school district. You will have an advantage over your competition because you will already be familiar with the school's unique programs, needs, and culture. Even if a position doesn't open up while you are teaching there, if you keep in touch with a teacher or administrator at the school, you can find out when a position becomes available.

Publications

Review job listings in publications from education organizations and other education-related publishers. For example, *Education Week*, a weekly newspaper published by Editorial Projects in Education, Inc., has an extensive list of job openings in teaching and administration. Also check the local newspapers where you wish to teach; districts often list job openings in the local want ads. *The New York Times* publishes a special section of education-related job openings (not part of the regular want ads) every Sunday in New York and nationwide. Become familiar with the format of the advertisements you read, so you can quickly find the information that is relevant to your own particular job search. While you can find teaching jobs advertised throughout the entire year, you will probably find that newspapers have the most teacher ads in them during the months of April through July.

Give 'Em What They Want!

If you are answering an advertisement for a position, *follow all the directions* given in the ad. Include everything requested—copies of certification, self-addressed and stamped envelopes, letters of reference, and unofficial transcripts. Most applicants will be asked to complete applications right away, but if you don't submit everything as requested, your resume will end up in an "I'll get to it later pile" and will not be processed until someone gets around to calling you about the missing documentation.

Job Fairs

Job fairs are becoming a popular way for public school districts to meet, and in some cases, hire on the spot, qualified teachers looking for work. In some areas, one school district will hold a job fair, in others, several school districts in one region will get together to sponsor a job fair. For example, a job fair in California recently had 30 different school districts in participation.

Each district had a booth set up where district representatives (human resources administrators, principals and experienced teachers) provided employment applications and district information to prospective teachers, such as salary schedules, class size, projected vacancies, and so on. Job fair attendees could leave resumes and/or portfolios with the districts of their choice. Some districts conducted brief interviews during the job fair.

In addition to job fairs sponsored by school districts, many colleges and universities hold teacher placement days, usually in the spring of the year—these placement days are often called campus job fairs. As demand outstrips supply in certain areas of certification, some school districts are finding it necessary to travel to colleges in other states to recruit teachers. You may be able to meet with administrators or human resource directors from many different school districts at a campus job fair.

Both kinds of job fairs are an excellent source of information about available job openings in a particular area or region, and you can sometimes even get hired during a job fair. You can find out about job fairs from your college placement office, your college's education department, or your local newspaper.

Steps to Achieving Success at a Job Fair

1. *Register in Advance*

   Signing up for a job fair in advance lets employers pre-screen applicants and possibly set up interviews the day of the fair. It's not a guarantee you will get noticed, but it may give you an advantage.

2. *Do Your Homework*

   Obtain a list of the schools who will be in attendance prior to the event and highlight those you wish to visit. By narrowing the field, you will increase your chances of meeting specific employers that interest you, as opposed to aimlessly walking among booths. After picking your top choices, research each school, so when you speak to one of their representatives, you appear knowledgeable and well informed.

3. *Dress for Success*

   You should dress professionally, as if you were interviewing for a job. Since you will be on your feet for several hours, wear comfortable shoes. If you are given a nametag, display it prominently, so your name is easily visible as you meet and greet people. If possible, put your nametag on the right side of your chest, so that people's eyes are led right to your nametag as you shake their hands.

4. *Bring Several Copies of Your Resumes*

   Bring plenty of copies of your resume with you to the job fair. If you have more than one job objective, such as two different secondary education certifications, make sure you bring enough of each version of your resume and keep them organized, so when you meet different school representatives you have the appropriate one in hand.

5. *Get Organized*

   Arrive early and survey the fair layout before it's flooded with eager job seekers like yourself. If you feel nervous, try approaching a school that is not one of your top picks, so you can practice talking about your skills and job interests and build up your confidence. You can make yourself more memorable by re-visiting the schools on your "top choices" list before leaving. Thank their representatives again for their time and reinforce your interest in having a formal interview on-site.

6. *Plan Ahead So You Feel Prepared*

   Plan what you want to say ahead of time by focusing on the type of work you are seeking, your background, experience, and professional objectives. Be quick, decisive and concise, especially at the booths of popular school districts where many job seekers are vying for attention. You only have a few minutes to sell yourself, so don't be afraid to ask what you need to do to obtain a formal interview.

7. *Networking Works*

Job fairs are a great way to meet fellow colleagues, exchange job information and leads, and talk to members of professional organizations. Print up simple business cards with your name and contact information, and bring plenty of them to hand out to people you meet. You never know what kind of job opportunities may result from networking.

8. *Follow-Up When It's Over*

Don't procrastinate in doing your follow-up work after the job fair. Send a letter to everyone you met whose address you obtained during the fair. Briefly restate your interest in the school and your qualifications for the position, as well as your interest in an on-site interview.

Teacher Sign-On Bonuses

If your area of specialization is in math, science, foreign languages, or special education, you are at a distinct advantage because of the nationwide shortage of teachers in these areas. Your job search will focus more on getting the best deal for yourself rather than having to focus exclusively on the best deal for the school. After you research some schools and find ones that you feel would be a good fit, you may want to investigate the perks they offer to lure new teachers into their schools. For example, some schools are handing out generous signing bonuses if you sign a contract to teach at their school, while others are offering gift certificates or other gestures that demonstrate their eagerness to hire the teachers who are in demand. For example, in California, many school systems offer housing bonuses and assistance for teachers as incentives to join their schools. Denver, Colorado school systems offer tax credits, property tax relief, and reduced-cost housing to teachers. Other states are providing greater tuition assistance for teachers who want to pursue continuing education or masters degrees. In Las Vegas, Nevada, local universities have partnered with the district to offer options to help professionals and stay-at-home parents with college degrees to change careers and become teachers.

The Internet

One of the best new resources for job hunters is the Internet. You may have heard of some of the most popular job searching websites, such as Monster.com. These sites boast millions of visitors every year and list hundreds of thousands of job openings for all different types of careers. While these mega sites offer education listings that can be searched by locality and other search criteria, they aren't geared specifically for teachers. The good news is that there are several other websites that are. Here are several examples of websites where you can post your resume and view job postings specifically geared for teachers and other education professionals. All sites offer free career information and free resume posting services to job hunters, unless otherwise noted.

www.recruitingteachers.com

This site has a huge list of links for nationwide job bank websites that list teacher vacancies. The National Teacher Recruitment Clearinghouse, hosted by Recruiting New Teachers, Inc. (RNT), is a resource for prospective teachers seeking jobs—and for school districts and states seeking qualified teachers. RNT is a national nonprofit company, established in 1986 to help build a qualified and diverse corps of teachers for America's schools.

www.teachers-teachers.com

Teachers-Teachers.com offers a job placement service for teachers. You can register to use their resume builder to create an online version of your resume. Then, you can list your job specifications, indicating in which states, subjects and type of school (public/private) you would like to teach. If there are job openings that match your specifications, you will receive an e-mail notification. If you find a job opening that appeals to you, you can log on to your personal home page on their site to more thoroughly view the open position. From there, you click on the school's name to view their website. If you want to apply for the job, you can save your cover letter online and email it with the click of a button. The site is quite sophisticated and streamlined, and it is affiliated with the American Association of Colleges for Teacher Education. In addition to their website, you can contact them by calling 503-690-7988 or by writing to 26 West Pennsylvania Avenue, Towson, MD 21204.

www.k12jobs.com

This site lists job postings at kindergarten, elementary schools, junior high, and high schools. Each job posting includes school name, location, application deadline, salary, contact information, and the school's e-mail and website addresses. You can search by job title, category, school name, or state that the job opening is located in.

www.cec.sped.org/cc/cc.htm

Career Connections is operated by The Council for Exceptional Children (CEC) and claims that it is the only job bank on the Internet devoted exclusively to special education professionals. This Internet job posting service is an online bulletin board listing job vacancies. Employers post job vacancies on the Internet-based job bank that is accessible only through the CEC website. The Resume Referral Service is a database of resumes that employers can search to find appropriate applicants. Job seekers can gain access to the database and search it by geographical location, job title, or other key words. There is no fee for searching the database. You can also call 614-529-0429 for more information.

www.hireed.net

You can use HireEd.net to post your resume, search job openings online, and even set up a search agent so that HireEd.net will conduct automatic searches and notify you via e-mail about job postings that match your qualifications and interests. HireEd.net's (Job Seeker) services are free for all members of the Association for Supervision and Curriculum Development (ASCD). If you're not a member, you can still post your resume and search the job listings for free but you will be charged a fee for setting up a search agent and having HireEd.net search for jobs for you. To get started, click on Job Seeker on the page's left-hand scroll bar, register, and begin your job search.

www.teacherjobs.com

This educational placement service places educators in public, private, and parochial schools on the elementary, secondary, and college levels throughout the nation. It claims to be "the largest teacher placement service in the United States." While there is no registration fee or cost to use this placement service, there is a fee if you land a job through a contact gained from their service. So, if you secure employment through information provided by their company, you will pay a fee (usually a percentage of your first year's salary.) You can also contact this company by writing to Educational Placement Service, 90 S. Cascade, Suite 1110, Colorado Springs, CO 80903.

www.edweek.org/jobs.cfm

This site is the Marketplace section of *Education Week* on the Web. The Marketplace consists of a wide range of administrative and teacher vacancies across the United States and abroad. You can browse through the ads by region or by job title. These listings are updated weekly and provide you with all the information you need to apply for a position. Many of the nation's top school districts, universities, and educational organizations advertise in The Marketplace. You can browse their listings for free.

www.privateschooljobs.com

At the Private School Employment Network's website, you can view job openings at private schools nationwide. The job openings are searchable by job title for free. If you want to place your resume online at this website, you can do so for a fee of $25. Access to the database of resumes is free to the private schools who want to search it.

www.careers.education.wisc.edu/ProjectConnect/MainMenu.cfm

To access teaching vacancies at *Project Connect: Connecting Schools and Teachers in the Information Age*, you need to get a username and password from the college or university where you received your teacher education degree. You can search the website address listed above to find state-by-state listings of educational institutions to see if your college is connected.

www.education-world.com/jobs

This education employment center offers free services for those seeking teaching jobs. You can browse job listings and other people's posted resumes as well as submit your own resume online.

www.greatteacher.net

Click on the link "Job Classifieds" to see a listing of available jobs. Positions are categorized by location (state, country, or region) and can be found in the category-scroll-down box under "select a location." Each ad has a job description along with contact information. When you click the "contact" button, a response form appears which can be emailed directly to the employer by clicking "send."

www.school-jobs.net

This site offers a bulletin board where job seekers and schools can find each other. You can search job openings nationwide by salary, location, or area of expertise. When you find a position that interests you, you can contact the school directly to apply. In addition, you can post your resume for free on this site. If a school is interested in your resume, they will contact you directly.

www.ihiresecondaryteachers.com

This job posting site is free to prospective teachers. You must register as a new candidate and complete the profile information in order to view the job ads. You apply for a job based upon the information supplied in the ad. The employer may then respond if interested. After you have registered, completed the profile, and submitted your resume, iHire will send you an e-mail when you have been matched to a position. You can then return to the website and login. When you arrive at the candidate menu page, select "view potential job matches" to see the list of matched jobs. Click on the job ID# and the job information will appear. If you would like to apply for a position, answer the requirement section and hit the "submit" button. This will allow the employer to view your application and resume. Job ads are posted for 60 days only. The employer has three options when they review your resume. They may keep it under review, disapprove it, or send you an e-mail notification to contact them for an interview. The status will be listed next to the Job ID# on your list of jobs responded to.

Creating Your Own Network

Networking can be just as powerful and productive as more formal job searches. Essentially, it is just talking to people you already know or meeting new people to talk about some aspect of teaching. For example, you can network with your friends, relatives, and acquaintances to find out if they know of a school that is hiring teachers. Your network may include:

▶ professional contacts made during your teacher education program
▶ friends and family, especially those who are in education-related jobs
▶ teachers and administrators you met during your internship or student teaching
▶ friends and acquaintances from other settings such as religious, civic, and professional organizations and social clubs

How many times have you heard the statement, "It is not *what* you know, but *who* you know"? The reality is that it can be advantageous to know *the right people*, or those who can help you get an interview for the position you want. Tell people that you are looking for a teaching job, ask them to pass your name along, or ask whether they know of any available teaching positions. Ask these people for permission to use their names as references. You can gather a lot of information in a casual way, just by talking to as many people as you can. After your conversations, try to take a few moments to jot down notes to yourself because the more people you talk to, the more jumbled the names, places, and facts can become. Organize your notes so you can easily refer back to them if one of your networking contacts eventually gives you a lead. Networking can be a powerful tool, and it just may help you get an interview and, ultimately, a job.

PREPARING YOUR RESUME

Once you determine where the jobs are, the next step is to contact the school(s) in which you would like to teach. The usual way to make this contact is to send a cover letter and a resume, which is a written summary of your work experience and academic preparation. As in face-to-face meetings, *first impressions count*, and a resume must make a good impression on the reader. One principal in a small Midwestern high school initially sorts resumes into two piles to determine which ones to review more closely. Any resume that contains the slightest mistake in spelling or grammar, has typographical errors, or is excessively long is considered unacceptable.

Knowing the appropriate format and critical information to include on a resume will not guarantee that you get an interview; however, if you do not present yourself professionally in writing chances for job search success are reduced.

What Goes into a Resume?

When it comes to landing a job, your resume is one of your most important sales and promotional tools. Using just one side of an 8.5"x 11" sheet of paper, you must convince a potential employer that you're the perfect candidate for the job opening that's available. Your resume has to be powerful, positive, attention getting, yet truthful. It should shout out to the employer, "Hire me!" not "File me!"

Most potential employers want to know the same basic things about you: your name, address, education, certification, and work experience. You might also include your specific job objective, the professional organizations you belong to, and your professional references. The rest of this chapter will explain how to organize and present this information.

Even if you choose to hire a professional resume writer or resume preparation service to create your resume, he or she will require the majority of this information in order to do a good job creating a resume on your behalf. The same holds true if you purchase off-the-shelf resume creation software for your computer. Keep in mind, the majority of these resume writing tips and strategies apply to traditional printed resumes as well as to electronic resumes that you submit online.

The first section of any resume includes information about how a potential employer can contact you. The details you will want to provide include:

Contact Information
    Full Name: _____
    Permanent Street Address: _____
    City, State, Zip: _____
    Daytime Telephone Number: _____
    Evening Telephone Number: _____
    Pager/Cell Phone Number (Optional): _____
    FAX Number (Optional): _____

E-mail Address: —————————————————————————

School Address (if applicable): —————————————————

Your Phone Number at School (if applicable): ———————————

If you live at school or if you are thinking of moving soon, include a permanent address as well as your current information.

Do not include personal information in the resume. You could endanger your chances of getting hired if you include information about your religion, marital status, race, or other personal details.

The following questions will help you pinpoint the specific types of information that needs to go into the various sections of your resume and/or cover letter. Cover letters are discussed in Chapter 6. By answering these questions, you will also get to know yourself better, so you can find the job opportunities you will prosper in and that you will enjoy. For more information on creating your resume, be sure to read Jason R. Rich's *Great Resume* (New York: LearningExpress, 2000).

Job Objective(s)

Many resumes begin with a career goal or objective. It doesn't have to be profound or philosophical; just list the job you want to obtain. The purpose of the objective is to assure potential employers that they are about to read a relevant resume.

Now Starring . . .

Your degree(s) and certification(s) are the stars of your resume. Make sure they are easy to find (that is, located near the beginning of the resume) and clearly written.

The first things that a human resources director, supervisor, or principal hiring a new employee looks for on a resume are the degree(s) and certification(s) of the applicant. How the applicant's information matches the hiring needs determines whether the remaining information on the resume will be read.

In the space that follows, write a short description of the job you're seeking. Be sure to include as much information as possible about how you can use your skills to the employer's benefit. Later, you will condense this answer into one short sentence.

What is the job title you're looking to fill? (i.e. elementary teacher)

Educational Background and Certification

List the specific type(s) of certification you have and the state(s) in which that certification was granted: _____

_____

When listing your educational background, start with your most recent school and work backward. List your degree or certificate, the name and location of the school, and the date you graduated. Also include special programs or teacher-related continuing education courses you have completed.
   List the most recent college or university you've attended:

_____

City/State: _____

What year did you start? _____

Graduation month/year: _____

Degree(s) and/or award(s) earned: _____

Your major(s): _____

Your minor(s): _____

List some of your most impressive accomplishments, extracurricular activities, club affiliations, etc.: _____

List specialized education courses you've taken that help qualify you for the job you're seeking: _____

Grade point average (GPA): _____

Other colleges/universities you've attended: _____

City/State: _____

What year did you start? _____

Graduation month/year: _____

Degree(s) and/or award(s) Earned: _____

Your major: _____

Your minor(s): _____

List some of your most impressive accomplishments, extracurricular activities, club affiliations, etc.: _____

List specialized education courses you've taken that help qualify you for the job you're seeking: _____

Grade point average (GPA): _____

High school attended: _____

City/State: _____

Graduation date: _____

Grade point average (GPA): _____

List the names and phone numbers of two or three current or past professors, teachers, or guidance counselors you can contact about obtaining
a letter of recommendation or list as a reference:

_____

_____

Work/Employment History

List all your experience working with children, even if it isn't specifically as
a teacher, such as summers spent as a mother's helper. For career-changers,
also list all managerial experience you have; every job requires skills interacting with people. Summer employment or part-time work should be labeled
as such, and you will need to specify the months in the dates of employment
for positions you held for less than a year.

If you just finished your teacher education program, you might feel like you
don't have much experience to list in a resume. This is not true! Think back
to those grueling college projects. Getting a grade on a project was only half
the project's value. You can use it now in place of experience you have not yet
gained in the workplace. List special projects with their title, a description,
and lessons learned.

Most recent employer: _____

City/State: _____

Year you began work: _____

Year you stopped working (write "Present" if still employed): _____

Job title: _____

Job description: _____

Reason for leaving: _____

What were your three proudest accomplishments while holding this job?

1. _____

2. _____

3. _____

Contact person at the company who can provide a reference:

_____

Contact person's phone number: _____

Annual salary earned: _____

Employer: _____

City/State: _____

Year you began work: _____

Year you stopped working: _____

Job title: _____

Job description: _____

Reason for leaving: _____

What were your three proudest accomplishments while holding this job?

1. _____

2. _____

3. _____

Contact person at the company who can provide a reference:

_____

Contact person's phone number: _____

Annual salary earned: _____

For special school projects, list the title of the project:

_____

Description of special project: _____

_____

Lessons learned from project: _____

_____

For special school projects, list the title of the project: _____

_____

Description of special project: _____

_____

Lessons learned from project: _____

_____

Military Service (if applicable)

Branch of service you served in: _____

Years served: _____

Highest rank achieved: _____

Decorations or awards earned: _____

Special skills or training you obtained: _____

Professional Organizations

List any professional organizations that you are a member of:

_____

_____

Hobbies and Special Interests

List any hobbies or special interests you have that are not necessarily work-related, but that potentially could separate you from the competition. Can any of the skills utilized in your hobbies be used for coaching or leading any extracurricular activities at a school?

What nonprofessional clubs or organizations do you belong to or actively participate in?

References

Employers interested in hiring you may want to speak to people who can accurately (and favorably) vouch for your ability to do the job. These people are called references. Make a list of everyone you feel would be a good reference—those who would highly recommend you to an employer. However, don't include your family members; this list should be made up of former supervisors, teachers, or other adults you have worked or dealt with in the past and who know you well. Make sure you get permission from your references before listing them.

You can include your list of references with each resume you send out, or you can simply state at the bottom of the resume that your references are available upon request. If you are responding to an advertisement, read it carefully to see if you are supposed to send references. If the ad does not mention them, you probably don't need to send them with your resume. List your references on a sheet of paper separate from your resume, but remember to include your name, address, and phone number on your reference list too.

Personal/Professional Ambitions

Take some time to reflect on the questions in this section because your answers to many of these questions can help you not only in the preparation of your resume but also in your broader career planning activities.

What are your long-term goals? _____

Personal: _____

Professional: _____

For your personal and professional goals, what are five smaller, short-term goals you can begin working toward achieving right now that will help you ultimately achieve each of your long term goals?

_____

_____

Short Term Personal Goals: _____

1. _____
2. _____
3. _____
4. _____
5. _____

Short Term Professional Goals: _____

1. _____
2. _____
3. _____
4. _____
5. _____

Will the job(s) you will be applying for help you achieve your long-term goals and objectives? If *yes*, how? If *no*, why not?

_____

_____

_____

Describe your personal and professional situation right now:

_____

_____

_____

What would you most like to improve about your life overall?

_____

_____

_____

What are a few things you can do, starting immediately, to bring about positive changes in your personal or professional life?

_____

_____

_____

Where would you like to be personally and professionally five and ten years down the road? _____

_____

_____

What needs to be done to achieve these long-term goals or objectives?

_____

_____

_____

What are some of the qualities about yourself, your appearance, and your personality that you're most proud of? _____

_____

_____

What are some of the qualities about yourself, your appearance, and your personality that you believe need improvement?

_____

_____

_____

What do others most like about you? _____

_____

_____

What do you think others least like about you? _____

_____

_____

If you decided to pursue additional education, what would you study and why? How would this help you professionally? _____

_____

_____

If you had more free time, what would you spend it doing? _____

_____

_____

List several accomplishments in your personal and professional life that you're most proud of. Why did you choose these things?

1. _____

2. _____

3. _____

4. _____

5. _____

What do you believe is your biggest weakness? Why wouldn't an employer hire you? _____

_____

What would be the ideal atmosphere for you to work in? Do you prefer a large public school atmosphere, or a small private school campus?

_____

_____

_____

List five qualities about a new job that would make it the ideal teaching assignment for you:

1. _____
2. _____
3. _____
4. _____
5. _____

What did you like most about the last place you worked? _____

_____

_____

What did you like least about the last place you worked? _____

_____

_____

What work-related tasks are you particularly good at? _____

_____

_____

What type of students would you prefer to have? _____

_____

_____

When it comes to work-related benefits and perks, what's most important to you? _____

_____

_____

When you're recognized for doing a good job, how do you like to be rewarded? _____

_____

_____

If you were to write a "help wanted" ad describing your ideal teaching job, what would the ad say? _____

_____

_____

Using the information in the previous questionnaire, you should be able to begin piecing together content for your resume. In terms of choosing the best possible wording to convey your information and then formatting your resume, follow the guidelines in this book or consult another book that specifically contains dozens of sample resumes which you can use to obtain ideas from. One good example is *101 Grade A Resumes for Teachers, 2nd Edition* by Rebecca Anthony and and Gerald Roe (New York: Barrons Educational Series, 1998). Whatever you do, however, never simply copy your resume right out of a book. Use the sample resumes provided in this book and in other resumes books as a guide, but be sure the content is 100% accurate and customized to you.

THE ELECTRONIC RESUME

If you plan to use the Internet to apply for teaching jobs, your resume will require special formatting so it can be read electronically.

An electronic resume can be created and distributed in a variety of ways. Keep in mind, there are no standard guidelines to follow when creating an electronic resume, since employers use different computer systems and software. Thus, it's important that you adhere to the individual requirements of each online job site you visit—use their specific formatting, saving, and sending formats when at their site. The majority of employers who work with online job services prefer to receive resumes in ASCII or Rich Text Format, however, some may accept .doc files (documents saved in Word format), for example.

In order to keep incoming resumes consistent in terms of formatting, many websites designed for recruiting insist that all electronic resumes be created using a pre-defined template. While online, you can complete a detailed form that requests all pertinent resume information. You will be prompted for each piece of information separately in pre-defined fields. The website then formats the information automatically to meet the employer's requirements.

When completing an online-based resume form, be sure you fill in all fields with the appropriate information only. Be mindful of limitations for each field. For example, a field that allows for a job description to be entered, for example, may have space for a maximum of only 50 words, so the description you enter needs to provide all of the relevant information (using keywords), but also be written concisely. Since an electronic resume is as important as a traditional one, consider printing out the online form first and then spend time thinking about how you will fill in each field (or answer each question).

Don't attempt to be clever and try adding information that wasn't requested in a specific field in order to provide more information about yourself to an employer. For example, if you're only given space to enter one phone number, but you want to provide a home *and* cell phone number, don't use the fields for your address to enter the second phone number.

Be sure to proofread your electronic resume carefully before hitting the send button. Just as with a traditional resume, spelling mistakes, grammatical errors or providing false information won't be tolerated by employers. When creating an electronic resume to be saved and submitted in an ASCII format, follow these general formatting guidelines:

▶ Set the document's left and right margins to 6.5-inches of text displayed per line. This will ensure that the text won't automatically wrap to the next line (unless you want it to).

▶ Use a basic, 12-point text font, such as Courier or Times Roman.

▶ Avoid using bullets or other symbols. Instead of a bullet, use an asterisk (*) or a dash (-). Instead of using the percentage sign (%) for example, spell out the word percent. (In your resume, write 15 percent, not 15%).

▶ If one is available, use a spellchecker to help you proofread your electronic resume and then proofread the document carefully yourself.

▶ Avoid using multiple columns, tables, or charts within your document.

▶ Within the text, avoid abbreviations—spell everything out. For example, use the word "Director," not "Dir." or "Vice President" as opposed to "VP." In terms of degrees, however, it's acceptable to use terms like "MBA," "B.A.," "Ph.D.," etc.

Properly formatting your electronic resume is important; however, what you say within your resume is what could ultimately get you hired. According to Rebecca Smith, M.Ed., author of *Electronic Resumes & Online Networking* (Franklin Lakes, NJ: Career Press, 2000) and companion website (www.eresumes.com), "Keywords are the basis of the electronic search and retrieval process. They provide the context from which to search for a resume in a database, whether the database is a proprietary one that serves a specific purpose, or whether it is a Web-based search engine that serves the general public. Keywords are a tool to quickly browse without having to access the complete text." Keywords are nouns and phrases that highlight your professional areas of expertise; they include industry-related jargon, projects, achievements, special task forces and other distinctive features about your work history.

Select and organize your resume's content in order to highlight those keywords. The idea is to identify all possible keywords that are appropriate to your skills and accomplishments that support the kind of job you are looking for. But to do that, you must apply traditional resume writing principles to the concept of extracting those keywords from your resume. Once you have written your resume, then you can identify your strategic keywords based on how you imagine people will search for your resume.

The keywords you incorporate into your resume should support or be relevant to your job objective. Some of the best places within your resume to incorporate keywords is when listing:

▶ job titles
▶ responsibilities
▶ accomplishments
▶ skills

Industry-related buzzwords, job-related technical jargon, licenses, and degrees are among the other opportunities you will have to come up with keywords to add to your electronic resume. Keywords are the backbone of any good electronic resume. If you don't incorporate keywords, your resume won't be properly processed by the employer's computer system. Choosing the right keywords to incorporate into your resume is a skill that takes some creativity and plenty of thought. Instead of using action verbs, use nouns or adjectives to describe your skills, job responsibilities, and qualifications. For example, instead of using the action word "managed," use the word "manager" or "management." Also, be sure to include the keywords listed by the employer within the job description or help wanted ad you're responding to.

One excellent resource that can help you select the best keywords to use within your electronic resume is the *Occupational Outlook Handbook* (published by the U.S. Department of Labor). This publication is available, free of charge, online (www.stats.bls.gov/oco/oco1000.htm), however, a printed edition can also be found at most public libraries. This resource contains keywords used in many different careers.

Resume Creation Tips

No matter what type of resume you're creating, here are some useful tips and strategies that will help ensure your finished document has the most impact possible when a potential employer reads it.

► Always use standard letter-size ivory, cream, or neutral-color paper. Brightly colored papers do not copy well and look unprofessional.
► Include your name, address, and phone number on every page if you use more than one page.
► Make sure your name is larger than anything else on the page (example: your name in 14-point font, the rest in 12-point).
► Use a font that is easy to read, such as 12-point Times New Roman, Century Schoolbook, Arial, or Courier.
► Do not use more than three fonts in your resume. You want it to look like a resume, not a ransom note.
► Edit, edit, edit. Read it forward and backward. Have friends with good proofreading skills read it. Even if you have a grammar and spellchecker on your computer, you still need to review it. For instance, a spellchecker would not catch any of the errors in the following sentence: *Their are two many weighs too make errors that a computer does nut recognize.*
► Use bullet points for items in a list. If someone is glancing at your resume, it helps highlight the main points.
► Use keywords in your industry.

▶ Avoid using excessive graphics such as boxes, distracting lines, and complex designs.

▶ Be consistent when using bold, capitalization, underlining, and italics. If one company name is underlined, make sure all are underlined. Check titles, dates, and so on.

▶ Don't list your nationality, race, religion, birth date, marital status, or gender. Keep your resume as neutral as possible. Your resume is a summary of your skills and abilities.

▶ One page is best, but do not crowd your resume. Shorten the margins if you need more space; if it's necessary to create a two-page resume, make sure you balance the information on each page. Don't put just one section on the second page. Be careful about where the page break occurs.

▶ Keep your resume updated. Don't write "12/99 to present" if you ended your job two months ago. Do not cross out or handwrite changes on your resume.

▶ Understand and remember everything written on your resume. Be able to back up all statements with specific examples.

Spending extra time on your resume is an excellent investment in your future. Pay careful attention to detail, and make sure that your resume promotes you in the best possible way. To assist in formatting and designing your resume, consider using specialized resume creation software, like Resume Maker Deluxe Edition (www.individualsoftware.com), for PC-based computers. The design and formatting of a resume is important, so check out one of the many books available that explain and demonstrate the resume creation process. Successful job seekers spend many hours creating multiple drafts of their resume, fine-tuning each sentence to make sure every word makes a positive impact. A resume is a one-page composition designed to sell your skills, work experience and educational background to a potential employer. Taking short cuts when creating this extremely important document can have disastrous results.

To ensure your resume will be seriously considered by a potential employer, avoid making these common errors:

▶ Stretching the truth. A growing number of employers are verifying all resume information. If you're caught lying, you won't be offered a job, or you could be fired later if it's discovered that you weren't truthful.

▶ Including any references to money. This includes past salary or how much you're looking to earn within your resume and cover letter.

▶ Including on your resume the reasons why you stopped working for an employer, switched jobs, or are currently looking for a new job. Also, do not include a line in your resume saying, "unemployed" or "out-of-work" along with the corresponding dates in order to fill a time gap.

▶ Having a typographical or grammatical error in a resume. If you refuse to take the time necessary to proofread your resume, why should an employer assume you'd take the time needed to do your job properly if you're hired?

▶ Using long paragraphs to describe past work experience. Consider using short sentences, phrases, or a bulleted list instead. Most employers will spend less than one minute initially reading a resume.

Before submitting your resume to a potential employer, read the job description carefully to ensure you have the skills, experience, and educational background the employer is looking for. If you have specific and highly marketable skills, be sure they're clearly listed. As you write, edit, and proofread your resume, make an effort to keep all of the information short, to the point, and totally relevant. Remember, any less important information can be discussed during a job interview. The purpose of your resume is to get an employer interested enough in you so you get invited for an interview.

Creating a powerful resume will take time and effort. Don't be afraid to write and then rewrite your resume multiple times until you're confident it has the impact needed to set you apart from the competition.

A Less-Than-Convincing Sample Resume

Julia Rose Stearn

15 Allemeda Blvd.

Anywhere, California 54321

OBJECTIVE:

To become a leader for today and tomorrow

TEACHING EXPERIENCE:

Student Teaching, Anywhere, CA, Schools, 2001

Summer School Volunteer Teacher, Anywhere, CA, Schools, 2000

EDUCATION:

University of Southern California, B.S. in Education, 2001

GPA: 3.2/4.0

ACTIVITIES:

Member—Student National Education Association

Vice President—Delta Delta Delta Sorority

HONORS:

Collegiate Academic All-American, Who's Who in American Education, Future Leaders in Education Meeting Invitee and Dean's List—USC.

AREAS OF CERTIFICATION:

English (K–6), Special Reading (K–12), and BD (K–8)

PROFESSIONAL WRITINGS:

Understanding the BD student in the Regular Classroom (published).

REFERENCES:

Available upon request

A High-Quality Sample Resume

ROSS BEARLEY

5555 S. Hope Street

Anywhere, Nebraska 12345

555-555-5555

CAREER OBJECTIVE

Secondary English Teacher

CERTIFICATION

English, 7–12

Reading, K–12

EDUCATION

B.S. Education	University of Nebraska–Lincoln, 2001
	GPA 3.5/4.0, cum laude; minor, Spanish
Blaine High School	Anywhere, Nebraska, 1997

EXPERIENCE

Student Teacher, Glendale High School, September 2000–January 2001

- Worked with English courses in grades 9, 11, and 12.
- Planned and implemented units on English literature and writing.

University of Nebraska–Lincoln, Student Teacher Advisory Committee

- Created orientation and debriefing sessions for students beginning and completing their student teaching assignments.
- Implemented a peer-review board for student teachers.

Blaine High School, Student Assistance Team Counselor

- Planned and directed weekly meetings with administrators, teachers, and students promoting a drug-free school.
- Revised the high school's drug-free student's manifesto.

Blaine High School, Site Council

- Chaired a subcommittee for improving the learning environment by lessening class disruptions and increase time on task.
- Assisted the vice principal with planning a community-based volunteer literacy program.

ACTIVITIES

Co-captain, Varsity Soccer

Member, Spanish Club

REFERENCES

Available upon request

THE INSIDE TRACK

Who: Marcia Patillo
What: Third Grade Teacher
Where: Middletown, Connecticut

INSIDER'S STORY

I really think networking is the best way to find a job. People who know you and know your work can give you good and realistic advice on schools, and they can also speak on your behalf. I know that a lot of teaching jobs come about this way; in fact, I got my most recent job by networking. I spread the word to everyone I could think of that I was looking for a job, so as many people as possible knew about it. My church choir director, who also teaches music at a private school, told me about an opening at her school. I immediately called and set up an interview. I went, taught a class, had an interview, and got the job. Also, I had a lot of recommendations from other teachers I had been working with when I was substituting in local public schools. I think it was these recommendations that helped put me ahead of other candidates.

My advice is simple: It pays to get to know as many professionals in your field as possible. Work with them, and do your best to impress them. I've met other teachers at workshops, conferences, and classes, and I make it a priority to get their contact information for the future. It also helps to get into a good school district and work in whatever position is open at the time, even as a teacher's aide or as a substitute teacher. After you have made a good impression on other teachers and principals, you are in a good position to apply for a full-time position.

I have the privilege of working with some wonderful teachers in my present school. The professional, caring atmosphere makes each day a pleasure. In addition, the effort that each teacher puts in to her work with children is a constant energy and moral boost.

Networking will also help you when you are planning lessons, or thinking of next year's curriculum. I've found my most helpful sources of information to be other teachers and librarians; they always have great suggestions. Parents are also good sources of information; sometimes they are experts in something you are teaching, or know someone, or work somewhere that's a great place for a field trip to supplement class work.

Plus, there should be a strong link between home and school, so it's good to establish rapport and trust with your parents. Their support and hands-on help will make your job a lot easier and you will get much better results when there is a problem to address.

When I first started teaching, I didn't have children of my own. After I had my own children, I had a whole new perspective on teaching and the importance of involving parents.

Teaching is a wonderfully fulfilling profession and it is all consuming. I spend a lot of time thinking and planning when I am away from school. Somehow I just can't "leave it at the office." It is really not like a regular nine-to-five job and I hope it never will be!

CHAPTER six

COVER LETTERS AND INTERVIEWS

Now that you've created a terrific resume, it's time to craft an engaging cover letter to accompany your resume. This chapter also shows you how to prepare for each job interview you get invited to, and explains the different types of questions you will most likely be asked. Sample questions and tips for topics to avoid are also included.

WRITING YOUR cover letters and promoting yourself in interviews can be stressful, but each can be done well if you prepare in advance. This chapter aims to reduce job search anxiety by outlining the steps you will need to take to craft a professional cover letter and present a polished and qualified image at your interviews. You'll also gain some inside information on what employers look for during interviews.

WRITING A COVER LETTER

After you get your resume completed, it's time to turn your attention to creating the cover letters that will accompany each resume you send out to potential employers. Like the resume, the text of the cover letter must be *relevant to your purpose*, which is to obtain a job within a specific school or school district. In other words, you should tailor each cover letter to the individual needs and requirements of each particular school for which you are applying. That's why it's important for you to do some research on the schools or school districts where you intend to apply. The purpose of a cover letter is to catch the employer's attention and encourage him or her to read the enclosed resume.

Take the time to find out to whom you should address your cover letter. Resumes sent to a specific individual's attention are always more successful that those with generic addresses. You can call the school directly and ask for the hiring person's name, or if they don't give out names, you should at least be able to get the person's formal job title so you can use that instead. If the school has a website, you may be able to obtain the hiring person's name from their site. If it is a public school, you can address your letter to the principal. If it is a private school, address the letter to the headmaster.

Always keep the purpose of your writing in mind; it will direct your thoughts and keep you on task. Try to focus in on at least one area where your skills and the needs of a particular school coincide. For example, if you took electives in instructional technology and you know that a school just obtained several new computers in their lab, you could highlight that connection in your cover letter by saying something like, "During my instructional technology courses, I designed several teaching units on how to introduce computers to elementary students. Twenty-four students out of a class of twenty-five passed the computer proficiency test at the end of my unit."

Five Steps to a Complete Cover Letter

- Introduce yourself and explain your reason for writing.
- Clearly specify which job you are applying for and state how you found out about the position.
- Be brief, but show that you know something about the position, express interest in the position, and describe how your abilities match the qualifications for the position.
- Demonstrate that you know something about the school and/or the district.
- Indicate that you would like to come in for a formal interview.

While you don't want to get bogged down in repeating everything that appears in your resume, you can use the cover letter to draw attention to the most important aspects of your work, experience, or education. If you are a career-changer, you can use the cover letter to highlight your transferable skills and to portray your commitment to teaching. If you have any experience working with children or young adults or in training in general, here is the place to emphasize how these experiences relate to the teaching job you want. Even if you don't have any experience that seems directly relevant, think about each skill you've used in previous jobs—you may find that you have more transferable skills than you thought. For example, working with the public, customer service, oral and written communication skills, explaining complicated procedures or codes to others, working on a computer, and organizing workloads and files are all useful and vital skills for a new teacher.

Tips for Formatting Cover Letters

Follow a standard business letter format; don't appear to be overly friendly or cute even if you know the person to whom you are sending the letter on a personal level. You never know who else might see the letter. In addition:

- Avoid using contractions in your cover letter.
- Never write a cover letter that is more than one page long.
- Use wide margins, so there is plenty of white space on the page. You don't want your letter to appear crowded or cluttered.
- Use a standard size and type of font—the same one you use for the body of your resume.
- Use a standard color of paper, preferably white or ivory, and always the same color and weight of the one you use for your resume.

An example of a good cover letter is shown at the end of this chapter. Many different and equally appropriate examples are available in other books that focus on resume writing and cover letters. Just as with the resume, don't ever copy a cover letter out of a book, just use the samples as a guide to create your own unique letter. The last step in creating a successful cover letter is to proofread it carefully for spelling, grammar, and typing errors.

FILLING OUT AN APPLICATION

If you are asked to complete an application, follow the general guidelines for writing a resume. Here are some additional pointers:

▶ If you hand-write your application, *do it neatly!*
▶ If possible, type the application so it will be easier to read.
▶ Answer every relevant question. Write N/A if a question is not applicable, so it is clear that you didn't just overlook it.
▶ List as many references as are requested and include the specific way to contact them that is requested. If the application asks for the phone numbers of your references, don't write in their addresses. If you know their e-mail addresses, go ahead and include them.
▶ List your hobbies, if asked. They may correspond to extracurricular activities in the school.
▶ Answer as many questions as possible in complete sentences.

If you are given a page to write your "philosophy of education," use the entire page. Explain why you responded the way you did. Support your answer with specific experiences, facts, and examples. Your writing is a mirror of who you are, so be careful and thoughtful in your response to any type of question about teaching.

HOW TO ACE THE JOB INTERVIEW

It is likely that you will be very nervous at your first professional job interview. In fact, few other experiences produce such high levels of anxiety. To complicate the situation, many people are uncomfortable talking about themselves to others and fear coming across as too shy or too egotistical. Don't worry—your best defense is to get prepared! You can do several things to get ready for an upcoming interview. The first step is to learn more about the interview process, then you can find out about specific parts of an interview and how to answer the different types of questions that are likely to surface during the meeting.

The interview is usually a multiple-step process, not a one-time experience. Many districts require a candidate to interview with several different individuals. Some interviews are conducted by a single school representative, and others are conducted by a team or panel of interviewers, which may include classroom teachers, curriculum specialists, special teachers, administrators, and even parents.

Do Your Homework

Before you go for an interview, research the school district and school. Many school districts will provide you with information about the school system. Another tactic is to contact a local real estate agent in the school district. Real estate agents may have information about schools for prospective homebuyers and might share it with you, too. Local libraries also have demographic information about surrounding school districts. You might also take a drive around the school district to see what the community looks like.

These days, many school districts and private schools now have websites where they post information about student achievement, curriculum, and staffing, so don't overlook the Internet as a valuable research tool. You can simply type the name of the school into any major search engine on the Web, or you can visit some of the job bank websites mentioned in Chapter 5 to see if a particular school has a website link on them. Additionally, most of the state education departments have website links for each of their school districts.

Tips for a Successful Interview

The following tips can reduce your anxiety and help you focus on presenting your qualifications to the interviewer.

Be Yourself

This statement seems obvious, but many candidates believe they have to put on an act to be hired. If you want to act, join the theater; if you want to teach, be yourself! Your personal happiness depends on finding the right match between your personality, strengths, and skills and the school or school district. That decision is complex and involves many factors; do not complicate it by not being true to yourself.

Prepare, Prepare, and Prepare Some More

The best thing you can do to ensure a successful interview is prepare yourself as well as possible. What does this mean?

Keep the purpose of the interview in mind. This exercise helps you organize your thoughts. Then, anticipate the kinds of questions the interviewer will ask during the session, and practice your responses with a friend.

Review your qualifications. Recall experiences that support your qualifications for the position, and rehearse answers to practice questions.

Think of ways to dissipate the stress of the interview. Sit up straight, breathe deeply and slowly, and smile! Teachers work in a stressful environment in which they are expected to manage student behavior, respond to multiple stimuli, and communicate well. Your composure during the interview reflects how you might handle the stress of your classroom.

Speak Confidently

Concentrate on exuding confidence when you greet your interviewer and give him or her an enthusiastic smile when you first meet. Speak with confidence throughout your interview and phrase your comments as if you assume you will be getting the job. For example, phrase your questions this way: "Where would my classroom be located?" "How many students would be in my class?" Try to elaborate on your answer rather than just curtly saying *yes* or *no*. Giving an example or telling a short anecdote about a previous teaching experience to amplify your answer is a great interview tactic. However, don't ramble on too long answering any one question. Some hiring administrators will ask scenario questions that don't have a right or wrong answer; they just want to evaluate your problem-solving skills and see how quickly and intelligently you can answer their questions.

Focus on Knowledge, Skills, and Experiences

The interviewer's main goal is to determine whether you can teach. When you answer questions, provide relevant information that demonstrates you have what it takes to be a good teacher.

If you are asked, "How would you teach reading to a second grade class of at-risk students?" do not respond with "Well, I was student teacher of the year," or "I attended the International Reading Association's state conference and sat in on a workshop about at-risk readers." These answers do not answer the question. Being named student teacher of the year is nice, and attending a conference may be important in acquiring new knowledge and skills, but this information is not relevant to the question. An appropriate response would be, "When I was student teaching, I used _____, which was successful with these second grade at-risk students. Other methods that were successful in the classroom were _____." Responding to specific questions by *citing personal experiences* demonstrates your knowledge and teaching skills.

Dress for Success

Interviewers expect you to be at your best, in terms of both appearance and presentation. Therefore, it's worth the time and money needed to purchase and maintain at least two professional-looking suits. You may need more than one outfit because you may be called back for a second or third interview at the same school. Your best bet is to be conservative in terms of clothing and accessories. Your credentials will get you the interview, but your interview will get you the job!

Use Proper English

You make an impression on the interviewer, or committee, during the interview. As mentioned previously, one of the characteristics of an effective teacher is to be able to communicate well. School districts are under increasing pressure to produce graduates who can read, write, and compute at grade level. Teachers are the key models of effective communication skills for students.

A sure way to end an interview quickly is to speak English poorly or to use slang. Think through your response before answering a question. If speaking in grammatical English sentences is difficult for you, spend some time before the interview working on your speaking skills. Have friends or family members ask you mock interview questions, and tape your responses. Play them back, listening for errors in grammar—get someone else to listen with you if you need help—and then plan and practice a better answer. That way, you will be prepared with grammatically correct answers to many of the questions you might be asked. This will make you more relaxed and confident when facing the questions you *didn't* anticipate.

Be Aware of Current Events

Many interviewers like to start off an interview with general chit-chat to warm up the atmosphere. They may do so by discussing current news events. Therefore, on the morning of your interview, read a local newspaper or watch a morning news program so you will be aware of the day's news events. It's good to appear knowledgeable about what's happening in the world around you.

What to Do While You're Waiting

If you're asked to sit in a waiting room until your interview begins, use the time to compose yourself, review your research notes, or pick up and glance through any free newsletters or educational brochures. Or you may want to use that extra bit of time to visualize yourself succeeding in the interview. In your mind, see yourself confidently walking into the interview room and calmly answering all the questions you are asked. If you've done your preparation work, you already have an idea about what questions will be posed to you, how you plan to answer them, and what questions you want to ask the hiring administrators.

Act Professionally

It's important to put on your professional persona right away on the day of your interview. Even when you are driving into the parking lot and getting out of your car, you never know who is looking at you. Perhaps the administrators are taking a break from interviewing candidates and are glancing out their window as you drive up. What will they see? Hopefully, a poised and professional person stepping calmly from the car, not someone who looks harried and frenzied struggling to get a big bag out of the car with papers spilling out of it.

Remember to be polite to everyone, including department secretaries and receptionists. They may be asked for their opinion in the hiring process; even just an informal negative comment from them could cause you to be passed over.

When you are in the actual interview, focus on how you are sitting in your chair. You want to sit up straight rather than slouch. Listen carefully to each question posed to you, take a moment or two to think about each answer, and then answer using complete sentences. Words like, "yeah," "nope," and "umm" should be avoided during your interview.

Throughout the entire interview, in addition to what you say, you will be evaluated based on how you conduct yourself and use body language. Prior to your interview, spend the necessary amount of time learning to control your nervous habits. If you know what your nervous habits are, they will be easier to control in stressful situations. Focus on acting and speaking in a calm, clear, and professional manner.

The Interview Process

Thinking about the interview ahead of time and having an idea of what to expect will help quell your anxiety. While every interview is going to be different, there are some basic things you can do to prepare yourself. Becoming familiar with the types of questions you will be asked will help you to come across as a confident and capable candidate during your interview.

The Questions

Listen carefully, and answer each question directly. Supporting information, such as a short anecdote, adds color and interest to your response and provides a clue to the interviewer as to what kind of teacher you might be in the classroom. However, do not ramble on, and do not fake answers. If you do not know the answer, just say so. Ask the interviewer to repeat any question that you don't understand.

If you say you are familiar with a program or philosophy of education, then be prepared to answer additional questions about it. Be prepared for open-ended questions such as, "If you were walking and came to a fork in the path and one way led to a lower path and the other led to a less-traveled higher path, which one would you take, and why?" You may also be expected to answer difficult questions about yourself and your teaching philosophy.

Interview Advice from a Principal

Phil Carolan, an experienced and respected elementary principal in a suburban school district on Long Island, New York, reveals the intensity of the interview process. He instructs student teachers to anticipate certain questions from an interviewer. You should anticipate at least a few questions at this level of specificity:

- How do you get parents on your side?
- Are you familiar with the content and performance standards for your state?
- How do you know what to teach? How do you teach it, and how do you know when students have learned it?
- What will your classroom look like, and why?
- Say that a parent complains to you at a conference that her child is not reading. What is reading, and how do you teach it?

Phil encourages student teachers to give elaborate answers that can be used as springboards to other questions. You should weave your beliefs, values, and educational philosophy into your answers.

Sample Interview Questions

Take some time to think about how you would answer the following questions. If time allows, role-play with a partner and practice answering the questions your partner asks. If you can videotape or audiotape yourself during the role-play, you will have an added advantage of evaluating and finding ways of improving your performance.

- ▶ Tell me about yourself.
- ▶ What are the greatest strengths that you will bring to this position, and how will you compensate for your weaknesses?
- ▶ What would you do if you truly believed in involving parents in your classroom, but your colleagues told you not to because it made them look bad?
- ▶ How would you construct a lesson on a particular piece of content in your subject area?
- ▶ What is your philosophy of teaching and learning?

▶ Why did you decide to become a teacher?

▶ What do you like best about teaching?

▶ What books have you read recently about the teaching profession and what did you think of them?

▶ What is the biggest lesson you learned during your student teaching experience?

▶ What is your philosophy of education?

▶ How would you set up a new classroom?

▶ Describe your methods for managing students' behavior.

▶ What do you know about our school district?

▶ What do you believe are the essential skills of a successful teacher?

▶ How would you motivate students in your classroom

▶ What would you say if a parent told you that you gave out too much homework?

▶ What type of after-school activities are you interested in sponsoring?

▶ How would you integrate computers into your classroom?

▶ What do you think about cooperative learning techniques?

▶ What are your professional goals for the next 5–10 years?

▶ What educational periodicals do you read on a regular basis?

▶ What are your plans for professional development?

▶ What would you do if one of your students failed a test?

▶ What would you do to prepare for parent-teacher conferences?

▶ Why should we hire you?

Scenario Questions

Some interviews for new teachers may include a segment on asking each applicant scenario questions, also known as hypothetical situation questions. These are different from the specific questions listed above because they set up a scenario in which you pretend to address a particular type of problem. For example, "What would you do if one of your student's parents arrived at your door during a class session loudly demanding to take his or her child home?" You would need to come up with an answer that sounds practical and sound, given the constraints of your limited experience. If you face a scenario that you really have no idea how to handle, you can just say so and hope they ask you another one that you can answer. Or you can say you would seek the advice of your principal or other administrator in such a situation.

Many scenario questions that are asked during an interview are related to conflict management—either with parents, colleagues, or students. Here are a few more examples of the types of scenario questions you might be asked:

What would you do if:
▶ Two of your students start fighting during class?
▶ One of your students threatens you?
▶ You suspect one of your students of cheating on a test?
▶ A parent becomes verbally abusive during a conference?
▶ A parent writes you a note complaining her child is not learning anything in your class?
▶ The music teacher consistently arrives late to your class to teach her lessons?
▶ The department secretary lost one of your lessons instead of making copies of it?

Keep in mind that many scenario questions have more than one right answer. The interviewers may not be looking for one specific response; they may just want to see how you react to difficult situations and how you perform under pressure.

Illegal Questions

Interviewers cannot legally ask you questions pertaining to specific aspects of your personal life. These areas include:

▶ national origin or citizenship
▶ age
▶ marital/family status
▶ affiliations
▶ personal (physical characteristics)
▶ disabilities
▶ arrest record
▶ military record

There are ways that interviewers can find out such information without asking you these specific questions. For example, whereas the interviewer cannot ask whether you are married or if you have children, the interviewer may ask whether you are able to fulfill after-school responsibilities such as sponsoring a club or coaching a team. You must choose whether to answer or to respectfully decline. Sometimes casual conversation will lead you into these areas. You must decide in advance how you plan to respond; if you become defensive, the outcome of the interview may be affected.

Ask Your Own Questions

The interview also is an opportunity for you to ask questions about the position and the school. Usually, toward the end of the interview, the interviewer will invite you to ask questions. Do not ask off-the-cuff questions. By researching the school district and the position you are applying for in advance of the interview, you can prepare your questions ahead of time. Ask questions that will help you decide whether you want to teach in that particular school. If you don't ask any questions, the interviewer may think that you aren't that interested in the position. Asking good questions can clearly differentiate you from the other candidates.

Questions NOT to Ask!

Some questions that are usually inappropriate to ask in an interview are:

- What is my salary?
- Do teachers have to take work home with them?
- Who do I have lunch with?
- When is my conference/preparation time?
- How do you feel about teacher unions?
- How many sick days do I get?

Ask questions that your research has suggested about the student body, about relationships with parents, or about the educational philosophy or policies of the administrators or board of education. For example, if you know that the school you are interviewing at is a charter school or magnet school, you might want to ask something like, "Where are the students drawn from who attend this school?" or "How are students selected to attend this school?" Other questions might include:

▶ Could you please tell me more about the student body here at your school?

▶ What is the level and type of parental involvement in this school?

▶ What particular challenges does this school face in the upcoming year?

▶ How is standardized testing viewed at this school?

▶ What extracurricular activities or clubs need teacher sponsorship? (Or ask specifically about the area(s) you are interested in sponsoring).

▶ What standards are your curriculum aligned with?

▶ Does this school have computers in the classroom or in a computer lab?

▶ What type of professional development opportunities are offered to teachers here?

▶ What new programs has the school or district implemented recently?

▶ Is there a mentor teacher program at this school?

If you are given an opportunity to tour a facility and meet staff members, be prepared to ask them, too, about the operation of the school. Some appropriate questions you might want to ask them:

▶ How many students do you have in your classroom?

▶ Can you get additional supplies if they are needed?

▶ What kind of equipment is available for teacher use?

Interview Mistakes You Can Avoid

To stay ahead of your competition, avoid making the following common interview mistakes.

Don't just wing it once you land an interview. Before the interview, spend time doing research about the school, its students, and the administrators you will be meeting with.

Don't be late for an interview. To avoid this, drive to the interview location sometime during the week before your interview, so you can find out exactly how to get there and how long it takes.

Don't dress sloppy. First impressions are crucial in an interview. Make sure your clothing is wrinkle-free and clean, that your hair is well groomed, and that your make-up (if applicable) is conservative. Always dress for success at an interview.

Not asking any questions during an interview sends a very negative message. Therefore, prior to the interview, use your research to compile a list of intelligent questions to ask. These questions can be about the school, its students, its educational philosophy and the job responsibilities of the job you're applying for.

Don't discuss salary, benefits, or vacation time during an initial interview. Wait for the interviewer to mention your salary. Of course, if it comes down to the time of the offer and you still don't know the salary, you will have to politely inquire about it before you accept the job.

During the interview, control your nervous habits. For example, if you're someone who drums your fingers on the table when you're nervous, make sure you're aware of your habit so you can control it.

Your Teaching Portfolio

The interview is an appropriate time to support your answers using a portfolio. A portfolio is evidence of your teaching qualifications presented in a scrapbook format. Some teacher education schools require that you develop a portfolio as a part of your student teaching experience. A portfolio may include any of the following items to showcase your teaching experience and talents:

- ▶ brief table of contents
- ▶ evaluations from your supervisors and teachers
- ▶ photographs from student teaching
- ▶ samples of lessons and units you have developed
- ▶ worksheets or other materials you have created for the classroom
- ▶ for high school teachers, instructor evaluations by students
- ▶ a personal statement describing your teaching philosophy and goals
- ▶ professional letters of reference
- ▶ extra copies of your resume
- ▶ list of references and their contact information
- ▶ letters of recommendation

The size of your portfolio will depend on which of the items you want to include to showcase your talents, but generally speaking, portfolios range in size from six to fifteen pages. It's important to be selective when considering what to include in your portfolio. Select items that highlight your specific teaching strengths or that illustrate your successful use of particular teaching methods—the use of manipulatives, for example, especially for teaching math or science. Your portfolio should not contain all your lesson plans.

The actual portfolio you use can be anything from an accordion-style file to a leather-looking presentation three-ring binder. You may want to browse through some office supply stores to find just the right organizing system. Organize your portfolio into sections, so you can immediately turn to the section of the portfolio that is needed during an interview. If you include photographs in your portfolio, be sure to add captions that are easily seen from a short distance so you don't have to peer down at each page while in an interview.

You can use examples in your portfolio to support your answer to an interview question. Principal Phil Carolan likes to see portfolios that contain pictures of candidates working with children in a positive manner and in an educational setting. He believes the portfolio is a symbolic representation of who the candidate is as a person.

Even if you don't spend much time talking about your portfolio during an interview, just the fact that you brought one with you may impress the interview committee.

A Writing Sample

Be prepared to provide a sample of your writing to the interviewer. Although many schools do not include a writing sample as a part of their interview process, there are a few out there who do. It's better to be over-prepared than under-prepared when it comes to the sometimes stressful process of interviews. Be aware that some school districts require that you write an essay on the topic of their choice as part of the interview process. You may have to sit down at a table and hand-write it right then and there during a specified time frame. Just being mentally prepared for this eventuality can help you tremendously. Once you have the topic, carefully organize your thoughts before writing. Many topics revolve around your teaching philosophy, so if you've prepared a teaching philosophy statement for your portfolio, you will have a head start on this project. Writing is an important skill for a teacher. Since teachers expect their students to write well, they must be able to model that process for their students.

Teaching a Demonstration Lesson

Many districts require you to develop and teach a demonstration lesson. You may actually teach the lesson to a class of students or you may present the lesson to a group of administrators, teachers, and parents. In the Half Hollow Hills School District in Dix Hills, New York, you are told the grade, time, subject, class, and regular teacher assigned to the class. You are encouraged to consult with the classroom teacher for guidance in preparing the lesson. How you handle this assignment is a defining part of the interview process. You can get a tremendous amount of help from the classroom teacher. However, information will not be volunteered—you must ask for it. Teacher candidates who show up five minutes before class time with a "canned activity" will not be as successful as those who take time to carefully prepare a lesson.

If you want to be prepared to teach a quality demonstration lesson, the first step is to call the school and speak with the secretary. School secretaries know everything that is going on. Ask when the teacher of the class that you will be teaching your lesson to is available. Some of the questions you should ask are:

- ▶ What topic is the class studying?
- ▶ What was taught before this lesson?
- ▶ What are the children like?
- ▶ Do the children have special needs?
- ▶ Is this a heterogeneous class?
- ▶ Can I bring nametags with me for the children?
- ▶ Who will be observing the lesson?
- ▶ When can I come in to meet the children?

Your goal is to look like you belong in the class. The more you know about the children and what they have been doing, the more comfortable you all will be. Some candidates spend an entire day in the school, before teaching the lesson, to get a feeling for the students. You are not expected to be perfect, but you are expected to be engaging and connect with the students.

The observers are looking for a person who is professional, caring, and knowledgeable. Plan to *teach something new* to the children, based on their needs. Also bring copies of a formal written lesson plan to give to each of the observers.

FOLLOW UP AFTER YOUR INTERVIEW

It is advisable to follow up with a letter thanking the interviewer for his or her time and consideration during the interview. Try to write and send the letter the same day you have your interview, or at the latest, the next day. You want the letter to be received before any decision is reached to hire a particular candidate so your letter can work in your favor. The letter should briefly re-emphasize some of your best qualifications for the position and your interest in the position and be as concise and focused as your cover letter and resume. Try to mention at least one issue that you discussed in your interview to help the interviewer remember your particular interview. You want to differentiate yourself from the other candidates being considered for the position. A sample follow-up letter appears at the end of this chapter. In addition, a thank-you letter to the classroom teacher is a nice touch if you taught a demonstration lesson in his or her class at some point during the interview process.

The interview itself is like the big game of the season. All the preceding preparation is for nothing if you cannot effectively communicate your qualifications to the interviewer. Remember, by the time you meet your interviewer, you have been well-prepared academically, you have learned from experiences in the classroom, and you have reflectively prepared for the interview. With all of this preparation, you will do fine, so relax!

Sample Cover Letter

5555 S. Hope Street

Anywhere, Nebraska 12345

April 13, 2001

Dr. John Dunn

555 South Benton

Klamath Falls, Oregon

RE: English teacher position

Dear Dr. Dunn:

I am applying for the position of secondary English teacher at Rodeo High School. I learned about this position at the University of Oregon "Career Placement Day," held on April 10, 2001. I believe my education, experiences, and interests meet the expectations for this position.

This position requires someone with not only excellent credentials to teach English but also excellent writing skills. My resume indicates that I have been published in a variety of journals and that I have conducted many workshops for other college students on ways to improve their writing skills. I also served as a volunteer student tutor in a learning center for at-risk students at a local high school. Documentation of these students' work indicates substantial improvement in their grades when they returned to traditional English courses.

While in high school and college, I was very active in a variety of organizations and activities. These experiences complement my academic preparation. I would be very interested in sponsoring student activities in your school.

I believe my academic preparation, school-related activities, and career goals match the requirements for this position. I am confident that I will be an asset to your school and that this position can fulfill my professional and personal needs as well. I am hoping to hear from you soon to schedule an appointment for an interview. Please call me at 555-555-5555.

Thank you for considering my qualifications.

Sincerely,

Ross Bearley

Ross Bearley

enclosure: resume

Sample Interview Follow-Up Letter

5555 S. Hope Street

Anywhere, Nebraska 12345

May 15, 2001

Dr. John Dunn

555 South Benton

Klamath Falls, Oregon

RE: English teacher position

Dear Dr. Dunn:

Thank you for meeting with me today to discuss the position you have available for a secondary English teacher.

I was very happy to learn that Rodeo High School has recently purchased computers for use in the English classes since I have considerable experience using a variety of software and editing tools for writing on the computer. As we discussed during our meeting, the use of computers to compose essays in English classes can help students achieve the new standards the school district has put in place. It will be rewarding to see how quickly students can improve their writing skills by using the new computers.

Again, thank you for allowing me to participate in a stimulating interview. I am very interested in your school district and would be proud to be a teacher at Rodeo High School. I look forward to hearing from you soon.

Sincerely,

Ross Bearley

Ross Bearley

THE INSIDE TRACK

Who: Anita Hernandez

What: Art Teacher

Where: Detroit, Michigan

INSIDER'S STORY

I teach art in a private school in Detroit. My students' problems are very different from those of typical inner-city children. The parents I deal with are very involved in their children's educations, the school has money for facilities and equipment, and is situated in a well-to-do neighborhood. I also teach very small classes (from four to thirteen kids), while most public school teachers struggle to deal with classes of 25 students and up. I teach in one of the school's three well-equipped computer labs and have access to the newest equipment and software.

The school also has an attitude towards certain aspects of education. For example, we don't give grades, which fits in with my teaching philosophy. Instead, we write written evaluations and checklist reports for our students, which is much more time consuming, but also more helpful to both students and parents than just assigning students an A, B, or C. With these evaluations, students receive specific feedback about their strengths and weaknesses. The school is very focused on the arts, which helps spur creativity and independent thought. It's great for my teaching budget, and it provides me with a lot of room to come up with really interesting and creative projects for the kids.

Because I teach an elective, and therefore am required *not* to give homework or too many quizzes/tests, my workload outside the classroom is light. Most of the time I spend working outside of the classroom is on creating lesson plans and thinking up activities for the students that are engaging, yet instructive. As such, my job leaves me with more time and energy to pursue other outside interests than most new teachers I know. I have enough time for side pursuits, such as continuing my own education at night, doing my own art, and working in freelance graphic design.

I encourage new or prospective teachers to search out all the possibilities for teaching that are out there. It's a very rewarding profession, and there are definitely jobs out there for people like me who need flexibility. Because I applied to many different schools and took the time to research the many different job openings available to me, I ended up in just the right position for me.

CHAPTER seven

HOW TO SUCCEED ONCE YOU'VE LANDED THE JOB

Now that you've landed your first teaching job, it's time to focus on how to manage your relationships with other teachers, staff, the principal, and parents, as well as how to succeed in the classroom. This chapter gives you tips for being successful during your first year on the job.

YOU HAVE secured your dream job, and you are ready to begin your teaching career. Taking out your education manuals, you start to plan the first lessons. You collect all the teacher's editions and manuals available and read all the students' records in the guidance files. You think you are ready to start, but one major ingredient must be added to the mix: Input from senior staff members.

The key to your happiness and success as a teacher often depends on your interaction within the school community—your working relationships with your colleagues. Building these relationships is the most important first step to take when starting any new job. Every school has a culture. Your job is to learn this culture and become part of it. Doing this will help you succeed as a teacher and can determine your ultimate success in the classroom.

SCHOOL CULTURE AND FITTING IN

A school is a complete community—self-contained in many ways, yet part of another community, that is, the district that encompasses the building. The school district (the official hiring agency) defines the set of rules and regulations that structure your workday. These regulations often appear in a policy manual and provide specific prescriptions for handling problems, expectations for your teaching day, and general "do's and don'ts" set by the board of education. In addition, there may be a teacher contract from your union or professional association that explains the specific details of your job. However, the *unwritten code* of behavior within your particular building is what you want to "capture" before you begin to teach.

Unwritten Expectations

The time you should arrive at school may be listed in the teacher handbook, in the union contract, or in the board of education policy book. Although the requirements are defined, they do not tell you what really happens. For example, the teacher workday may be listed as seven hours, beginning at 8:20 A.M. Because the children do not arrive at the building until 9:00 A.M., when the buses pull in, this may seem logical to you. On the first day of school, you leave your house expecting to arrive right on time at 8:20 A.M. However, when you get to the school, you find a parking lot completely filled—you are the last one in! Are you on time? Technically, yes. Culturally, for this school, no.

In this particular school, many faculty members come in earlier than required to have breakfast together, socialize, copy materials, or complete professional work assignments. This culture can differ dramatically among schools within a district. It is your job to learn and interpret these small nuances that are part of the school culture. Social arrangements for weekend or after-school gatherings may be made during these times, and you should be a part of them. To belong to a school community, you must have shared experiences that bind you to other staff members and make you part of the culture.

Your first task is to be a good detective and learn who the players are. Listen carefully to the clues presented by colleagues during casual conversations, and learn to ask questions that will help you understand the culture of the school.

Make Friends with the Secretaries and Support Staff

In your school building, several people run the operation. The secretaries are the most visible. The front office is a gathering place for staff members, so the secretaries know all the personnel and the staff hierarchy. *Get to know the secretaries!* Learn what they do, because they will point you in the right direction when you need information. They know who is in charge of what curriculum area and how to get what you need for your classroom.

Listen to Other Teachers—and the Administrators

Your colleagues are extremely important to your success. To begin with, they already know the culture of the building because they are not only part of it, but they probably also know how to create the changes they see as necessary. Before you even walk into your classroom, find out who else is in your department or on your grade level. You can ask a secretary or your administrator, a department chairperson, an assistant principal, or whoever your principal has put in charge of your area. If your school is a "one-person operation," go to that person: The principal. Never be afraid to ask pertinent questions of your administrators or colleagues.

Consult with Other Professional Staff

Many staff members can help you adjust to the school. Within every school setting, there are support personnel who work with your children regularly. For example, in elementary school, children may have the same art, music, physical education, technology, and library science teachers throughout their elementary school experience. These teachers may have already worked with your students (unless you teach kindergarten) for one or more years and may be able to share some interesting information with you to help guide your instruction. They also have specific skills that can assist you in the classroom and enhance your curriculum. These teachers can work with you to integrate the curriculum by supplementing the course of study in art, music, or physical education. The librarian can prepare materials for you and work with your children on a research project. A collegial approach is a healthy way for you to integrate yourself into the staff culture.

Other staff members also work cooperatively with classroom teachers to help selected students. Like the curriculum teachers described above, many of these teachers may already know some of your students. If they are going to work with your students, then you must work with them, too. Be assertive; seek them out, because they can be great sources of information and support to you. Often supplying mandated services to children who need extra help, these teachers include:

- ▶ remedial reading teacher
- ▶ remedial mathematics teacher
- ▶ teacher of the gifted
- ▶ resource room teacher
- ▶ speech and language teacher
- ▶ psychologist
- ▶ guidance counselor

The entire school community is your resource, and the more you expand your network to include all staff members, the easier your transition and integration will be.

Take the time to learn who your colleagues are, what their strengths are, and how you can engage them in your personal growth as a teacher. Once you become a part of the process, you, too, will be asked for advice.

Questions to Ask Fellow Teachers

Begin to establish relationships with your colleagues by asking questions. If you get your assignment during the summer before the school year starts, ask the secretaries for home telephone numbers or e-mails of teachers in your school or department. Do not be afraid to call or draft a brief e-mail to introduce yourself.

Here is a list of questions to ask your fellow teachers. Some of these questions seem obvious, but the only way to learn what the culture is and how to become part of it is to *ask*.

▶ Are the other members of my grade level or department getting together over the summer? Would it be possible for me to attend?

▶ How do you begin the first day of school?

▶ What are the procedures the first day and week of school?

▶ Are these procedures different from the rest of the school year?

▶ What kinds of materials are used in addition to prescribed textbooks?

▶ When is planning time?

▶ How is planning time used? Do grade levels plan curriculum together?

▶ Can I see a plan book that has been used, which spells out the development of the curriculum?

▶ How do you determine the length of time spent on a unit?

▶ Is there a common or agreed-upon length of time to spend in each area or on each unit?

▶ What time do the teachers normally arrive at school?

▶ What time do the teachers go home?

▶ Do all of the teachers eat together? If not, where do the staff members in my unit or grade level go for lunch?

▶ How often do you contact parents?

▶ Is parent contact done by phone or in writing?

▶ Do you keep records of parent contact?

▶ Do you meet with every parent who requests a conference?

▶ How do you record test grades and other marks?

▶ How do you determine student grades? What constitutes an A, B, C, or D (or whatever marking system is in place)?

▶ What happens if I fail a student?

▶ What do you do when you have to be absent? Do you leave specific plans, or is the substitute responsible for carrying on with a general outline?

▶ Is there a specific substitute my grade level prefers to use?

▶ Would you mind helping me out with. . . . ? (Any number of issues can be filled in here.)

Be Humble

A first-year teacher has this information to share about his experience as a new teacher. Tracey Loller, a third grade English teacher in eastern Pennsylvania, has the following to say about starting out. "Fitting in was hard. Since I had done my student teaching at the school, I felt comfortable with my mentor teacher, but it took awhile for the other teachers to accept me and get to know me. I asked a lot of questions, especially from the other teachers at my grade level. They were very open with me, and shared their lessons and advice. It's important to let the other teachers know when you don't know something. You can't pretend you know something if you don't, and if people don't know what you don't know, then they can't help you. By not asking for help, you are in danger of isolating yourself and struggling alone. One strategy that helped me was going to the prior grade teachers to ask for family histories of students. I met with the school psychologist, and he shed light on some situations that ended up being really helpful for me. Also, it is important to smile. People will be helpful if you look sincere, friendly, and approachable. Make friends with everybody, the teachers, the secretaries and the janitors. And don't forget to treat everybody with respect."

In order to have a successful first year, be inquisitive and enthusiastic. A new teacher must take a tremendous amount of time to prepare for lessons, and everything will be easier if you have the friendship, cooperation, and assistance of your colleagues.

If you are a career-changer, you may have spent several years in the business community or in another position in the school system. But in your new job, you're no more experienced than a recent college graduate. Remember that you are "the new kid on the block" until you prove yourself in the classroom. Be respectful of the teachers who have been teaching for years, and seek their wisdom.

Teacher Jacinta Perini advises eating lunch in the faculty room—no matter how busy you are. It's tempting to stay in your room to catch up on grading papers and getting things organized for the afternoon. But there is a great deal of sharing that goes on during lunchtime, and new teachers can really benefit from the casual sharing environment among teachers at lunchtime.

First-Hand Advice to New Teachers

Setting up a new classroom can feel overwhelming. Find an experienced teacher in your grade and pick his or her brain for organization procedures and helpful routines. A mentor is so important for a new teacher. I can't emphasize that enough! Before school starts, you should be meeting with a mentor on a regular basis and then keep seeing that teacher regularly—discuss everything! A mentor is especially helpful for solving discipline problems.

WORKING WITH YOUR SUPERVISORS

One of the most important keys to your success as a teacher at any level is to be able to get what you need to help the students in your class. You will need supplies, information, cooperation, and assistance from many "interested parties," including your supervisors. Indeed, the first person to consider when you need help is your immediate supervisor.

Getting to Know the Hierarchy

Your immediate supervisor and your principal almost certainly took part in the decision to hire you to teach the specific class you're teaching, and they want you to succeed. So, it is in your best interest to get to know your supervisors, who may include any or all of the following:

▶ principal or headmaster
▶ vice or assistant principal
▶ curriculum supervisor
▶ director

A hierarchy of supervisors may work with you along the road to success, and each individual will play an important role at some point. Seek them out, and begin a congenial relationship that allows you to have regular conversations with these administrators.

The Principal's Job

The principal or headmaster is in charge of the entire school building. The ultimate responsibility for everyone and everything comes back to his or her desk. He or she must answer to the members of the board of education, who make the policies that guide the district; to the superintendent, who is responsible for the achievement of all schools within a district; and to the parents of every student in the school community. Your job as a teacher is to provide the best educational opportunities and instruction for each and every one of your students. For your principal to succeed, he or she must provide you with the guidance and materials that allow you to do that. There may be an intermediary supervisor between you and the principal, but if so, this person usually keeps your principal informed of what's going on.

The principal monitors attendance (including yours), enrollment, hiring and placement of all kinds of personnel, and custodial and transportation issues; prepares budgets; orders supplies; implements curriculum; conducts after-school activities; and works with parent groups. If you have any questions about the school, the principal will advise you, point you in the right direction to find an answer, or otherwise help you handle a problem.

The Principal as Problem Solver

Some people try to avoid letting their supervisor know when something has gone wrong. They may be embarrassed and try to "fix it themselves." This approach can really backfire. In fact, it usually makes things worse, rather than better, and complicates the situation.

Keep your principal "clued in," or "in the loop" of what is going on with your students and their parents. As a new teacher, you do not have the background or experience to make informed decisions about difficult situations. Your colleagues may be able to help guide you through a specially requested parent conference, for example, but your principal has a long-term history of decision making and should be the first person you go to for advice.

How to Handle a Parent Problem

Parents may request to see you because they are concerned about their child's progress. The parents may claim, "You are not challenging my child." (Don't be offended, but parents sometimes request not to have a beginning teacher, because they fear that your inexperience will have a negative effect on their child's instruction.)

Your principal has weathered situations like this before. He or she may know these parents well, having heard the same complaint from them before. The principal can help you plan the conference and perhaps suggest words you can use to calm the parents' fears. If you plan ahead, you are more likely to have the parents on your side by the end of the meeting.

Meet with your principal again after the conference. The principal will respect your careful handling of the situation; he or she would much rather counsel you ahead of time than have to clean up an unpleasant situation afterward.

How Not to Handle a Parent Problem

Picture the same example given above handled another way. You arrange the conference yourself; the parents are unimpressed with the outcome and go straight to your principal. The principal is caught off guard, cannot respond to the parents immediately (because he or she does not have the information needed to make a judgment), and can only temporarily "calm the waters." The parents are angry or frustrated; the principal has to arrange to meet with you to find out what happened and why, and *then* plan another meeting with the parents to resolve the problem.

What could have been one preliminary meeting between you and the principal has instead turned into three or four stressful interactions involving you and the parents. "Why didn't you come to me first?" is the question any principal would ask. The principal will not question your judgment if you ask, "How should I handle this?" or "Do you have any suggestions or information for me to help with this conference?" Your judgment *will* be questioned, however, if you continue to operate in a manner that causes your administrator extra stress.

Being Observed

Your supervisors will want to watch you work in the classroom. Formal observations are expected several times each year. These lessons are sometimes carefully planned, and teachers may use "bells and whistles" to "wow" the supervisors. Supervisors know this happens, but they want to see *the real you.* Informal pop-ins on your class and spontaneous conversations with you provide that insight.

During a class observation, your supervisor will "scan" your classroom and note the answers to the following questions:

- Does the classroom reflect the student's work?
- How does the teacher manage discipline?
- What systems or routines does the teacher have in place that demonstrate his or her guidelines for student performance?
- How do students interact with each other when they are with the teacher?
- How does the teacher speak to the students?
- Does the teacher listen to the students?
- Are the plans listed in the teacher's plan book being implemented?
- What materials is the teacher using?
- Are the teacher's instructional strategies varied and appropriate for the students?
- Is the room organized?
- Is the room clean?
- Is active learning going on?
- Is the room safe?

Some of these items may seem silly to you, but the answers tell a story about you and your students. They indicate who you are and how you work. The better your supervisor knows you, the better you will be supported when you ask for supplies or assistance.

Know What the Principal Wants

All the advice you get may not be good. One teacher may say, "Everyone does it this way," yet you truly believe that another method would be more comfortable for you. Talk with your principal or immediate supervisor about it. The administration may have actively sought a teacher who could take a stand and use a new technique or method.

Reading, for example, was taught for many years with a *basal approach*. Students read together from a basal reader, completed exercises in phonics and practice books, and worked only with students on a similar reading level. Several years ago, a new philosophy called *whole language* was introduced. This method was different in that teachers worked from complete novels, with students of varying ability, and connected the reading exercise to a writing assignment. Teachers using this instructional pattern required knowledge of whole-language strategies and an understanding of how to assess student progress with these methods.

You may have been hired because you have training in a technique that the principal wants introduced into the curriculum. Other teachers may be doing things differently, but that is irrelevant. Find out what the *principal* wants. Change within a school is often needed but hard to do. One way for a principal to make it happen is to hire candidates who demonstrate interest or proficiency in the needed area. If you are questioned or even confronted, you must let people know that you have the support of the administration.

It is also important that you never compromise your belief in a child. You are his or her advocate for that year, and you must follow through and follow up on that child's behalf. If you are unhappy about how one of your students was spoken to or reprimanded, handle it carefully with the other staff member, but handle it. You must speak out, even if you are new. Your principal can suggest words to diplomatically keep your colleagues engaged while continuing to implement your project, program, or philosophy.

Finding a Mentor

As a beginning teacher, you often will need someone to turn to for immediate answers. Who should you approach, and whom should you trust? Your administrator can point you in the right direction and help you find positive role models who are doing a good job and are successful in the classroom. Asking for help in identifying a mentor can only enhance your performance, and it helps you establish a relationship with the administration—especially if you follow their suggestions. Once you are in the building for a while, you can add to your cadre of advisors.

Some districts have a formal mentor program. Experienced teachers are paid a stipend to assist the newest faculty members, and time is set aside to plan and to review specific lessons and general plans. In Missouri, for instance, this support system is mandated by law; individual districts also may formalize such a plan. The teachers selected to be mentors have been judged by administrators to be outstanding teachers. In other districts, retired teachers are hired to observe the classrooms of the new teachers and to assist in the development of lessons, instructional groups, and student behavior modification programs. Again, master teachers are worth listening to.

When you feel established in the school and have gotten to know your colleagues, you will be in a better position to choose your own mentor. When you first begin teaching, however, work with whomever your principal recommends or your district assigns. You need someone who can give you answers when you need them. If your assigned mentor isn't a "perfect fit," look for someone whose style or personality better matches your own after you become more established.

MAKING THE MOST OF YOUR UNION

In the United States, there are two major national unions that work with teachers to assist and guide them during their career and sometimes into retirement: the American Federation of Teachers (AFT) and the National Education Association (NEA). The purpose of both of these organizations is to assist teachers. Therefore, membership in one of these groups can be useful in your career.

How the Union Works

You may have very little contact with the national level of AFT or NEA; the local or state affiliate affects your daily life much more than the national organization. If you decide to join a union, you join the "local," just like any other union worker. Each local association gets information and advice from the state and national levels of the organization.

In some school districts, both organizations are represented in one school. In that case, each teacher chooses whether to join one union or the other or neither. In other districts, only one of these two organizations is represented on the staff. Some districts are "union shops," which means that every teacher hired *must* join the union. In that case, dues are deducted automatically from your paycheck, and you become a union member as soon as you become a staff member. Some districts may not belong to a national organization but have one or two state and local groups that provide a service for you.

Check Out these Websites for More Information about Unions

American Federation of Teachers at www.aft.org

National Education Association at www.nea.org

Whether the AFT or the NEA dominates and whether you are under obligation join varies within districts, counties, and states. When you have a choice of organizations to join, find out the benefits of each. If everyone in your building belongs to one organization, though, it is smart to go with the crowd. You do not want to stand alone on issues, and differences may arise later that you cannot predict now. You will jeopardize your ability to fit in to the culture if you are the solitary member of a national teacher organization in your building.

What the Union Does for You

In some districts, one union negotiates and handles your contract. Elected officials such as a president and vice president represent your interests and the interests of all the teachers in the school community. The local officials bargain for a contract and work with the board of education to determine your salary, health insurance benefits, and working conditions.

Working with Union Representatives

Local union representatives may be valuable sources of advice. After all, they were elected by the other faculty; they must be respected by their peers. They often are knowledgeable senior staff members, so they can help you answer questions and handle problems that arise when dealing with issues within your school and district. They can help you navigate the maze of confusion that comes with being a new teacher. Unions can provide information and assistance about some of the following areas:

▶ opportunities for professional growth
▶ your retirement system
▶ your health plan and/or options
▶ group insurance for your household
▶ legal assistance (at a group rate)
▶ understanding your contract (if you are bound by one)
▶ filing papers to go on leave or retire
▶ opportunities to purchase items at a discount
▶ solving problems in a large bureaucratic system

Mary Taverna-Ali, a teacher and union representative in an elementary school, believes that her role is that of a "sounding board." She will listen to a problem and offer advice for handling the situation. She says, "I must always maintain confidentiality so the teachers will trust me. I always have the best interest of my colleagues in mind, and I can encourage them to stay professional when they are upset."

Unions are designed to assist you and enhance your professional well-being. It is up to you to make the most of the opportunities they offer.

THE IMPORTANCE OF CLASSROOM MANAGEMENT

You may become frustrated because situations keep arising in class that were not addressed in any of your teacher education courses in college. A principal or any other supervisor who has been a classroom teacher knows that it takes many years to become a *master teacher*. A master teacher starts to build a portfolio of ideas as the years progress. These experiences form the basis for making decisions about instruction, curriculum, students, parents, and staff members.

Unfortunately, there is no quick and easy way to amass the knowledge and skills that experienced teachers have. However, you can gain insights early in your teaching career that will help you immensely.

One of the keys to your success as a teacher is your classroom management skills. This area is seldom covered thoroughly enough (or at all) in traditional teacher education programs; however, it is an area that can make or break your success as a new teacher. One fourth grade teacher had a student teacher who had to plan and execute the lessons for the class during the last week of his internship. The lessons were written up, and one by one, they fell into place. Then one day, mid-lesson, several girls came back from lunch and recess upset and angry at each other. This situation disrupted the lesson, and the student teacher couldn't bring it to closure. An emergency call went out to the master teacher. In about one minute, she assessed what was going on and moved it into another domain, so the lesson could resume. "What happened?" the student teacher asked. "How did you defuse that so quickly?" It turns out that 25 years in the classroom can provide experience that no one textbook can teach. Again, all new teachers should access the master teachers among them for professional advice and guidance.

The issue of classroom management often plagues new teachers, as shown in an article appearing in the *Washington Post* on August 7, 2001, which describes a career-changer who became a new teacher at the age of 50. As with many new teachers, maintaining control is her biggest challenge. Even after five weeks, there's a constant tension between learning and disruption. She said, "I can get the kids to learn something, but not as much as I would like because of the classroom management issue. . . . I have had good days. I know good days are attainable." She learned some effective strategies from a mentor teacher, which helped her, such as distributing tokens to reward good behavior, posting a list of consequences for failing to obey the classroom rules that hang on the wall, and sharpening her voice to sound more like a strict disciplinarian. There are several different effective strategies you can try in your own classroom, based on the age and type of students you teach, so don't become discouraged by this issue.

For specific classroom management questions, you may want to ask a mentor teacher or even one of the school administrators, depending on the nature of the problem. For general guidance in classroom management, you can find a wealth of information from one or more of these helpful and practical books:

- Emmer, Edmund T., Carolyn M. Evertson, and Murray E. Worsham. *Classroom Management for Secondary Teachers* (Needham Heights, MA: Allyn & Bacon, 1999).
- MacKenzie, Robert J. *Setting Limits in the Classroom: How to Move Beyond the Classroom Dance of Discipline* (Rocklin, CA: Prima Publishing, 1996).
- Rubinstein, Gary. *Reluctant Disciplinarian: Advice on Classroom Management From a Softy Who Became (Eventually) a Successful Teacher.* (Fort Collins, CO: Cottonwood Press, 1999).
- Watson, George. *Classroom Discipline Problem Solver: Ready-To-Use Techniques & Materials for Managing All Kinds of Behavior Problems* (West Nyack, NY: Center for Applied Education Research, 1998).

Classroom management is a skill that is often needed most by new teachers, especially with so many children coping with hyperactivity or inattentiveness. Gaining practical information about this key area will help you tremendously during your first few years as a teacher.

Professional Development

You took classes, got first-hand experience, and spent time and money preparing for your profession. You learned many things in school, but once you start to teach, you discover that there are many things yet to learn. Some are incorporated into your routines by watching and learning from your supervisors, colleagues, and senior staff. Other ideas are found in teacher journals. But that is not enough.

A teacher's professional growth must be continuous, so many state departments of education expect you to attend formal workshops and take courses to maintain certification. In addition, many states require a master's degree to get permanently certified.

For example, the New York State Education Department has proposed new professional development standards to be effective as of 2004: In order to maintain professional teacher certification, teachers will be required to complete 175 hours of professional development over a five-year period. This professional development can take many different forms, such as courses and other learning opportunities delivered by institutions of higher education, teacher centers, school districts, and independent professional development service providers. Work done mentoring, performing action research projects, peer coaching, curriculum planning and development, creating and assessing teacher portfolios, and participating in fellowship programs can all count toward this professional development requirement.

School districts sometimes join forces with neighboring communities and share staff development services. They bring in some of the best instructors and presenters available. Often, master teachers run the in-service courses, providing an opportunity for you to meet and work with these experts in concentrated curriculum areas.

It may be hard to summon up the energy to take courses, pay attention, and bring what you learn back into the classroom because new teachers spend quite a bit of time preparing for their lessons. Many teachers are in their school buildings at 7:00 A.M., preparing lessons and materials, and they often stay until early evening. But the good news is that when a school district offers courses, there usually is no fee. College courses often cost several hundred dollars per credit, and courses are three or more credits. They are an expensive way to maintain your professional growth. When the district offers continuing education, you can get your credit for free.

Some districts sponsor courses for college credit. In the Half Hollow Hills District on Long Island, New York, special arrangements were made with a local college to confer degrees in technology to program participants. Sessions were conducted after school, mainly within the district, at reduced fees. Many teachers have taken advantage of this opportunity by enrolling in the courses over the years. Consistently, teachers have found the learning environment exciting and brought their new skills back the classroom. They have become very valuable resources for the school community.

Some school districts have a staff development committee that can be very helpful for new teachers. Often, they team up a veteran teacher and new staff member who have the same interests. They can attend workshops together and develop a common teaching method. It helps connect staff members within a building and it enables them to work toward fulfilling a school's mission statement and building goals. Staff can bring in new methods and share with others. The newer teachers learn from the experienced staff, and the veteran staff members become more receptive to listening to suggestions from the newer teachers.

Sometimes, staff development funds are set aside—within the building or the district—to provide teachers with an opportunity to select and pursue topics of interest. Flyers advertising one- to three-day workshops are sent to schools, often posted on a staff bulletin board or in the faculty room. You should take the initiative to find out who is in charge of administering these programs at your school and how to apply for these sessions.

During the summer, districts often offer week-long courses in a technique or skill that staff members need. Every district is accountable for student achievement, and this success depends on staff training. Because many states are currently implementing new state standards to improve student performance, many districts are offering courses to help staff members learn how to implement this plan. To help you evaluate the professional development programs at a particular school, take a look at the following list.

Professional Development Should

- focus on teachers as central to student learning, yet include all other members of the school community.
- concentrate on individual, collegial, and organizational improvement.
- respect and nurture the intellectual and leadership capacity of teachers, principals, and others in the school community.
- reflect the best available research and practice in teaching, learning, and leadership.
- enable teachers to develop further expertise in subject content, teaching strategies, uses of technologies, and other essential elements in teaching to high standards.
- promote continuous inquiry and improvement embedded in the daily life of schools.
- be planned collaboratively by those who will participate in and facilitate that development.
- require substantial time.
- be driven by a coherent long-term plan.

Other ways you can continue your professional development is to join professional associations, attend professional teacher workshops, and take additional education courses on your own. For example, the Association for Supervision and Curriculum Development (ASCD) offers professional workshops and institutes, video and audio tapes for teachers, and short multimedia online tutorials on topics such as classroom management, standards, multiple intelligences, curriculum integration, year-round schooling, and mentoring. You can access their tutorials and other information at their website, www.ascd.org.

Integrating Technology into the Classroom

One of the most popular areas within professional development is technology. Of course the most obvious form of technology is the personal computer, and some schools have programs in place to help teachers integrate the use of computers into their classrooms. However, other schools expect their teachers to gain experience in technology on their own. Today's students spend many hours watching television and playing video games, so their familiarity with technology is often quite high. Teachers who can reach out to these students by using computer-assisted instruction are in high demand. Teachers who use technology as another method of teaching a lesson can help students excel in this vital area. Using computers in school can help students learn problem-solving skills, use reasoning skills, and explore solutions to real-life issues.

According to an article appearing in *Education Week* in August 2001, schools have greatly multiplied the number of instructional computers available to students. In fact, the "national student-to-computer ratio improved from 125-to-1 in 1984 to just 4.9-to-1 in 2000. And, even students attending the country's poorest schools are not far from the national average, with one computer for every 5.3 students. But looking at the figures on more sophisticated technology, such as Internet access, the digital divide persists. For example, while in well-off schools, 82% of classrooms are connected to the Internet, only 60% of classrooms in the poorest communities have Internet access."

The National Center for Education Statistics has been tracking the rate at which public schools and classrooms are gaining access to the Internet since 1994. You can access a May 2000 report on their findings at their website, www.nces.ed.gov/pubsearch/pubsinfo.asp?pubid=2001071. Additionally, you can read a Report on Americans' Access to Technology Tools, October 2000, entitled *Falling Through the Net: Toward Digital Inclusion* prepared by the U.S.

Department of Commerce at the website, www.search.ntia.doc.gov/pdf/ fttn00.pdf.

Some teachers may be eligible for grants or fellowships to enable them to learn more about integrating technology into their classrooms. In 1999, the Department of Education earmarked 135 million dollars in grant money to train 400,000 new teachers on using technology in the classroom. Many of these grants will focus on the needs of low-income communities and rural areas. For more information on these grants, visit the website, www.ed.gov/ teachtech.

Other ways to gain experience in technology is through teacher workshops, institutes, and conferences. An example of one such course is offered by Media Workshop. K–8 Educators from schools in Washington Heights, in New York City, participated in a 12-week course that explored various ways in which new media and technology can be integrated into curriculum using student-centered, collaborative, and inquiry-based strategies for teaching and learning. During the course, each educator created a digital portfolio that included various elements, such as interdisciplinary teaching resources, examples of student produced work, learning activities that integrated technology, and outlines for professional development workshops. Most of the teaching resources were created in Microsoft PowerPoint, a software program that can be downloaded to a local computer. You can view these portfolios at the organization's website, www.mediaworkshop.org.

Another online resource for learning about technology is www.lightspan. com. Lightspan, Inc. provides curriculum-based educational software and Internet products and services for teachers and students. At this site, you can search and share lesson plans utilizing the Web, learn about classroom themes, and even help your students enter a Cyberfair. The Cyberfair is set up to help you engage your students in an online collaborative project. Your students can learn and practice their technology skills, such as Web research, finding and using digital images and sounds, and other Web publishing skills.

For more information about technology in education, you can visit the website of the International Technology Education Association at www. iteawww.org.

MANAGING PARENT RELATIONSHIPS

When you are hired to work with students, there is an *unwritten* agreement that you will also work with their parents and other community members. Parents trust that the schools will "do the right thing" for their children, and it is your job to keep them informed about school achievement. This includes exchanging information with parents, involving parents in decision-making, asking parents to help out at school, and providing ways for families to collaborate in their child's learning process. When parents and families are involved in their child's education, children do better in school, teachers are happier, and schools improve as well.

The First Meeting

The first time you meet the parents of your students is very important, because they want to know who you are. They want to be sure that you know what you are doing and that their child will flourish with you. This is a normal reaction, and it has little to do with you, your skill level, or your training. When you meet parents in person, they will be able to put a face with a name and build a partnership with you regarding their child's academic success.

Many districts have a "Back to School Night" or "Meet the Teacher Night" at the beginning of the school year. You have a limited time, with a large group of parents, to present yourself positively and professionally. Middle schools and high schools often ask parents to follow a student schedule, and you will have only ten to fifteen minutes to get your message across to each group of parents. Elementary teachers may get up to an hour to present the curriculum to their audience. In either scenario, you must be positive and clear. These events usually do not devote time to individual parent concerns. If parents confront you with questions that are personal to their child or otherwise inappropriate, thank them for their interest and invite them to schedule a private appointment with you. If you are flustered or angered by a question, maintain your composure, smile, and say, "We can discuss that privately." Stay calm and in control, and move on with your presentation.

Report Cards

Another way you interact with parents is through report cards, which formally present student achievement in an organized format. Your job is to get the message of student progress or shortcomings across clearly and concisely. Entire books have been written to help you write and organize comments, such as *Quick Tips: Writing Effective Report Card Comments* by Sharon Shafer (New York: Scholastic Trade, 1999). Some parents just look for grades; others want to read the supporting commentary with it.

First and foremost, find something positive to say about each child. You not only want the parent on your side, but your interest is in truly teaming with the parent to help the child. If the child is not doing well, you must convey that message to the parent, but in such a way that the parent will be able to work with you, not against you. Comments such as, "He doesn't do his work, and when it's done, it is sloppy" will not get you what you need from the parent. This comment should be rephrased to, "John seems to have a difficult time completing assignments. I have confidence he is capable of doing the work, and if he slows down, his work will be neater and more organized." Basically, this comment says the same thing but sends a very different message to the parents. It shows that you see positive attributes in the child, and that you are confident that the child can improve and grow. It also lets the parents know that their child is not completing the work and is careless. Taking the time to carefully compose your comments will enable you to foster positive parent-teacher relationships and allow you to teach more effectively.

Keep the Lines of Communication Open

Being accessible to parents makes it easier for the parents to be accountable for student performance *with* you, as your partner. Problems are prevented when small issues are addressed at the outset, before they become big issues. If they are not addressed early on, the parent-teacher relationship can become adversarial, rather than collegial, which can interfere with the student's progress.

Bear in mind that parents' expectations are not always clearly communicated to their children's teachers. They want to trust the teacher, and they want the teacher to be responsive to their child's individual needs. Shelley Obletz, a parent of middle school twins, explained, "I want to work as a team with the teachers. I want to know what is going on. I don't want a 'once a year' meeting. If my child has a need, I want to know about it. The relationship should never be adversarial with the child in the middle. Parents and teachers must work together as a team for the benefit of the children."

Involving Parents: When and How?

The report card should not be the first time a parent hears from you. You have many opportunities to send messages and to interact with them early in the school year. Here are some suggestions.

- Begin early. Send a letter home to both the parent and the child before school begins. Tell them what the school year will be like and what your expectations are. Children *love* to receive mail, and it sets a very positive tone for interactions with the parents.
- Send home a weekly or monthly newsletter to let parents know what is going on in the classroom. You may want to do this via e-mail.
- Invite parents for a special event such as a science demonstration, a reenactment of a civil war battle, or a poetry reading.
- Ask parents to sign work that is sent home. Leave a space for them to write any comments or concerns they have.
- Call or e-mail parents to let them know that students are doing well.
- Call or e-mail parents to let them know that students are not completing work as expected.
- Attend PTA meetings or other school events to interact with parents informally.
- Tell parents when they can reach you at work if they want to contact you directly, and encourage them to e-mail you via the school.

Parent Groups

Your school probably has a parent association—sometimes called PTA (Parent Teacher Association), PTO (Parent Teacher Organization), or PTSA (Parent Teacher Student Association). These organizations run functions that raise funds that go back to the school in some form. Materials may be purchased for classroom use, or assembly programs may be brought in for entire grade levels. It is to your benefit to attend and participate in these activities. It sends a message to the parents that you are part of their community, and they appreciate your presence.

THE BOARD OF EDUCATION

An important community group to know about is the local board of education. The members are volunteers who are elected by community to set school policy. You probably do not see them on a regular basis, but you may be invited to speak at a meeting or host them in your school. They may have even been part of your interview committee. They are the ones who actually vote "yes" or "no" to hire you after the superintendent recommends you for the position. These people often are the eyes and ears of the community and will know quite a bit about what goes on in individual classrooms.

Remember, the trustees of the board of education are residents when you see them in the community; they only become an official governing body when they are in session. When you approach individuals with personal teaching issues, you are putting them "on the spot." It is unprofessional to do this. Rather, if you have an issue at school, go to your mentor, your assistant principal, or your principal first, and hopefully, the problem will get rectified in a satisfactory manner. Should you have a rare problem reaching beyond the scope of the principal's office, only then should you include the board—after all in-school methods of conflict resolution have been exhausted. Also, it should be done in writing and following guidelines specified at your Board of Education for such issues.

CHALLENGES FACING TEACHERS

The role of a teacher has changed dramatically over the past several years. Many of the challenges that face today's teachers just didn't exist decades ago. Here are several challenges you will most likely come across, to some degree, based on where you teach and what type of students you have.

Violence in Schools

This is one of the most distressing challenges facing today's teachers and one that has appeared quite prominently in the news media. Violence in the schools received even more widespread attention after two students from Columbine High School went on a killing rampage, murdering 13 people and then fatally shooting themselves. While incidents like this one are rare, they nevertheless cause great concern for many teachers across the nation. According to a 1998 report from the U.S. Department of Justice entitled *Indicators of School Crime and Safety*, every hour more than 900 teachers are threatened, and 40 teachers are physically attacked on school grounds.

The good news is that some forms of school violence have actually declined recently. For example, in the last half of the 1990s, the *2000 Annual Report on School Safety* states there was a steady decline from 17 to 12 in the percentage of students in grades nine through twelve who reported carrying a weapon to school on one or more days during the previous month.

According to Ronald D. Stephens, the Executive Director of the National School Safety Center, "no greater challenge exists today than creating safe schools." He lists eight key strategies that teachers and other school leaders must implement to achieve this goal:

1. Establish clear behavior standards.
2. Provide adequate adult presence and supervision.
3. Enforce the rules fairly and consistently.
4. Supervise closely and sanction offenders consistently.
5. Cultivate parental support.
6. Control campus access.
7. Create partnerships with outside agencies.
8. Believe you can make a difference.

Many institutions, school districts, and federal government agencies have created programs aimed at reducing school violence. To learn more about these programs and to see how you can get involved, contact one or more of these organizations:

Center for the Prevention of School Violence
313 Chapanoke Road, Suite 140
Raleigh, NC 27603
800-299-6054
www.ncsu.edu/cpsv

This Center's mission is to enable every student to attend a school that is safe and secure; one that is free of fear and conducive to learning. While it is located in North Carolina, its services and information have reached out to help interested parties in other states too. You can access a wealth of information at their website, including statistics, solutions to violence, and links to other programs.

The National School Safety Center
141 Duesenberg Drive, Suite 11
Westlake Village, CA 91362
805-373-9977
www.nssc1.org

The National School Safety Center (NSSC) is a nonprofit organization that was created by presidential directive in 1984 to meet a need for additional training and preparation in the area of school crime and violence prevention for local school districts. NSSC provides technical assistance and legal and legislative aid to support programs that help to improve student discipline, attendance, achievement and school climate. This center has worked with representatives in all 50 states, so its reach is truly national.

U.S. Department of Education: Safe and Drug Free Schools Program
202-260-3954
www.ed.gov/offices/OESE/SDFS

The Safe and Drug-Free Schools Program is the federal government's primary vehicle for reducing drug, alcohol and tobacco use, and violence, through education and prevention activities in the nation's schools. They offer two major programs: state grants for drug and violence prevention programs and national programs.

The National Youth Gang Center
www.iir.com/nygc/maininfo.htm

This organization was formed by the Office of Juvenile Justice and Delinquency Prevention (OJJDP) as a response to the gang problems in large and small cities, suburbs, and even rural areas over the last two decades.

Overcrowded Schools

For the sixth consecutive year, a record number of students are expected to enroll in public and private elementary and secondary schools this fall, according to a report published August 16, 2001 by the U.S. Department of Education's National Center for Education Statistics. According to this report entitled *Projections of Education Statistics to 2011*, over 53.1 million students will enter K–12 classrooms this fall, which is the most ever recorded. This surge in the number of students has many school districts scrambling to find additional space, supplies, and in some cases, teachers to accommodate the extra students in their schools. In many overcrowded schools, it is not uncommon to see students sitting on top of desks or overflowing into the hallways during the first week of school.

Some school districts have turned to year-round schooling to help ease the overcrowded schools in that district. Students in these districts attend school the same number of days—180—as students on the traditional nine-month calendar, but their schedule includes several short vacations rather than one three-month long summer vacation. According to an article in the Educational Resources Information Center entitled *Year-Round Education: A Strategy for Overcrowded Schools—ERIC/CUE Digest Number 103*, "by switching to the year-round calendar, districts can fit more students into existing school buildings, saving millions of dollars in construction costs." The article goes on to explain that in this system, some students are attending school while others are on their short vacations. Therefore, using this method, a school in a building built for 750 students can serve as many as 1,000 students. You may find out that you prefer a year-round schedule, or it may turn out to be a problem for you. It is something to keep in mind because many schools are moving in this direction.

For more information about reducing class size, contact the advocacy group called Reduce Class Size Now, 2888 Ponce de Leon Court, Gulf Shores, AL 36542, 334-540-7012. Their website (www.reduceclasssizenow. org) has a wealth of information about class size reduction plans, supporting candidates who are for reducing class size, content of relevant research studies about class size, and answers to critics.

Standardized Testing

As the public demands more accountability from teachers and schools, more administrators are finding the need to increase the role of standardized testing in their schools. Currently, all 50 states now have some statewide testing policies in place. Many parents feel that holding teachers responsible for their students' achievement will result in better education. However, many educators agree that this single-minded emphasis on test scores has serious limitations. Many teachers complain that they must now "teach to the test," which means that they focus their lesson plans on preparing students to take one or more standardized tests instead of teaching the critical thinking skills students need for higher-level learning. They feel that they are devoting too much classroom time preparing for these multiple-choice tests. According to an *Education Week* survey during the year 2000, over 66% of teachers think state tests are forcing them to concentrate too much on what's tested to the detriment of other important topics, and nearly half said they spend "a great deal of time" helping students prepare for tests.

In many states, the student's scores on these tests are directly linked to the quality of instruction given to them by their teachers, even though some educators claim this is not a valid link. For example, in the state of Florida, schools are given a grade A–E based on the scores of their students on the state's standardized test called the Florida Comprehensive Assessment Test (FCAT). Teachers in "A" schools often receive cash bonuses. Therefore, the incentive to teach to the test is great even if other academic areas must fall by the wayside. For the 2000–2001 school year, 568 schools in Florida achieved an "A", and another 629 schools improved their grades by at least one letter grade. All will receive a bonus of $100 per student as part of the state's school recognition program.

Another example of bonus money going to schools and teachers is in the state of California, where the governor earmarked bonuses totaling $227 million for the Governor's Performance Award program for 2001. These bonuses are to reward schools whose test scores rose enough to meet state growth targets. Under the bonus program, which is open only to low-performing schools, schools must show exceptional improvement on state tests. Out of a list of roughly 1,200 schools that are eligible; the bonuses will likely be awarded to educators at only a portion of those schools. Approximately 1,000 certified staff members at the schools with the most improvement stand to receive bonuses of $25,000 each, while 3,750 more are slated to get $10,000 each, and an additional 7,500 are to receive $5,000 each.

On the federal level, President Bush signed into law his plan for education, called the *No Child Left Behind Act of 2001*, in January 2002. A section of his plan, entitled "Achieving Equality Through High Standards and Accountability," explains his idea for mandatory testing in grades 3–8. You can access this report online at www.ed.gov/inits/nclb/part3.html.

For additional information on standardized testing and other types of student assessment, you can visit the library portion of the ERIC Clearinghouse on Assessment and Evaluation website at www.ericae.net/ftlib.htm. This library contains links to full-text books, reports, journal articles, newsletter articles, and papers on the Internet that address educational measurement, evaluation, and learning theory.

Another good source of information on student assessment can be found at www.cse.ucla.edu, the website of the National Center for Research on Evaluation, Standards, and Student Testing. This organization is funded by the U.S. Department of Education and the Office of Educational Research and Improvement. It conducts research on important topics related to K–12 educational testing.

THE PAYOFF

The first few years of teaching are difficult because you spend endless hours planning lessons, preparing for class, and trying to fit in with your colleagues. Is it worth it? Rewards come at the most unexpected times. One day, a fifth-grade special education teacher unexpectedly received a bouquet of flowers and this note:

> Dear Mrs. Jackson,
>
> Yesterday, my son Max read to me from a book and I was overwhelmed by his newly acquired ability to read. I just want to say thank you. Your teaching skills have absolutely made a difference in my son's life.
>
>   Regards,
>   Sally Halpern

The entire school cheered for the success of this learning-disabled child who had struggled for so long, and his mother's letter brought smiles to everyone on the staff. This kind of recognition reminds all teachers why we work so hard and why we continue to put forth extra effort and endless time.

Teaching is a profession for the bright, the energetic, and the caring. We can't think of a better way to have a rewarding and enriching professional career.

Good Luck!

THE INSIDE TRACK

Who:	Mary McKeown
What:	Elementary School Teacher
Where:	Berkeley, California

INSIDER'S STORY

My mother was a teacher and she absolutely loved everything about teaching. She enjoyed the children, the curriculum, the planning and all that being a teacher entailed. I heard classroom stories over dinner, our whole family would grade math papers when she was under time pressure, and all of us were involved with her classes. We knew the kids and laughed and worried over the incidents and happenings in her classroom. I knew forever that I wanted to be a teacher too, and I have never regretted the decision.

My own teaching experience has been varied. In my 28 years of experience, I've taught in both public and private schools, in a variety of districts, and in a variety of states. I've taught many different subjects and many different grades, from junior first (for students that were too immature for first grade but also too bright to repeat kindergarten) through the fourth grade, although I've spent the most years teaching third grade. Like my mother before me, I love teaching, not only because of the students, but also, in a large part, due to my teaching colleagues.

The teachers with whom I've been on staff were an extremely valuable connection. The colleagues I have met at seminars, classes, and in-service gatherings were also an invaluable resource. And although I moved to several different states over the years, I maintained contact with former colleagues. In fact, when my school burned down during the enormous fire in the Oakland and Berkeley Hills, all of my professional files were lost. Friends and colleagues from other locations sent material that had been shared with them, so almost all my files were replaced.

My advice to teachers who are just starting out is to make connections with as many people in teaching as possible. Attend conferences, professional-development classes, and observe other teachers' classes to supplement your own experiences. The more educators you know, the more sources of creative inspiration and problem-solving techniques you can call on when you need help.

Appendix A

Professional Associations

Membership in a professional association is expected in most professional fields. This directory helps you locate the general teaching associations as well as organizations for your specialty or specialties that can help you be the best teacher you can be!

The organizations listed in this directory provide information related to the teaching profession in general or specifically to your certification or area of specialization. These associations can keep you informed about continuing education courses, new teaching methods, or job opportunities that can enhance your performance in your current position or help you find a new job.

American Association for Employment in
  Education
3040 Riverside Drive, Suite 125
Columbus OH 43221-2550
614-485-1111; FAX: 614-485-9609
www.aaee.org

American Alliance for Health, Physical
  Education, Recreation, and Dance
1900 Association Drive
Reston, VA 20191
703-476-3400; 800-213-7193
www.aahperd.org

American Association for Girls and Women
  in Sport
1900 Association Drive
Reston, VA 20191
703-476-3400
www.aahperd.org

American Association for Health Education
1900 Association Drive
Reston, VA 20191
703-476-3400
www.aahperd.org

Association for Supervision and Curriculum
  Development
1703 North Beauregard Street
Alexandria, VA 22311-1714
703-578-9600; 800-933-ASCD
www.ascd.org

American Association of Physics Teachers
1 Physics Ellipse
College Park, MD 20740
301-209-3300
www.aapt.org

American Association of Teachers of French
University of Illinois
57 East Armory Avenue
Champaign, IL 61820
www.aatf.utsa.edu

American Council on the Teaching of Foreign
 Languages
Six Executive Plaza
Yonkers, NY 10701
www.actfl.org

American Federation of Teachers
555 New Jersey Avenue, NW
Washington, DC 20001
www.aft.org

American String Teachers Association
1806 Robert Fulton Drive, Suite 300
Reston, VA 22091
703-476-1316; FAX: 703-476-1317
www.astaweb.com

American Vocational Association
1410 King Street
Alexandria, VA 22314
800-826-9972
www.avaonline.org

Association for Childhood Education
 International
17904 Georgia Avenue, Suite 215
Olney, MD 20832
www.udel.edu/bateman/acei

Association for Educational Communications
 and Technology
1025 Vermont Avenue, NW, Suite 820
Washington, DC 20005-3516
202-347-7834; FAX: 202-347-7839
www.aect.org

Association of Teacher Educators
1900 Association Drive
Reston, VA 22091-1502
703-620-3110; FAX: 703-620-9530
www.siu.edu/departments/coe/ate

Association of Teachers of Spanish and
 Portuguese
P.O. Box 6349
Mississippi State, MS 39762
www.aatsp.org

Council for Exceptional Children
1920 Association Drive
Reston, VA 22091
888-232-7733
www.cec.sped.org

International Reading Association
P.O. Box 8139
800 Barksdale Road
Newark, DE 19714
302-731-1600
www.reading.org

International Society for Music Education
International Office
University of Reading, Bulmershe Court
Reading RG6 1HY
United Kingdom
(+44) 1734-318856
www.isme.org

Music Educators National Conference
1806 Robert Fulton Drive
Reston, VA 20191
703-860-4000; 800-336-3768
www.menc.org

National Art Education Association
1916 Association Drive
Reston, VA 20191-1590
703-860-8000
www.naea-reston.org

National Association for Bilingual Education
Union Center Plaza
810 First Street, NE, 3rd Floor
Washington, DC 20002
www.nabe.org

National Association for Gifted Children
1707 L Street, NW, Suite 550
Washington, DC 20036
202-785-4268; FAX: 202-785-4248
www.nagc.org

National Association for Sport and Physical Education
1900 Association Drive
Reston, VA 20191
800-213-7193, ext. 410
www.aahperd.org/naspe/naspemain.html

National Association of Biology Teachers
12030 Sunrise Valley Drive, Suite 110
Reston, VA 20191
703-264-9696; 800-406-0775
www.nabt.org

National Association of State Directors of
Teacher Education and Certification
39 Nathan Highway
PMB #134
Mashpee, MA 02649
508-539-8844; FAX: 508-539-8868
www.nasdtec.org

The National Board for Professional
Teaching Standards
www.nbpts.org

Arlington Office
1525 Wilson Boulevard, Suite 500
Arlington, VA 22209

Southfield Office
26555 Evergreen Rd, Suite 400
Southfield, MI 48076

Southeast Regional Office
3301 Woman's Club Drive, Suite 130
Raleigh, NC 27612

National Business Education Association
1914 Association Drive
Reston, VA 20191
703-860-8300; FAX: 703-620-4483
www.nbea.org

National Catholic Education Association
1077 30th Street, NW, Suite 100
Washington, DC 20007-3852
202-337-6232; FAX: 202-333-6706
www.ncea.org

National Child Care Association
1016 Rosser Street
Conyers, GA 30012
800-543-7161
www.nccanet.org.

National Clearinghouse for Bilingual Education
2011 Eye Street NW, Suite 200
Washington, DC 20006
www.ncbe.gwu.edu

National Clearinghouse for Professions in
    Special Education
1110 North Glebe Road, Suite 300
Arlington, VA 22201
800-641-7824; FAX: 703-264-1637
www.special-ed-careers.org

National Commission on Teaching &
    America's Future Teachers College,
    Columbia University
525 West 120th Street, Box 117
New York, NY 10027
212-678-4153; FAX: 212-678-4039
www.nctaf.org/

National Council for the Social Studies
3501 Newark Street, NW
Washington, DC 20016
202-966-7840
www.ncss.org

National Council of Teachers of English
1111 Kenyon Rd.
Urbana, IL 61801
www.ncte.org

National Council of Teachers of Mathematics
1906 Association Drive
Reston, VA 22091
www.nctm.org

National Council on Economic Education
1140 Avenue of the Americas
New York, NY 10036
800-338-1192; FAX: 212-370-1793
www.nationalcouncil.org

National Education Association
201 16th Street, NW
Washington, DC 20036
www.nea.org

National Middle School Association
2600 Corporate Exchange Drive, #370
Columbus, OH 43231
800-528-NMSA
www.nmsa.org

National School Orchestra Association
307 Eleventh Street
Port Clinton, OH 43452
www.astaweb.com

National Science Teachers Association
1840 Wilson Boulevard
Arlington, VA 22201-3000
703-243-7100
www.nsta.org

Phi Delta Kappa
P.O. Box 789
Bloomington, IN 47402
www.pdkintl.org

Teachers of English to Speakers of Other
    Languages, Inc. (TESOL)
700 South Washington Street, Suite 200
Alexandria, VA 22314
703-836-0774
www.tesol.org

Appendix B

Additional Resources

The following directory will point you in the right direction to find out the information you need to achieve your goals and become a great teacher. For more information about specific topics discussed in Chapters 1–7, search through the following extensive list.

BOOKS AND WEBSITES FOR TEACHERS

Art Education

Books

Bates, Jane K. *Becoming an Art Teacher.* (Belmont, CA: Wadsworth Publishing, 2000).

Dobbs, Stephen Mark. *Learning In and Through Art: A Guide to Disipline Based Art Education.* (New York: Oxford University Press, 1998).

Hume, Helen D. *A Survival Kit for the Elementary/Middle School Art Teacher.* (Center for Applied Research in Education, 2001).

Online

Eyes on Art
www.kn.pacbell.com/wired/art2

Web Museum
www.sunsite.unc.edu/wm

Bilingual and ESL Education

Books

Cloud, Nancy, et. al. *Dual Language Instruction: A Handbook for Enriched Education* (Boston, MA: Heinle & Heinle, 2000).

Mohamed, Jeff. *Teaching English Overseas: A Job Guide for Americans and Canadians* (Pittsburg, CA: English International, 2000).

Watkins-Goffman, Linda. *Lives in Two Languages: An Exploration of Identity and Culture* (Ann Arbor, MI: University of Michigan Press, 2001).

Online

ESL Center
www.member.aol.com/eslkathy/esl.htm

Teachers of English to Speakers of Other Languages
www.tesol.org

Clearinghouse for Multicultural/Bilingual Education
www.Weber.edu/MBE/htmls/mbe.html

Career Resources for Teachers

Books

Calhoun, Florence J. *Choosing a Career in Teaching* (New York: Rosen, 2000).

Eberts, Marjorie, et al. *Opportunities in Education* (New York: McGraw-Hill, 2000).

Echaore-McDavid, Susan. *Career Opportunities in Education* (New York: Checkmark, 2000).

Feirsen, Robert et al. *How to Get the Teaching Job You Want: The Complete Guide For College Graduates, Returning Teachers and Career Changers* (Sterling, VA: Stylus, 2001).

McKinney, Anne, Editor. *Real Resumes for Teachers* (Fayetteville, NC: PREP Publishing, 2000).

Moffatt, Courtney and Thomas. *How to Get a Teaching Job* (Needham Heights, MA: Allyn & Bacon, 1999).

VGM. *Resumes for Education Careers* (New York: McGraw-Hill, 1999).

Online
Academic Employment Network
www.academploy.com

Chronicle of Higher Education Career Network
www.thisweek.chronicle.com/jobs

50 States' K-12 Employment Opportunities
www.uky.edu/Education/TEP/usajobs.html

National Teacher Recruitment Clearinghouse
www.recruitingteachers.org

Colleges and Financial Aid

Books
Antonoff, Steven R. *College Match; A Blueprint for Choosing the Best School for You.* 7th Edition (Alexandria, VA: Octameron Associates, 2001).
Cassidy, Daniel J. *The Scholarship Book* (Upper Saddle River, NJ: Prentice Hall, 2002).
Kaplan, Benjamin R. *How to Go to College Almost For Free* (Glendon Beach, OR: Waggle Dancer Books, 2000).
Phillips, Vicky. *Never Too Late to Learn: The Adult Student's Guide to College* (New York: Random House/Princeton Review Books, 2000).
The Scholarship Advisor, 2001 Edition (Princeton, NJ: Princeton Review, 2000).
2002 Scholarships, Grants & Prizes (Princeton, NJ: Peterson's Guides, Inc., 2000).

Online
College is Possible
www.collegeispossible.org

Office of Postsecondary Education Programs
www.ed.gov/offices/OPE

Early Childhood Education

Books

Gonzalez-Mena, Janet. *Foundation: Early Childhood Education in a Diverse Society* (Mayfield, CA: Mayfield Publishing, 2000).

Isbell, Rebecca, et al. *Early Learning Environments that Work* (Beltsville, MD: Gryphon House, 2001).

Online

Early Childhood Care and Development
www.ecdgroup.com

Early Childhood Educator's Web Corner
www.users.sgi.net/~cokids

Elementary Education

Books

Gipps, Caroline, et al. *What Makes a Good Primary School Teacher?: Expert Classroom Strategies.* (New York: Routledge Fulmer, 2001).

Kellough, Richard D., Patricia Roberts. *A Resource Guide for Elementary School Teaching; Planning for Competence* (Upper Saddle River, NJ: Prentice Hall, 2001).

Klein, M. Diane, Deborah Chen. *Working with Young Children from Culturally Diverse Backgrounds* (Albany, NY: Delmar Publishers, 2001).

Wong, Harry, Rosemary Trip Wong. *The First Days of School: How to Be an Effective Teacher.* (Mountain View, CA: Harry K. Wong Publishing, 1998).

Online

A World of Kindergartens
www.iup.edu/~njyost/KHI/KHI.htmlx

Electronic Elementary Magazine: The E-Link
www.inform.umd.edu/MMS+State/MDK12_Stuff/homepers/emag

First Year Guides

Books

Kronowitz, Ellen. *Your first Year of Teaching and Beyond* (Reading, MA: Addison Wesley Longman, 1998).

Williamson, Bonnie, et al. *A First-Year Teacher's Guidebook, Second Edition* (Sacramento, CA: Dynamic Teaching Co., 1998).

Wong, Harry K. and Rosemary Tripi Wong. *The First Days of School: How to be an Effective Teacher* (Westminster, CA: Teacher Created Materials, 1998).

Language Arts

Books

Appleman, Deborah. *Critical Encounters in High School English; Teaching Literary Theory to Adolescents* (New York: Teachers College Press, 2000).

Cramer, Ronald L. *Creative Power: The Nature and Nurture of Children's Writing* (Reading, MA: Addison Wesley Longman, 2000).

Jago, Carol. *With Rigor for All: Teaching the Classics to Contemporary Students* (Westport, CT: Heinemann, 2000).

Online

Children's Literature Web Guide
www.ucalgary.ca/~dkbrown

Write Site
www.writesite.org

Reading
www.reading.org

Math Education

Books

Muschal, Judith A., Gary Robert Muschla. *The Math Teacher's Book of Lists* (Upper Saddle River, NJ: Prentice Hall, 1999).

Online

Math Archives–Topics in Mathematics
www.archives.math.utk.edu

World Wide Web Virtual Library-Math
www.euclid.math.fsu.edu/Science/math.html

Music Education

Books

Haines, B. Joan E, Linda L. Gerber. *Leading Young Children to Music* (Upper Saddle River, NJ: Prentice Hall, 1999).

Philpott, Chris, Editor. *Learning to Teach Music in the Secondary School* (New York: Routledge Fulmer, 2001).

Online

K–12 Resources for Music Educators
www.isd77.K12.mn.us/resources/staffpages/shirk/K12.music.html

Music Education Launch Site
www.talentz.com/MusicEducation/index.mv

Science Education

Books

Chiappetta, Eugene L., Thomas R. Koballa. *Science Instruction in the Middle and Secondary Schools* (Upper Saddle River, NJ: Prentice Hall, 2001).

Online

Elementary Science Support Center
www.essc.calumet.purdue.edu

MAD Scientist Network
www.madsci.org

Secondary Education

Books

Kraut, Harvey. *Teaching and the Art of Successful Classroom Management: A How-to Guidebook For Teachers in Secondary Schools, 3rd Edition* (Staten Island, NY: Aysa Publishing, 2000).

Maloy, Robert W. and Irving Seidman. *The Essential Career Guide to Becoming a Middle and High School Teacher* (Westport, CT: Bergin & Garvey, 1999).

Marzano, Robert J., Debra Pickering, Jane E. Pollock. *Classroom Instruction That Works; Research-Based Strategies for Increasing Student Achievement* (Alexandria, VA: Assn for Supervision & Curriculum Development, 2001).

Tovani, Cris, Ellin Oliver Keene. *I Read It, But I Don't Get It: Comprehension Strategies for Adolescent Readers* (York, ME: Stenhouse Publishing, 2000).

Online

Classroom Discipline Resources
www.7-12educators.miningco.com/msub49.htm

Middle School Partnership
www.middleschool.com

Teacher Talk
www.education.Indiana.edu/cas/tt/v1i2/table.html

Social Studies/History Education

Books

Lindquist, Tarry. *Ways That Work: Putting Social Studies Standards into Practice* (Westport, CT: Heinemann, 1997).

Roupp, Heidi (Editor). *Teaching World History: A Resource Book (Sources and Studies in World History)* (Armonk, NY: M.E. Sharpe, 2001).

Online

Social Studies Lesson Plans and Resources
www.csun.edu/~hcedu013

CSS Journal: Computers in the Social Studies
www.cssjournal.com/welcome.html

Special Education

Books

Bullough, Robert V., Jr., Nel Noddings. *Uncertain Lives; Children of Promise, Teachers of Hope* (New York: Teachers College Press, 2001).

Sacks, Arlene. *Special Education: A Reference Handbook* (Santa Barbara, CA: ABC-CLIO, 2001).

Online

Classroom Management Special Education
www.pacificnet.net/~mandel/SpecialEducation.html

LD Online
www.ldonline.org

Substitute Teaching

Books

Manera, Elizabeth S., et al. *Substitute Teaching: Planning for Success* (Indianapolis: Kappa Delta Pi, 1996).

Technology Education

Books

Wilson, James M., Bena O. Kallick (Editor). *Information Technology in Schools: Creating practical Knowledge to Improve Student Performance* (San Francisco, CA: Jossey-Bass, 2000).

Online

Electronic School
www.electronic-school.com

Teaching & Learning on the WWW
www.mcli.dist.Maricopa.edu/tl

PERIODICALS FOR TEACHERS

Print and Online

American School Board Journal
www.asbj.com

Chronicle of Higher Education
www.chronicle.merit.edu

Creative Classroom
www.creativeclassroom.org

Early Childhood News
www.earlychildhood.com

Education Week
www.edweek.org

Elementary School Journal
www.journals.uchicago.edu/ESJ/home.html

The English Teacher's Assistant
www.etanewsletter.com

ESL Magazine
www.eslmag.com

New Teacher Page
www.geocities.com/Athens/Delphi/7862

The International Educator
www.tieonline.com

Instructor Magazine
www.place.scholastic.com/instructor

Online Teacher Magazine
www.teachermagazine.org

Teachers College Record
www.tcrecord.org

Teaching K–8
www.teachingk-8.com

Technology and Learning Magazine
www.techlearning.com

GENERAL RESOURCES FOR TEACHERS

Books

Fiersen, Robert and Seth Weitzman. *How to Get the Teaching Job You Want* (Sterling, VA: Stylus, 2000).

Hopkins, Timothy. *1001 Best Websites for Educators* (Sacramento, CA: Teacher Created Materials, Inc. 2001).

Lewin, Larry. *Using the Internet to Strengthen Curriculum* (Alexandria, VA: The Association for Supervision and Curriculum Development, 2001).

Moorman, Chick. *Spirit Whisperers: Teachers Who Nourish a Child's Spirit* (Merrill, MI: Personal Power Press, 2001).

Palmer, Parker J. *The Courage to Teach: Exploring the Inner Landscape of a Teacher's Life* (San Francisco, CA: Jossey-Bass, 1997).

Winebrenner, Susan, Pamela Espeland. *Teaching Gifted Kids in the Regular Classroom: Strategies and Techniques Every Teacher Can Use to Meet the Academic Needs of the Gifted and Talented (Updated Edition)* (Minneapolis, MN: Free Spirit Publishing, 2000).

Online

American School Directory
www.asd.com

AskEric Home Page (Educational Resources Information Center)
www.ericir.syr.edu

Busy Teacher's K–12 Website
www.ceismc.gatech.edu/busyt

bigchalk
www.bigchalk.com

Education Planet
www.educationplanet.com

Education Week on the Web
www.edweek.org

Gateway to Educational Materials
www.thegateway.org

National Library of Education
www.cde.ca.gov/iasa

New York Times Learning Network
www.nytimes.com/learning

PBS TeacherSource
www.pbs.org/teachersource

Route 66 A K–12 World Wide Web Project
www.web66.coled.umn.edu

Teachnet.com
www.teachnet.com

World Wide Web Virtual Library–Education
www.csu.edu.au/education/library.html

Appendix C

Sample Free Applicaiton for Federal Student Aid (FAFSA)

On the following pages you will find a sample FAFSA. Use this form familiarize yourself with the form so that when you apply for federal and state student grants, work-study, and loans you will know what information you need
to have ready. At print, this was the most current form. Although the form re-
mains mostly the same from year to year, you should check the FAFSA website (www.fafsa.ed.gov) for the most current information.

The FAFSA

July 1, 2001 — June 30, 2002
Free Application for Federal Student Aid

OMB # 1845-0001

Use this form to apply for federal and state* student grants, work-study, and loans.

Apply over the Internet with

FAFSA ON THE WEB

www.fafsa.ed.gov

1 If you are filing a 2000 income tax return, we recommend that you complete it before filling out this form. However, you do not need to file your income tax return with the IRS before you submit this form.

If you or your family has unusual circumstances (such as loss of employment) that might affect your need for student financial aid, submit this form, and then consult with the financial aid office at the college you plan to attend.

You may also use this form to apply for aid from other sources, such as your state or college. The deadlines for states (see table to right) or colleges may be as early as January 2001 and may differ. You may be required to complete additional forms. Check with your high school guidance counselor or a financial aid administrator at your college about state and college sources of student aid.

2 Your answers on this form will be read electronically. Therefore:

- use black ink and fill in ovals completely:

  Yes ● No ⊗ ⊘

- print clearly in CAPITAL letters and skip a box between words:

  | 1 | 5 | | E | L | M | | S | T |

- report dollar amounts (such as $12,356.41) like this:

  $ | 1 | 2 | , | 3 | 5 | 6 | **no cents**

Green is for students and purple is for parents.

If you have questions about this application, or for more information on eligibility requirements and the U.S. Department of Education's student aid programs, look on the Internet at **www.ed.gov/studentaid** You can also call 1-800-4FED-AID (1-800-433-3243) seven days a week from 8:00 a.m. through midnight (Eastern time). TTY users may call 1-800-730-8913.

3 After you complete this application, make a copy of it for your records. Then send the original of pages 3 through 6 in the attached envelope or send it to: Federal Student Aid Programs, P.O. Box 4008, Mt. Vernon, IL 62864-8608.

You should submit your application as early as possible, but no earlier than January 1, 2001. We must receive your application no later than July 1, 2002. Your school must have your correct, complete information by your last day of enrollment in the 2001-2002 school year.

You should hear from us within four weeks. If you do not, please call 1-800-433-3243 or check on-line at www.fafsa.ed.gov

4 **Now go to page 3 and begin filling out this form.**
Refer to the notes as needed.

STATE AID DEADLINES

AR   April 1, 2001 *(date received)*
AZ   June 30, 2002 *(date received)*
*^ CA   March 2, 2001 *(date postmarked)*
* DC   June 24, 2001 *(date received by state)*
DE   April 15, 2001 *(date received)*
FL   May 15, 2001 *(date processed)*
HI   March 1, 2001
^ IA   July 1, 2001 *(date received)*
IL   First-time applicants – September 30, 2001
        Continuing applicants – July 15, 2001
        (date received)
^ IN   For priority consideration – March 1, 2001
        (date postmarked)
* KS   For priority consideration – April 1, 2001
        (date received)
KY   For priority consideration – March 15, 2001
        (date received)
LA   For priority consideration – April 15, 2001
        Final deadline – July 1, 2001
        (date received)
^ MA   For priority consideration – May 1, 2001
        (date received)
MD   March 1, 2001 *(date postmarked)*
ME   May 1, 2001 *(date received)*
MI   High school seniors – February 21, 2001
        College students – March 21, 2001
        (date received)
MN   June 30, 2002 *(date received)*
MO   April 1, 2001 *(date received)*
MT   For priority consideration – March 1, 2001
        (date postmarked)
NC   March 15, 2001 *(date received)*
ND   April 15, 2001 *(date processed)*
NH   May 1, 2001 *(date received)*
^ NJ   June 1, 2001 if you received a
          Tuition Aid Grant in 2000-2001
        All other applicants
          – October 1, 2001, for fall and spring terms
          – March 1, 2002, for spring term only
        (date received)
*^ NY   May 1, 2002 *(date postmarked)*
OH   October 1, 2001 *(date received)*
OK   For priority consideration – April 30, 2001
        Final deadline – June 30, 2001
        (date received)
OR   May 1, 2002 *(date received)*
* PA   All 2000-2001 State Grant recipients and all
          non-2000-2001 State Grant recipients in
          degree programs – May 1, 2001
        All other applicants – August 1, 2001
        (date received)
PR   May 2, 2002 *(date application signed)*
RI   March 1, 2001 *(date received)*
SC   June 30, 2001 *(date received)*
TN   May 1, 2001 *(date processed)*
*^ WV   March 1, 2001 *(date received)*

Check with your financial aid administrator for these states: AK, AL, *AS, *CT, CO, *FM, GA, *GU, ID, *MH, *MP, MS, *NE, *NM, *NV, *PW, *SD, *TX, UT, *VA, *VI, *VT, WA, WI, and *WY.

^ *Applicants encouraged to obtain proof of mailing.*
* *Additional form may be required*

STATE AID DEADLINES

Notes for questions 13–14 (page 3)

If you are an eligible noncitizen, write in your eight or nine digit Alien Registration Number. Generally, you are an eligible noncitizen if you are: (1) a U.S. permanent resident and you have an Alien Registration Receipt Card (I-551); (2) a conditional permanent resident (I-551C); or (3) an other eligible noncitizen with an Arrival-Departure Record (I-94) from the U.S. Immigration and Naturalization Service showing any one of the following designations: "Refugee," "Asylum Granted," "Indefinite Parole," "Humanitarian Parole," or "Cuban-Haitian Entrant." If you are in the U.S. on only an F1 or F2 student visa, or only a J1 or J2 exchange visitor visa, or a G series visa (pertaining to international organizations), you must fill in oval c. If you are neither a citizen nor eligible noncitizen, you are not eligible for federal student aid. However, you may be eligible for state or college aid.

Notes for questions 17–21 (page 3)

For undergraduates, full time generally means taking at least 12 credit hours in a term or 24 clock hours per week. 3/4 time generally means taking at least 9 credit hours in a term or 18 clock hours per week. Half time generally means taking at least 6 credit hours in a term or 12 clock hours per week. Provide this information about the college you plan to attend.

Notes for question 29 (page 3) — Enter the correct number in the box in question 29.

Enter **1** for 1st bachelor's degree
Enter **2** for 2nd bachelor's degree
Enter **3** for associate degree (occupational or technical program)
Enter **4** for associate degree (general education or transfer program)
Enter **5** for certificate or diploma for completing an occupational, technical, or educational program of less than two years

Enter **6** for certificate or diploma for completing an occupational, technical, or educational program of at least two years
Enter **7** for teaching credential program (nondegree program)
Enter **8** for graduate or professional degree
Enter **9** for other/undecided

Notes for question 30 (page 3) — Enter the correct number in the box in question 30.

Enter **0** for 1st year undergraduate/never attended college
Enter **1** for 1st year undergraduate/attended college before
Enter **2** for 2nd year undergraduate/sophomore
Enter **3** for 3rd year undergraduate/junior

Enter **4** for 4th year undergraduate/senior
Enter **5** for 5th year/other undergraduate
Enter **6** for 1st year graduate/professional
Enter **7** for continuing graduate/professional or beyond

Notes for questions 37 c. and d. (page 4) and 71 c. and d. (page 5)

If you filed or will file a foreign tax return, or a tax return with Puerto Rico, Guam, American Samoa, the Virgin Islands, the Marshall Islands, the Federated States of Micronesia, or Palau, use the information from that return to fill out this form. If you filed a foreign return, convert all figures to U.S. dollars, using the exchange rate that is in effect today.

Notes for questions 38 (page 4) and 72 (page 5)

In general, a person is eligible to file a 1040A or 1040EZ if he or she makes less than $50,000, does not itemize deductions, does not receive income from his or her own business or farm, and does not receive alimony. A person is not eligible if he or she itemizes deductions, receives self-employment income or alimony, or is required to file Schedule D for capital gains.

Notes for questions 41 (page 4) and 75 (page 5) — only for people who filed a 1040EZ or Telefile

On the 1040EZ, if a person answered "Yes" on line 5, use EZ worksheet line F to determine the number of exemptions ($2,800 equals one exemption). If a person answered "No" on line 5, enter 01 if he or she is single, or 02 if he or she is married.

On the Telefile, use line J to determine the number of exemptions ($2,800 equals one exemption).

Notes for questions 47–48 (page 4) and 81–82 (page 5)

Net worth means current value minus debt. If net worth is one million or more, enter $999,999. If net worth is negative, enter 0.

Investments include real estate (do not include the home you live in), trust funds, money market funds, mutual funds, certificates of deposit, stocks, stock options, bonds, other securities, education IRAs, installment and land sale contracts (including mortgages held), commodities, etc. Investment value includes the market value of these investments as of today. Investment debt means only those debts that are related to the investments.

Investments do not include the home you live in, cash, savings, checking accounts, the value of life insurance and retirement plans (pension funds, annuities, noneducation IRAs, Keogh plans, etc.), or the value of prepaid tuition plans.

Business and/or investment farm value includes the market value of land, buildings, machinery, equipment, inventory, etc. Business and/or investment farm debt means only those debts for which the business or investment farm was used as collateral.

Notes for question 58 (page 4)

Answer **"No"** (you are not a veteran) if you (1) have never engaged in active duty in the U.S. Armed Forces, (2) are currently an ROTC student or a cadet or midshipman at a service academy, or (3) are a National Guard or Reserves enlistee activated only for training. Also answer "No" if you are currently serving in the U.S. Armed Forces and will continue to serve through June 30, 2002.

Answer **"Yes"** (you are a veteran) if you (1) have engaged in active duty in the U.S. Armed Forces (Army, Navy, Air Force, Marines, or Coast Guard) or as a member of the National Guard or Reserves who was called to active duty for purposes other than training, or were a cadet or midshipman at one of the service academies, **and** (2) were released under a condition other than dishonorable. Also answer "Yes" if you are not a veteran now but will be one by June 30, 2002.

Page 2

Step One: For questions 1-34, leave blank any questions that do not apply to you (the student).

1–3 Your full name (as it appears on your Social Security Card)

1. LAST NAME	2. FIRST NAME	3. MIDDLE INITIAL
FOR INFORMATION ONLY	DO NOT SUBMIT	

4–7 Your permanent mailing address

4. NUMBER AND STREET (INCLUDE APT. NUMBER)

5. CITY (AND COUNTRY IF NOT U.S.)   6. STATE   7. ZIP CODE

8. Your Social Security Number   XXX – XX – XXXX

9. Your date of birth   ☐☐ / ☐☐ 1 9 ☐☐

10. Your permanent telephone number   (☐☐☐) ☐☐☐ – ☐☐☐☐

11–12 Your driver's license number and state (if any)

11. LICENSE NUMBER   12. STATE

13. Are you a U.S. citizen? Pick one. See Page 2.
- a. Yes, I am a U.S. citizen. ○ 1
- b. No, but I am an eligible noncitizen. **Fill in question 14.** ○ 2
- c. No, I am not a citizen or eligible noncitizen. ○ 3

14. ALIEN REGISTRATION NUMBER   A ☐☐☐☐☐☐☐☐

15. What is your marital status as of today?
- I am single, divorced, or widowed. ○ 1
- I am married/remarried. ○ 2
- I am separated. ○ 3

16. Month and year you were married, separated, divorced, or widowed   MONTH ☐☐ / YEAR ☐☐☐☐

For each question (17 - 21), please mark whether you will be full time, 3/4 time, half time, less than half time, or not attending. **See page 2.**

	Full time/Not sure	3/4 time	Half time	Less than half time	Not attending
17. Summer 2001	○ 1	○ 2	○ 3	○ 4	○ 5
18. Fall 2001	○ 1	○ 2	○ 3	○ 4	○ 5
19. Winter 2001-2002	○ 1	○ 2	○ 3	○ 4	○ 5
20. Spring 2002	○ 1	○ 2	○ 3	○ 4	○ 5
21. Summer 2002	○ 1	○ 2	○ 3	○ 4	○ 5

	Middle school/Jr. High	High school	College or beyond	Other/unknown
22. Highest school your father completed	○ 1	○ 2	○ 3	○ 4
23. Highest school your mother completed	○ 1	○ 2	○ 3	○ 4

24. What is your state of legal residence? STATE ☐☐

25. Did you become a legal resident of this state before January 1, 1996?   Yes ○ 1   No ○ 2

26. If the answer to question 25 is "No," give month and year you became a legal resident.   MONTH ☐☐ / YEAR ☐☐☐☐

27. Are you male? (Most male students must register with Selective Service to get federal aid.)   Yes ○ 1   No ○ 2

28. If you are male (age 18-25) and not registered, do you want Selective Service to register you?   Yes ○ 1   No ○ 2

29. What degree or certificate will you be working on during 2001-2002? See page 2 and enter the correct number in the box.   ☐

30. What will be your grade level when you begin the 2001-2002 school year? See page 2 and enter the correct number in the box.   ☐

31. Will you have a high school diploma or GED before you enroll?   Yes ○ 1   No ○ 2

32. Will you have your first bachelor's degree before July 1, 2001?   Yes ○ 1   No ○ 2

33. In addition to grants, are you interested in student loans (which you must pay back)?   Yes ○ 1   No ○ 2

34. In addition to grants, are you interested in "work-study" (which you earn through work)?   Yes ○ 1   No ○ 2

35. Do not leave this question blank. Have you ever been convicted of possessing or selling illegal drugs? If you have, answer "Yes," complete and submit this application, and we will send you a worksheet in the mail for you to determine if your conviction affects your eligibility for aid.   No ○ 1   Yes ○ 3   **DO NOT LEAVE QUESTION 35 BLANK**

Step Two:

For questions 36-49, report your (the student's) income and assets. If you are married, report your spouse's income and assets, even if you were not married in 2000. Ignore references to "spouse" if you are currently single, separated, divorced, or widowed.

36. For 2000, have you (the student) completed your IRS income tax return or another tax return listed in question 37?

  a. I have already completed my return. ○ 1   b. I will file, but I have not yet ○ 2   c. I'm not going to file. **(Skip to question 42.)** ○ 3
                                     completed my return.

37. What income tax return did you file or will you file for 2000?

  a. IRS 1040 .... ○ 1   d. A tax return for Puerto Rico, Guam, American Samoa, the Virgin Islands, the
  b. IRS 1040A, 1040EZ, 1040Telefile ...... ○ 2   Marshall Islands, the Federated States of Micronesia, or Palau. **See Page 2.** ...... ○ 4
  c. A foreign tax return. **See Page 2.** ...... ○ 3

38. If you have filed or will file a 1040, were you eligible to file a 1040A or 1040EZ? See page 2.   Yes ○ 1 No ○ 2 Don't Know ○ 3

For questions 39-51, if the answer is zero or the question does not apply to you, enter 0.

39. What was your (and spouse's) adjusted gross income for 2000? Adjusted gross income is on IRS Form 1040–line 33; 1040A–line 19; 1040EZ–line 4; or Telefile–line I. $ [ ][ ][ ] , [ ][ ][ ]

40. Enter the total amount of your (and spouse's) income tax for 2000. Income tax amount is on IRS Form 1040–line 51; 1040A–line 33; 1040EZ–line 10; or Telefile–line K. $ [ ][ ] , [ ][ ][ ]

41. Enter your (and spouse's) exemptions for 2000. Exemptions are on IRS Form 1040–line 6d or on Form 1040A–line 6d. For Form 1040EZ or Telefile, see page 2.   [ ][ ]

42-43. How much did you (and spouse) earn from working in 2000? Answer this question whether or not you filed a tax return. This information may be on your W-2 forms, or on IRS Form 1040–lines 7 + 12 + 18; 1040A–line 7; or 1040EZ–line 1. Telefilers should use their W-2's.

        You (42) $ [ ][ ][ ] , [ ][ ][ ]
    Your Spouse (43) $ [ ][ ][ ] , [ ][ ][ ]

Student (and Spouse) Worksheets (44-46)

44-46. Go to Page 8 and complete the columns on the left of Worksheets A, B, and C. Enter the student (and spouse) totals in questions 44, 45, and 46, respectively. Even though you may have few of the Worksheet items, check each line carefully.

  Worksheet A (44) $ [ ][ ][ ] , [ ][ ][ ]
  Worksheet B (45) $ [ ][ ][ ] , [ ][ ][ ]
  Worksheet C (46) $ [ ][ ][ ] , [ ][ ][ ]

47. As of today, what is the net worth of your (and spouse's) current investments? See page 2. $ [ ][ ][ ] , [ ][ ][ ]

48. As of today, what is the net worth of your (and spouse's) current businesses and/or investment farms? See page 2. Do not include a farm that you live on and operate. $ [ ][ ][ ] , [ ][ ][ ]

49. As of today, what is your (and spouse's) total current balance of cash, savings, and checking accounts? $ [ ][ ][ ] , [ ][ ][ ]

50-51. If you receive veterans education benefits, for how many months from July 1, 2001 through June 30, 2002 will you receive these benefits, and what amount will you receive per month? Do not include your spouse's veterans education benefits.

        Months (50) [ ][ ]
        Amount (51) $ [ ][ ][ ]

Step Three:

Answer all seven questions in this step.

52. Were you born before January 1, 1978? ....   Yes ○ 1 No ○ 2

53. Will you be working on a master's or doctorate program (such as an MA, MBA, MD, JD, or Ph.D., etc.) during the school year 2001-2002? ....   Yes ○ 1 No ○ 2

54. As of today, are you married? (Answer "Yes" if you are separated but not divorced.) ....   Yes ○ 1 No ○ 2

55. Do you have children who receive more than half of their support from you? ....   Yes ○ 1 No ○ 2

56. Do you have dependents (other than your children or spouse) who live with you and who receive more than half of their support from you, now and through June 30, 2002? ....   Yes ○ 1 No ○ 2

57. Are you an orphan or ward of the court or were you a ward of the court until age 18? ....   Yes ○ 1 No ○ 2

58. Are you a veteran of the U.S. Armed Forces? See page 2. ....   Yes ○ 1 No ○ 2

If you (the student) answer "No" to every question in Step Three, go to Step Four.

If you answer "Yes" to any question in Step Three, skip Step Four and go to Step Five.

(If you are a graduate health profession student, your school may require you to complete Step Four even if you answered "Yes" in Step Three.)

Step Four: Complete this step if you (the student) answered "No" to all questions in Step Three.

59. Go to page 7 to determine who is considered a parent. What is your parents's marital status as of today? (Pick one.)　Married/Remarried ○ 1　Single ○ 2　Divorced/Separated ○ 3　Widowed ○ 4

60–63 What are your parents' Social Security Numbers and last names?
If your parent does not have a Social Security Number, enter 000-00-0000

| 60. FATHER'S/STEPFATHER'S SOCIAL SECURITY NUMBER | XXX – XX – XXXX | 61. FATHER'S/STEPFATHER'S LAST NAME | FOR INFORMATION ONLY |
| 62. MOTHER'S/STEPMOTHER'S SOCIAL SECURITY NUMBER | XXX – XX – XXXX | 63. MOTHER'S/STEPMOTHER'S LAST NAME | DO NOT SUBMIT |

64. Go to page 9 to determine how many people are in your parents' household.

65. Go to page 9 to determine how many in question 64 (exclude your parents) will be college students between July 1, 2001 and June 30, 2002.

66. What is your parents' state of legal residence?　　STATE

67. Did your parents become legal residents of the state in question 66 before January 1, 1996?　Yes ○ 1　No ○ 2

68. If the answer to question 67 is "No," give the month and year legal residency began for the parent who has lived in the state the longest.　MONTH / YEAR

69. What is the age of your older parent?

70. For 2000, have your parents completed their IRS income tax return or another tax return listed in question 71?

a. My parents have already completed their return. ○ 1
b. My parents will file, but they have not yet completed their return. ○ 2
c. My parents are not going to file. (Skip to question 76.) ○ 3

71. What income tax return did your parents file or will they file for 2000?

a. IRS 1040 .... ○ 1
b. IRS 1040A, 1040EZ, 1040Telefile ..... ○ 2
c. A foreign tax return. See Page 2. ...... ○ 3
d. A tax return for Puerto Rico, Guam, American Samoa, the Virgin Islands, the Marshall Islands, the Federated States of Micronesia, or Palau. See Page 2. .... ○ 4

72. If your parents have filed or will file a 1040, were they eligible to file a 1040A or 1040EZ? See page 2.　Yes ○ 1　No ○ 2　Don't Know ○ 3

For questions 73 - 83, if the answer is zero or the question does not apply, enter 0.

73. What was your parents' adjusted gross income for 2000? Adjusted gross income is on IRS Form 1040–line 33; 1040A–line 19; 1040EZ–line 4; or Telefile–line I.　$ ___ , ___

74. Enter the total amount of your parents' income tax for 2000. Income tax amount is on IRS Form 1040–line 51; 1040A–line 33; 1040EZ–line 10; or Telefile–line K.　$ ___ , ___

75. Enter your parents' exemptions for 2000. Exemptions are on IRS Form 1040–line 6d or on Form 1040A–line 6d. For Form 1040EZ or Telefile, see page 2.　___

76–77 How much did your parents earn from working in 2000? Answer this question whether or not your parents filed a tax return. This information may be on their W-2 forms, or on IRS Form 1040–lines 7 + 12 + 18; 1040A–line 7; or 1040EZ–line 1. Telefilers should use their W-2's.

Father/Stepfather (76) $ ___ , ___
Mother/Stepmother (77) $ ___ , ___

Parent Worksheets (78-80)

78–80 Go to Page 8 and complete the columns on the right of Worksheets A, B, and C. Enter the parent totals in questions 78, 79, and 80, respectively. Even though your parents may have few of the Worksheet items, check each line carefully.

Worksheet A (78) $ ___ , ___
Worksheet B (79) $ ___ , ___
Worksheet C (80) $ ___ , ___

81. As of today, what is the net worth of your parents' current investments? See page 2　$ ___ , ___

82. As of today, what is the net worth of your parents' current businesses and/or investment farms? See page 2. Do not include a farm that your parents live on and operate.　$ ___ , ___

83. As of today, what is your parents' total current balance of cash, savings, and checking accounts?　$ ___ , ___

Now go to Step Six.

For Help — (800) 433-3243

Step Five: Complete this step only if you (the student) answered "Yes" to any question in Step Three.

84. Go to page to determine how many people are in your (and your spouse's) household.

85. Go to page to determine how many in question 84 will be college students between July 1, 2001 and June 30, 2002.

Step Six: Please tell us which schools should receive your information.

For each school (up to six), please provide the federal school code and your housing plans. Look for the federal school codes on the Internet at **www.fafsa.ed.gov**, at your college financial aid office, at your public library, or by asking your high school guidance counselor. If you cannot get the federal school code, write in the complete name, address, city, and state of the college.

86. 1ST FEDERAL SCHOOL CODE OR NAME OF COLLEGE / ADDRESS AND CITY — STATE

HOUSING PLANS
87. on campus ○ 1 / off campus ○ 2 / with parent ○ 3

88. 2ND FEDERAL SCHOOL CODE OR NAME OF COLLEGE / ADDRESS AND CITY — STATE

89. on campus ○ 1 / off campus ○ 2 / with parent ○ 3

90. 3RD FEDERAL SCHOOL CODE OR NAME OF COLLEGE / ADDRESS AND CITY — STATE

91. on campus ○ 1 / off campus ○ 2 / with parent ○ 3

92. 4TH FEDERAL SCHOOL CODE OR NAME OF COLLEGE / ADDRESS AND CITY — STATE

93. on campus ○ 1 / off campus ○ 2 / with parent ○ 3

94. 5TH FEDERAL SCHOOL CODE OR NAME OF COLLEGE / ADDRESS AND CITY — STATE

95. on campus ○ 1 / off campus ○ 2 / with parent ○ 3

96. 6TH FEDERAL SCHOOL CODE OR NAME OF COLLEGE / ADDRESS AND CITY — STATE

97. on campus ○ 1 / off campus ○ 2 / with parent ○ 3

Step Seven: Please read, sign, and date.

By signing this application, you agree, if asked, to provide information that will verify the accuracy of your completed form. This information may include your U.S. or state income tax forms. Also, you certify that you (1) will use federal and/or state student financial aid only to pay the cost of attending an institution of higher education, (2) are not in default on a federal student loan or have made satisfactory arrangements to repay it, (3) do not owe money back on a federal student grant or have made satisfactory arrangements to repay it, (4) will notify your school if you default on a federal student loan, and (5) understand that the Secretary of Education has the authority to verify information reported on this application with the Internal Revenue Service. If you purposely give false or misleading information, you may be fined $10,000, sent to prison, or both.

98. Date this form was completed.

MONTH / DAY / 2○1 or ○02

99. Student signature (Sign in box)

1 **FOR INFORMATION ONLY.**

Parent signature (one parent whose information is provided in Step Four) (Sign in box)

2 **DO NOT SUBMIT.**

If this form was filled out by someone other than you, your spouse, or your parent(s), that person must complete this part.

Preparer's name, firm, and address

100. Preparer's Social Security Number (or 101)

― ―

101. Employer ID number (or 100)

―

102. Preparer's signature and date

1

SCHOOL USE ONLY: Federal School Code

D/O ○ 1

FAA SIGNATURE

1

MDE USE ONLY:
Special Handle ―

For Help — www.ed.gov/prog_info/SFA/FAFSA

Notes for questions **59–83** (page 5) **Step Four:** Who is considered a parent in this step?

Read these notes to determine who is considered a parent for purposes of this form. Answer all questions in Ste about them even if you do not live with them.

If your parents are both living and married to each other, answer the questions about them.

If your parent is widowed or single, answer the questions about that parent. If your widowed parent has remarried as of today, answer the questions about that parent and the person whom your parent married (your stepparent).

If your parents have divorced or separated, answer the questions about the parent you lived with more during the past 12 months. (If you did not live with one parent more than the other, give answers about the parent who provided more financial support during the last 12 months, or during the most recent year that you actually received support from a parent.) If this parent has remarried as of today, answer the questions on the rest of this form about that parent and the person whom your parent married (your stepparent).

Notes for question **64** (page 5)

Include in your parents' household (see notes, above, for who is considered a parent):
- your parents and yourself, even if you don't live with your parents, and
- your parents' other children if (a) your parents will provide more than half of their support from July 1, 2001 through June 30, 2002 or (b) the children could answer "No" to every question in Step Three, and
- other people if they now live with your parents, your parents provide more than half of their support, and your parents will continue to provide more than half of their support from July 1, 2001 through June 30, 2002.

Notes for questions **65** (page 5) and **85** (page 6)

Always count yourself as a college student. Do not include your parents. Include others only if they will attend at least half time in 2001-2002 a program that leads to a college degree or certificate.

Notes for question **84** (page 6)

Include in your (and your spouse's) household:
- yourself (and your spouse, if you have one), and
- your children, if you will provide more than half of their support from July 1, 2001 through June 30, 2002, and
- other people if they now live with you, and you provide more than half of their support, and you will continue to provide more than half of their support from July 1, 2001 through June 30, 2002.

Information on the Privacy Act and use of your Social Security Number

We use the information that you provide on this form to determine if you are eligible to receive federal student financial aid and the amount that you are eligible to receive. Section 483 of the Higher Education Act of 1965, as amended, gives us the authority to ask you and your parents these questions, and to collect the Social Security Numbers of you and your parents.

State and institutional student financial aid programs may also use the information that you provide on this form to determine if you are eligible to receive state and institutional aid and the need that you have for such aid. Therefore, we will disclose the information that you provide on this form to each institution you list in questions 86–97, state agencies in your state of legal residence, and the state agencies of the states in which the colleges that you list in questions 86–97 are located.

If you are applying solely for federal aid, you must answer all of the following questions that apply to you: 1–9, 13–15, 24, 27–28, 31–32, 35, 36–40, 42–49, 52–66, 69–74, 76-85, and 98–99. If you do not answer these questions, you will not receive federal aid.

Without your consent, we may disclose information that you provide to entities under a published "routine use." Under such a routine use, we may disclose information to third parties that we have authorized to assist us in administering the above programs; to other federal agencies under computer matching programs, such as those with the Internal Revenue Service, Social Security Administration, Selective Service System, Immigration and Natural-ization Service, and Veterans Administration; to your parents or spouse; and to members of Congress if you ask them to help you with student aid questions.

If the federal government, the U.S. Department of Education, or an employee of the U.S. Department of Education is involved in litigation, we may send information to the Department of Justice, or a court or adjudicative body, if the disclosure is related to financial aid and certain conditions are met. In addition, we may send your information to a foreign, federal, state, or local enforcement agency if the information that you submitted indicates a violation or potential violation of law, for which that agency has jurisdiction for investigation or prosecution. Finally, we may send information regarding a claim that is determined to be valid and overdue to a consumer reporting agency. This information includes identifiers from the record; the amount, status, and history of the claim; and the program under which the claim arose.

State Certification

By submitting this application, you are giving your state financial aid agency permission to verify any statement on this form and to obtain income tax information for all persons required to report income on this form.

The Paperwork Reduction Act of 1995

The Paperwork Reduction Act of 1995 says that no one is required to respond to a collection of information unless it displays a valid OMB control number, which for this form is 1845-0001. The time required to complete this form is estimated to be one hour, including time to review instructions, search data resources, gather the data needed, and complete and review the information collection. If you have comments about this estimate or suggestions for improving this form, please write to: U.S. Department of Education, Washington DC 20202-4651.

We may request additional information from you to ensure efficient application processing operations. We will collect this additional information only as needed and on a voluntary basis.

Worksheets

Do not mail these worksheets in with your application.
Keep these worksheets; your school may ask to see them.

Worksheet A
Calendar Year 2000

For question 44 Student/Spouse		For question 78 Parent(s)
$	Earned income credit from IRS Form 1040–line 60a; 1040A–line 38a; 1040EZ–line 8a; or Telefile–line L	$
$	Additional child tax credit from IRS Form 1040–line 62 or 1040A–line 39	$
$	Welfare benefits, including Temporary Assistance for Needy Families (TANF). Don't include food stamps.	$
$	Social Security benefits received that were not taxed (such as SSI)	$
$ — Enter in question 44.		Enter in question 78. — $

Worksheet B
Calendar Year 2000

For question 45 Student/Spouse		For question 79 Parent(s)
$	Payments to tax-deferred pension and savings plans (paid directly or withheld from earnings), including amounts reported on the W-2 Form in Box 13, codes D, E, F, G, H, and S	$
$	IRA deductions and payments to self-employed SEP, SIMPLE, and Keogh and other qualified plans from IRS Form 1040–total of lines 23 + 29 or 1040A–line 16	$
$	Child support received for all children. Don't include foster care or adoption payments.	$
$	Tax exempt interest income from IRS Form 1040–line 8b or 1040A–line 8b	$
$	Foreign income exclusion from IRS Form 2555–line 43 or 2555EZ–line 18	$
$	Untaxed portions of pensions from IRS Form 1040–lines (15a minus 15b) + (16a minus 16b) or 1040A–lines (11a minus 11b) + (12a minus 12b) excluding rollovers	$
$	Credit for federal tax on special fuels from IRS Form 4136–line 9 – nonfarmers only	$
$	Housing, food, and other living allowances paid to members of the military, clergy, and others (including cash payments and cash value of benefits)	$
$	Veterans noneducation benefits such as Disability, Death Pension, or Dependency & Indemnity Compensation (DIC) and/or VA Educational Work-Study allowances	$
$	Any other untaxed income or benefits not reported elsewhere on Worksheets A and B, such as worker's compensation, untaxed portions of railroad retirement benefits, Black Lung Benefits, Refugee Assistance, etc. Don't include student aid, Workforce Investment Act educational benefits, or benefits from flexible spending arrangements, e.g., cafeteria plans.	$
$	Cash received or any money paid on your behalf, not reported elsewhere on this form	XXXXXXXX
$ — Enter in question 45.		Enter in question 79. — $

Worksheet C
Calendar Year 2000

For question 46 Student/Spouse		For question 80 Parent(s)
$	Education credits (Hope and Lifetime Learning tax credits) from IRS Form 1040-line 46 or 1040A-line 29	$
$	Child support paid because of divorce or separation. Do not include support for children in your (or your parents') household, as reported in question 84 (or question 64 for your parents).	$
$	Taxable earnings from Federal Work-Study or other need-based work programs	$
$	Student grant, scholarship, and fellowship aid, including AmeriCorps awards, that was reported to the IRS in your (or your parents') adjusted gross income	$
$ — Enter in question 46.		Enter in question 80. — $